Al Goldman

May fun & success
be yours in
all your racing
endeavours.

Rita M. Jeffi

Ask the Experts

RITA M. JEFFERIES

presents

ASK THE EXPERTS

Published by Jefferies Equine Consulting, Dune Haven Farm, R.R.
#1, Puslinch, Ontario NOB 2J0.

Cover is after a photograph of Dune, winner of the Governor
General's Cup, taken by Rita M. Jefferies. Photograph of Rita M.
Jefferies taken by Bob Rutter.

Photograph of Just Cruising (Chapter 1) courtesy of Randy Roy;
photographs accompanying 'A Lower Leg Bandage' (Chapter 5,
Question 3), and 'The Figure-Eight Splint Bandage' (Chapter 5,
Question 4), courtesy of 3M Canada Inc.; photograph of Dick Day
(Chapter 8) courtesy of Bruce Wilkinson; photograph of Mac Cone
(Chapter 9) courtesy of Mac Cone. Diagrams accompanying 'Lar-
yngeal Hemiplegia' (Chapter 10, Question 6), and the section title
photograph to Chapter 4 are courtesy of Raymond A. Pleau.

Balance of photographs throughout the book are by
Rita M. Jefferies.

ISBN 0-9694269-0-9

To Yuri, who gave me some of my happiest moments in life, looking at the world as framed by his two ears ...

To Dune, who gave me some of my winningest moments ...

To Dan's Harem, who gave me champions ...

To Battlestar Galactica, who taught me that there is always more to be learned ...

and to all the other four-footed members of my family, past and present, who have given me so much love and companionship through the years.

As we all know, riding is certainly one of the more challenging sports; in fact, it may be called an art. As such, it often presents us with problems that need to be solved, dilemmas that need to be resolved. Usually there is no one really knowledgeable close by.

Designed to help those who want to help themselves, this book provides answers to all those equine-oriented questions on feeding, stabling, training, veterinary developments and much, much more....

Contents

I. FINDING THE RIGHT HORSE

A champion show hunter (both in Canada and in the United States), Just
Cruising, epitomizes all the qualities an 'A' Circuit horse should have
says hunter / jumper judge Randy Roy.

The 'A' Circuit Horse

QUESTION: Could you describe the qualities that make a horse an 'A' Circuit hunter candidate? (What should an 'A' Circuit horse look like? What capabilities should he show? Where does the difference come between the 'A' Circuit horse and the Trillium Circuit horse?)

Also, there seems to be a wide range in horse prices. What would be a realistic minimal price for an 'A' Circuit horse and what factors would affect the price?

EXPERT: With both a Senior A.H.A. and a C.E.F. Judges Card, Randy Roy has officiated at every major hunter / jumper show in North America and he is the only Canadian who has ever been called upon to do so. He judges at two or three horse shows a month – a hectic schedule but one which does allow him some time free for training at the other shows. Roy also has a Hunter and Jumper Course Designer's Card.

Although he graduated from university with Honours in French and Sociology, Roy decided on a career with horses. He worked with George H. Morris for almost two years as a manager amidst such excellent riders as Mac Cone, Katy Monahan, Leslie Burr, Melanie Smith, and Buddy Brown. Then, along with Ian Millar, he trained at Dwyer Hill Farm for ten years, during which time the Dwyer Hill team captured almost every North American title in the hunter and jumper shows.

Roy currently resides with his wife, Cathy, in King Township at Hunter's Glen Farm, a private show stable. Cathy rides in the Amateur Owner Hunter Division and on Another Brother was Zone Champion last year and Amateur Owner Champion at the Royal Winter Fair. Their two children, Ryan and Paul, are also riders.

Along with Geoff Teall, Roy is a partner in an operation called 'North Run' in New York. The partnership enables Roy to train and ultimately sell horses in a top circuit.

Asked if he had ever had a particularly special horse, Roy replied,

'I would have to say it's Just Cruising who launched me. He's the greatest horse in the world! He captured all the awards in Canada. In the United States he was Champion at Devon and Champion on the Florida Circuit. We showed him until we couldn't afford to keep him any longer. I'm trying to work it out so that one day I can bring him back to my farm and retire him.'

ANSWER: The right looks, size, movement, attitude, manners, and style of jumping are all important ingredients in the making of an 'A' Circuit horse. Without these 'right' or suitable qualities, it is impossible to put in a winning performance in top level competition.

Unless he is showing in the Conformation Division, an 'A' Circuit horse does not have to have top conformation, but he does have to have eye-appeal. A refined head, sloping shoulders and good hindquarters are the type of characteristics which combine to form an attractive look that will be eye-catching enough to grab the attention of the judge.

Quality is really a key characteristic and is found most frequently in the Thoroughbred. Says Roy, 'The Thoroughbred is representative of the whole system. There's nothing that can outclass and outdo the beautiful Thoroughbred. He is a standout. He's a beautiful horse.' He adds however, 'If a European Warmblood puts in the best round of the day, then he's absolutely the winner. I'm not ever going to hurt the heavier horse in my judging.'

Size-wise, Roy likes a horse to be from sixteen hands to sixteen hands, two inches. He does not like really large horses because their big stride often makes it very uncomfortable for them to fit in the proper number of strides between fences and still hold themselves off of the jumps.

Conversely, he does not like the very small horses because they usually have to struggle to make the combinations and possibly hurry down the lines.

As far as movement is concerned, Roy emphasizes that the successful 'A' Circuit horse really needs to be able to shine as a hack. He favours 'daisy-cutters'; that is, horses with long, low, sweeping strides.

Temperament is often displayed in performance and Roy takes note of the horse's attitude when he is judging. Says Roy, 'I like a pleasant attitude. I don't like anything that's a little too strong or something that looks agitated or irritated with a lead change or whatever the rider happens to be doing. Their ears tell me where they're at. I don't like a horse that's too alert, so that he's spooky and suspicious, but I do like an attentive attitude.'

Roy is one of a growing number of professionals who has lost any prejudice he might have had against mares. He explains, 'All my life, I was one of those adamant gelding fans. I wouldn't go down the road to look at a mare. That was one of my priority questions, "Is it a mare or a gelding?" Now I never even ask!'

As far as form is concerned, Roy likes a beautiful style. He describes what he likes to see in an 'A' Circuit horse over a fence. 'I like "round" – round head and neck and round through the back. I like legs up and knees tidy, but not tucked away so tight that they're limited. I like to see a little air between the fence and the horse. That, I call scope. I like the hind end to follow straight along with the front end, neither swaying to the right nor swaying to the left. I like a nice big, round jumper.'

When it comes to the kinds of blemishes that so many horses have, Roy draws the line of acceptability between what can be noticed by the judge from a distance and what cannot. Any large blemish makes a horse less acceptable. Splints and curbs, for example, can rarely be seen from a distance, whereas some capped hocks are highly visible and others not.

Horses which show in the Conformation Division, on the other hand, need to be relatively blemish-free in order to win.

The price of an 'A' Circuit horse is a very difficult subject with which to deal. A young unschooled horse found 'off the beaten track' might be purchased for a few thousand. At the other end of the spectrum Zone Champions have been known to sell in the neighbourhood of a hundred thousand dollars if they are heading south of the border.

If you plan to search for a potential 'A' Circuit hunter on your own, try to keep in mind all of the characterists that Roy has suggested. Remember, factors such as appearance, size, movement, temperament, jumping style, training and show experience will all have a bearing on the price you have to pay. If money is a concern and you have to compromise a little, consider a horse with slight blemishes or perhaps one that does not move as exceptionally well as he might.

The one characteristic that Roy would never sacrifice is jumping style. When he is looking for hunter prospects, Roy always watches for a horse with a natural instinct to miss or clear the jump and to jump in quiet, round form.

Although it is not easy for the inexperienced horseperson to be able to tell whether or not an unschooled horse is going to have good form over a fence, you would be well advised to ask the owner to longe the horse over a small 'x' fence at a trot. This gait, coupled with the natural nervousness the horse would most likely feel on being confronted with a jump, should give some indication of what kind of athletic ability he has.

Once you have selected your 'A' Circuit horse and have him or her ready to show, Roy stresses the importance of making sure you have the animal turned out really well. Says Roy, 'I'm a very big person on turn out. I'll go out of my way to do the little extras so that maybe I can get the edge.'

He elaborates, 'When I'm judging I don't need to see *past* what he'll look like – I need to see what he looks like. I'm not going to say to myself, "The fifth place one in the model is the most beautiful one, but my God, the braids in the mane are poorly done, the feathers are still there – he's not trimmed right – he doesn't look the part at all." I'll just go to the one who does.' He sums up, 'We're talking top of the line competition. I need them to be turned out immaculately and beautifully.'

The 'A' Circuit and the Trillium: You ask about the difference between an 'A' Circuit show and a Trillium Circuit show. Basically the two circuits compliment each other. The 'A' Circuit is a little more demanding in quality and in form, whereas the Trillium Circuit, according to Roy, 'is a great new addition which takes the pressure off horses, riders, trainers and parents by allowing them to show at a level at which they can be competitive.' He explains, 'It's an excellent avenue to show horses that would be pointless and rewardless to show at the 'A' Circuit level. It's a perfect situation for numerous horses that don't jump or move with the best.' Roy also feels that it is a great circuit for starting young horses at a less difficult level and for other horses that need to step down to a more comfortable level.

The 'A' Circuit is also much more expensive a level at which to show. Showing costs are higher, as is the average cost of purchasing a horse suitable for that level.

Best Breed and Type for Trillium Shows and Hacking

QUESTION: Would you please send opinions, regarding best breed and type of hunters suitable for a small show or local schooling show?

Or, please send a list of breeders in Ontario who specialize in breeding and training hunters.

EXPERT: Allan Clarkson has been involved with breeding, training and showing horses since 1950. Well-known hunters such as Andora, who was Champion at the Canadian National Exhibition (CNE), Mr. Mort, who was Zone Champion Second Year Working Hunter, and On Target, who won the Canadian-bred and numerous other red ribbons at such shows as Bolton, the CNE, Barrie and the Royal Agricultural Winter Fair, are but three examples of hunters that Clarkson has developed successfully on the show circuit.

As well as hunters, Clarkson bred Spot Check, who was the Champion Open Jumper at the Royal with Hugh Graham riding, and developed Vince Dunn's Sea Hawk whom Jim Elder and later Beth Underhill rode. Sea Hawk has placed in international competition.

Clarkson was the first President of the prestigious Bolton Horse Show which started as a centennial Bolton project and since has become an annual event under other names. Clarkson, himself, judges extensively at horse shows across Canada and has also judged in Bermuda.

At his own stable, Pine Toft, he has been joined by his daughter, Carolyn, who rides the promising young horses Clarkson selects and trains.

With such an extensive background in the world of breeding, training, showing and judging, Clarkson is an ideal horseman to answer this question.

ANSWER: Clarkson assumes that by small shows you mean something on the Trillium Circuit and suggests that for such shows, you keep the following qualities in mind:

• First of all, because the distances are a little shorter between fences than on the 'A' Circuit, it is possible to win with a slightly less 'scopey' horse than you would need for the upper level circuit.
• The horse should be fairly correct in his conformation, but refinement is not as essential.
• At one time it was not necessary to have a good mover on the Trillium Circuit but nowadays, to do well, good movement is important.
• A solid colour horse rather than an Appaloosa or a Palamino is preferable. Clarkson points out that even though colour should not enter into placings, all other things being equal, it invariably does.
• You need a horse with a sensible disposition because at Trillium level shows, especially in areas where they are held at country fairs, the horse is often exposed to such things as ferris wheels etc. and it is important that he doesn't 'flake out'.
• A horse should have good form over a fence but he does not have to be so 'snappy' with his knees as he would have to be for the 'A' Circuit. As long as he is steady and 'gets his spots right', you should be able to win a ribbon.

Clarkson suggests that in this day and age such a horse would cost a minimum of six thousand, five hundred dollars. In this price range

Clarkson points out that. 'You have to sacrifice something!' and he is of the opinion that the best thing to sacrifice is size. He feels that you absolutely cannot buy a big horse that is correct for that amount of money and since a long stride is not really necessary, size is the logical sacrifice.

A personal note: As far as a list of breeders and trainers of hunters and jumpers is concerned, I suggest that you contact the following organizations: The Canadian Sport Horse Association, Box 520, Gormley, Ontario LOH I G0; and / or The Canadian Thoroughbred Horse Society (Ontario Division), Box 172, Rexdale, Ontario M9W 5L I.

Buying the Right Yearling for the Racetrack

QUESTION: I have been involved with horses for the past five years and would now be extremely interested in owning a Thoroughbred race horse.

I would appreciate receiving advice from one of your experts on acquiring a yearling at the Woodbine September Sales. As a novice to this side of the business, what exactly do I have to consider with regard to blood lines, conformation and anything else of significance?

Having attended the yearling sales on one occasion as a spectator, I noticed prices varied considerably. How do I determine the value of the horse and is it possible to obtain information in advance of the sale as to what kind of price the horse might go for?

EXPERT: Dr. George Badame, an equine veterinarian whose practice is centred on the backstretch at Woodbine and Greenwood, is also a skilled advisor in the selection of promising young stock.

For several years he acted as a consultant for Stafford Farms as well as for other owners and to quote from the Toronto Star, some time ago, columnist Jim Proudfoot stated, 'The man's record is phenomenal.' Proudfoot fantasized about taking 'George Badame, he of the keen eye, down to the Kentucky Sales' and having him 'select a promising steed.'

Badame's skills have developed from a lifetime spent with Thoroughbreds. Because his father was a trainer, the young Badame grew up around horses and that background, combined with his medical knowledge, has made him an astute horseman.

ANSWER: Obviously, when you plan on purchasing a yearling at Woodbine's September Sales or at any sale for that matter, price is going to be a major factor in determining the quality of the youngster you are able to buy. It *is* possible, however, to pay the same price for a yearling as the man next to you pays and yet end up with the better prospect. How? What makes one horse a preferred selection?

Pedigree, of course, has always been a very important consideration. A yearling out of a stakes winning dam by a leading sire is bound to be considered to have a fair amount of potential talent. In today's market though, there has been an ever-increasing awareness of the importance of conformation; that is, conformation as it relates to soundness. Buyers are becoming more sophisticated – more aware of the fact that if a horse does not stay sound, his pedigree or inherited talents may never have the chance to be realized.

Conformation: Badame outlines a number of conformation faults for which he would turn a horse down:

• A sway-back or conversely, a roach back: A severe concavity or a convex outline to the back limits the athletic abilities of the horse. Though he might win races, he is unlikely to be a really good horse. The back (from behind the withers to the top of the tail) should be as flat as possible.

• Bad feet: A bad foot is anything that deviates from a good one.
   a. *A concave hoof* is undesirable. The hoof should be convex; that is, it should gradually radiate out from the hairline to the base. The foot should spread out.
   b. *Rings on the hoof* are a bad sign. Rings signify gaps in nutrition

usually caused by sickness. (The minute that the body is under attack, all unnecessary expenditures such as hoof growth, stop. When things are returned to normal, hoof growth begins again but the gap show up as a ring thus indicating, if there are several rings, that the horse has been suffering recurring attacks.) One ring, however, is excusable.

c. *The higher the heel,* the more quarter crack trouble a horse will have. A low heel is preferable; in fact, the closer the hairline is to the ground, the better.

d. *Scaling on the feet* is not good. The periople (the layer of soft, light-coloured horn covering the outer aspect of the hoof) is needed to stop dehydration of the foot. Scaling indicates that the horse does not have a good periople or is not developing one. Blacksmiths sometimes create or worsen this problem by excessively rasping the foot.

• Hind leg problems: The horse should not have hocks that come too far underneath him. There should be a perpendicular line from the point of the hock to the back of the ankle.

True curbs are best avoided as are bog spavins.

• Bad joint alignment: Any type of misalignment is definitely undesirable and fairly self-explanatory.

• 'Round' front ankles: All horses should have basically square ankles. Roundness indicates that there is more than a normal amount of synovial fluid in the joint – nature's way of immobilizing it. Such a roundness reveals a predisposition to ankle problems.

• The inability to turn without stumbling: If a horse does not turn well or if he stumbles in the hind end, the problem signifies an ailment in the hind limbs. One stumble is acceptable.

• A tail that does not snap: Because the tail is the extension of the backbone, a good strong tail that snaps back when lifted is desirable.

• A neck that does not blend with the rest of the body: A good neck is one that balances everything else.

Although none of these faults stops a horse from running, Badame is quick to point out that even just one does affect how long the horse will be around to show the ability he might have.

23

When you examine the conformation of a horse, Badame suggests that you study each component part first and then put all these parts together to get a total picture of the animal.

And finally on the subject of conformation, Badame advises, 'Go to the races and study the winners of each race. Even better, study the top horses – the stakes horses – to get a good idea of what good conformation is all about.'

On the Subject of Blood Lines: Pedigree is so involved a topic it is impossible to discuss in detail here, but Badame does list two important 'rules of thumb':

• Be very hesitant about buying a yearling by a sire that never won a stakes unless that sire has already proven himself. It is always easy to make excuses as to why a stallion was never a stakes winner, but the bottom line is that it is wiser to wait until he is progeny-tested.

• It is good to have the dam be by a good brood mare sire and if she is, the fact that she might not have raced need not be a big concern. Naturally, the better the pedigree, the better the chances that the dam's progeny will have talent, but also the higher the price will be.

Brood mare sire lists are printed weekly in 'The Blood-Horse'.

In Summary: Badame makes some helpful suggestions for the neophyte buyer as well as the buyer on a limited budget:

• Subscribe to weekly or monthly periodicals and study bloodlines and sales figures. Be aware of the average price for which yearlings by a particular sire were purchased. Obviously if your budget limits you to fifty thousand dollars, yearlings by sires above this price would be out of your reach, unless one happened to be, as Badame puts it, 'a cripple'.

• Buy from a farm that has a track record of producing winners. These winners do not have to be stakes winners because if you are working on a 'short bankroll', Windfields and other top farms will be out of reach, but some farms just seem to do a better job than others of raising youngsters.

• If it is at all possible, visit the farms from which the yearlings you are interested in come. If the owners are doing a good job but are new to the business, you might be able to get a bargain because the farms or consignors have no track record.

• Have some idea of how much you can spend and do not waste time 'window-shopping'. Look at horses within your budget.

Finally, when asked what he would sacrifice for cost, Badame admits he would go for conformation and soundness and sacrifice a little pedigree. To quote Badame, 'I'd rather have a horse that's sound and has got good conformation and maybe a *little* less pedigree than one with a little more pedigree because I know one's going to make the races and the other one's not!'

2. UNDERSTANDING YOUR HORSE

'The horse is both endowed *and* encumbered with a lot of behaviour that is inherent.' *Dr. Andrew Fraser*

Intelligence and the Horse

QUESTION: I have now been involved with horses for the past four years and in this short time have come to believe that horses are very intelligent. More experienced horsemen seem to think otherwise. I would greatly appreciate any information your experts may have on this subject.

EXPERT: Some time ago, I had the opportunity to interview Andrew Fraser MRCVS MVSL FBIOL of the Memorial University in Newfoundland. Fraser is the Director of Animal Care and a Professor of Physiology. His favourite subject and one he has spent a great deal of time studying is equine behaviour.

To answer your question, following is an outline of Fraser's beliefs as discussed in the interview which was based on the question, 'Is the horse an intelligent animal?'

ANSWER: Fraser pointed out that the intelligence of the horse is difficult to measure but, using behaviour as the yardstick, he puts the intelligence of the horse on a par with that of the pig and of the dog – both of which he considers to be very intelligent. He cautions against judging an animal's intelligence solely by our human standards but recommends instead that we be aware of alternative forms of intelligence.

A great deal of the horse's behaviour is inherent; that is, it has become a part of the genetic make-up of the horse. As an established species, the horse has tremendous antiquity – dating back a good ten-million years – and behaviour which was necessary for the horse to live and adapt must have been part of its genetic code at that time. Thus the horse's tendencies towards suspicion, flight, etc., while not particularly necessary now, nor desirable, were originally essential for survival against predators.

Similar reactions today, based on these established patterns of behaviour which enabled the horse to be such a successful species, earn the animal the description of being 'stupid'. To use Fraser's words: 'The horse is both endowed *and* encumbered with a lot of behaviour that is inherent.'

Although the great bulk of behaviour in a horse has an inherited basis, the balance is learned through drill or consistent repetition. It is at this point that good training becomes essential. So much of a horse's time, talent and temperament can be spoiled by an inadequate handler who 'turns the horse off.' Even worse, a horse can become badly confused to such an extent that he never reaches his full potential.

How do we communicate our wishes to the horse? The processes used in teaching the horse are *positive reinforcement, negative reinforcement* and *conditioning* with an overall policy of *consistency* being vital.

A horse is capable of learning how to respond correctly to human vocabulary but only on a very limited basis. Fraser cites seven, as being the approximate number of human words that a horse can learn. A horse might know its name, the proper response to 'walk', to 'trot' and to 'canter', 'whoa' or 'stop', and perhaps 'come'. The tone we use when talking influences the horse: a loud angry voice can excite or upset; a calm, quiet voice can soothe.

Of course a horse also learns to respond to the physical requests of a human. A push with the hand to move over, a pressure of the legs to move forward, a resistance in the reins to slow down or stop are but three of the ways we can communicate our wishes physically. (Obviously horses have an extensive vocabulary which they use to communicate with each other.)

According to Fraser, the horse is capable of experiencing not only the primitive emotions of pain, hunger, fear and rage but also several others; for example, the horse shows a capacity for bonded pairing – a close association with another horse.

Fraser summarized ways in which horses show both human-type and biological intelligence as follows:

• The ability of horses to survive stands out as a major accomplishment in the animal kingdom. Survival for more than ten million years is no mean feat and certainly one which we humans might find very difficult to achieve.

• The ability to organize themselves into groups in a complicated but peaceful social system is definitely a form of intelligence.

• The extra sense of caution that horses display, while sometimes frustrating to humans, is very sensible. They often seem disinclined to make a decision but in reality it is their way of trying to protect themselves until they have examined a situation.

• The ability to reason (but only in circumstances where problems are related to their own natural circumstances of living) exists. (Horses do not reason well when problems have no relationship to their natural lifestyles.)

• A keen sense of judgement of distances, etc. is often shown.

• An economy of movement is evident when horses expend no more energy than necessary to accomplish a certain act.

We, as humans, can make use of the horse's intelligence to our advantage, not only in training but also in day to day handling. The horse's ability to learn through drill, his excellent memory, his keen judgement and economy of movement – all can make teaching the horse much easier as long as training is carried out skilfully. The horse's inherent tendencies to suspicion, 'spooking', flight, etc. should be considered and problems dealt with quietly and consistently.

3. FEEDING YOUR HORSE

Lactating mares have special nutritional requirements.

Watering and Feed Schedule
for the Working Owner

QUESTION: I have heard that it is best to water and to feed hay about an hour or two before grain is fed, for better digestion. No mention was made in the article as to optimum times for feeding and watering in relation to each other. I can only water the horses morning and evening and I want to know the order to feed and water to insure maximum digestion.

EXPERT: An Associate Professor of Animal Nutrition in the Department of Animal and Poultry Science at the University of Guelph, Dr. John Burton concentrates on the horse and the young bovine. At the undergraduate level he teaches two courses on horse production in North America, and in Ontario in particular. The course includes breeding, productive physiology, genetics, selection programmes, management of farms, use of facilities, exercise physiology and, of course, nutrition.

Burton did his undergraduate work at Guelph when it was part of the University of Toronto. He did his graduate work in Animal Metabolism at the world-famous Cornell University, from which he also obtained his PH.D.

One of Burton's personal interests is driving a Standardbred daily from 5:30 A.M. to 7:30 A.M. (He must be dedicated!) As well, he rides when he can find the time.

A highly regarded lecturer, Burton is frequently called upon to speak on horse nutrition to various groups and associations.

ANSWER: Burton recommends the following order for the watering and feeding of horses:

• Water the horses first. Because water goes through the digestive tract very, very quickly, it is not necessary to wait any specified amount of time before feeding.

35

- Give the horses a portion of their hay ration. Allow ten to fifteen minutes for hay consumption. This time lapse will give them a chance to fill up their stomachs a little and take the extreme edge off of their appetites. Thus it will discourage the bolting of their grain.
- Feed the grain to the horses.
- Give the horses the balance of their hay.

Burton cautions that a thirsty, somewhat dehydrated horse, if given dry food before being watered, could develop colic or a bit of the problem that triggers laminitis. (A performance horse on a high intake level of grain would be more susceptible than a horse on a low intake maintenance diet.) When the horse eats oats or prepared feed, the seed coats of these grains are going to be broken up and cracked and the carbohydrate is going to be readily digested. A horse that is a little on the dry side will have slightly less fluid secreted into the stomach when the dry diet is eaten and consequently the movement *out* of the stomach is not going to be as rapid. If a drink of water is taken after a 'good bit of grain' is in the stomach, there are two things that will happen: a more rapid expansion of the grain in the stomach itself and a more rapid flushing of the carbohydrates into the gut. It is this type of thing that can lead to health problems.

A personal note: Let horses eat their grain in peace. Noise or commotion at feed time agitates horses, particularly the less placid ones and thus interferes with their digestion.

Nutrition in Hay

QUESTION: I would like to know about the difference in quality of hay and alfalfa of this year's crop versus one that is one year old and one that is two years old. I know that the older the hay the less value it has, but where is the limit? Does for instance, a three-year-old hay which is very good with a lot of alfalfa equal fresh hay that is just so so?

To get the highest value, when should one cut? I mean what percentage of the hayfield should be in bloom?

EXPERT: Dr. John Burton (see preceding question and answer).

ANSWER: First of all, Burton points out that you speak of hay and alfalfa as two different things, whereas in actual fact, alfalfa, when dried and baled, *is* hay. Different types of hay are: alfalfa hay, grass hay, clover hay and legume / grass mixtures.

According to Burton there are *two* things which occur as hay ages:
• It tends to *dry* more, thus becoming more crumbly and more *dusty*.
  In feeding to horses, the dust is a problem and Burton does not recommend feeding hay that is over one year old inside the stable and definitely not inside to any horses that have respiratory problems. As he points out, at least outside, either the dust can blow away or the horse is able to move away from it.
• The vitamin content (particularly vitamins A and D) *decreases* with exposure to the air and to light so storage causes it to drop considerably. After six to eight months, only about one-half of the original amount of both of these vitamins is left in the hay. After a year's storage there is little left of either of these vitamins. Burton, however, does point out that vitamins A and D can be supplemented relatively easily in concentrates.

Nutrients remaining in the hay are *energy* (starchy type and cellulose), *protein* and *minerals*. The protein content may decrease very slightly simply because there is often a considerable leaf loss with older, dryer hay and the leaves are the location of most of the higher quality protein. To use Burton's words, 'In answer to the question, "Is hay that's two or three years old that has a fair proportion of alfalfa as good as the fresh hay that may be of lower quality or not so much alfalfa?", there is no straight "yes" or "no" answer. From the standpoint of energy and protein, probably the older hay might be better, but from the standpoint of total nutrition, including vitamins, it isn't likely to be as good.'

As far as the percentage of hay field in bloom or 'stage of cutting' is concerned, the *earlier* you cut it, the *higher* the *quality*. Unfortunately there is a conflict between quality and quantity because the earlier you cut the hay the lower the quantity will be. As a rule of thumb ten per cent in bloom is a good percentage. Burton adds that most of the nutrients will be in higher supply, more available and more digestible to the horse the earlier that the hay is cut.

As a good hay for horses, Burton recommends a grass / legume mixture of a fifty to fifty ratio. The grass may be brome, timothy or perhaps some orchard grass and the legume may be alfalfa or clover. Keep in mind if feeding a lot of alfalfa, that it is high in calcium and take this factor into account when calculating your calcium / phosphorous balance, which should be in a two to one ratio.

The colour of hay can serve as a guideline to the quality of hay. Generally, the greener and leafier it is, the better the quality. If hay is rained on before being baled, some of the greenness will go and although the quality may still be good, some of the nutrients will be leached out. (Soluble nutrients are protein, carbohydrates (energy) and minerals.)

Is Second Cut Hay Acceptable for Horses?

QUESTION: Is second cut hay okay for horses?

EXPERT: Dr. John Burton (see Chapter 3, Question 1).

ANSWER: 'Absolutely!' says Burton who is very much in favour of good quality second cut hay which he says can be used very effectively in an equine feeding programme. As a matter of fact, second cut hay is being exported from North America to Britain where it brings rather exorbitant prices.

What you must be aware of if you decide to feed second cut hay is that it consists of a lot of alfalfa or alfalfa and clover; in other words, it is predominantly legume hay rather than predominantly grass hay as is first cut.

Legume hay is higher in nutritional value than equal quality grass hay. It generally contains twice as much protein, three times as much calcium and higher quantities of vitamins. Of these nutrients, it is the high calcium content of which you should take particular note. It is vital that a horse's calcium intake should be within certain ratios to his phosphorous intake. The ratio range of calcium to phosphorous according to Burton can be as low as one and one-half to one, to as high as four to one. Good quality second cut hay often has a seven to one ratio, a quality which means that phosphorous *must* be added to your horse's diet if you are feeding second cut hay. Most cereal grains contain more phosphorous than calcium.

A personal note: When I feed my horses second cut hay, bran with a one to twelve calcium / phosphorous ratio is what I add to their feed.

How to Deal with Dust in Hay Fields and in Hay

QUESTION: I keep horses on my farm and my hay and pasture fields are bordering on a dirt road. The dust stirred up by traffic and blown by the wind onto the fields is quite extensive. Could any veterinarian advise what effect this condition over an extended period of time will have on the health of my animals? I am concerned and would very much appreciate your comments and advice.

EXPERT: Dr. Tim Ogilvie is a Professor of Veterinary Medicine at the Atlantic Veterinary College in Prince Edward Island where he is involved in lecturing and research. Previously, he was with the Ontario Veterinary College.

His particular field is the study of chronic respiratory diseases.

ANSWER: According to Ogilvie, dust is an irritant and, as with all irritants, the more you can do to keep it away from a horse, the better.

When excess road dust exists in hay, Ogilvie suggests the following:

- Cut the hay at a fairly early growth stage so that it is not dry, dusty and brittle in its own right.
- Bring the baled hay in as soon as possible.
- Break the hay bales apart in another part of the barn and shake the hay up before feeding it to the horse in the stall.
- Dampen the hay with water.

As for the dust which the horses encounter in the air outside, Ogilvie suggests that the dust is so diluted that it is unlikely to be harmful.

A personal note: If you are still concerned, try contacting the township to see if there is any chance of having the road or part of the road, oiled.

Feeding the Pregnant and Lactating Mare

QUESTION: Many a novice breeder has difficulty knowing what to feed pregnant mares and mares with young foals at their sides. Indeed, very often the importance of *having* to be careful with feeding frequencies, quantities and ratios is not even realized. Feeding breeding stock can thus become a question of trial and error. Unfortunately, such an approach may lead to irreparable damage either to the mare or the foal and possibly even to both.

To answer the numerous questions of *what, how often,* and *how much*, I approached a leading animal nutritionist. He outlined a basic feeding programme.

EXPERT: Dr. John Burton (see Chapter 3, Question 1).

ANSWER: Burton divided breeding feeding programmes into several sections:
- early gestation (with no foal at foot)
- late gestation
- early lactation
- creep feeding.

He stressed the fact that a well-balanced diet consists of a good quality, average amount of hay and trace-mineralized salt, supplemented, if necessary, by an appropriate amount of grain concentrate mix. Ample good fresh water should always be available.

Good quality hay, in Burton's opinion, is basically a grass hay or a grass hay with some legume in it. The hay should be in the nine to twelve per cent protein range. He suggests taking a sample of hay and having it analysed so that one can start from a knowledgeable basis. Although the University of Guelph no longer offers a hay analysis service, Agri Food Labs will analyse hay as will most feed companies.

Early Gestation (with no foal at foot): For the one thousand pound to eleven hundred pound mare who is in good condition Burton suggests the following:
• fifteen to twenty pounds of hay per day (about one-half a bale)
• trace-mineralized salt
• all the good, clean, fresh water desired.

Mares who need to improve their condition or who are hard keepers would need some grain concentrates. In such cases, Burton suggests the following addition: two to three pounds of oats or a normal concentrate grain mix that contains eleven to twelve per cent protein.

Mares that are being ridden would probably need a little more.

Late Gestation: At this stage, a twelve to fifteen per cent increase in energy and about a twenty per cent increase in protein is necessary. Burton, as a rule of thumb, suggests a twenty per cent increase in feed intake during the last three months.

It is important to remember that the rapidly developing fetus leaves less room in the abdomen for the digestive tract; therefore, the amount of hay that can be fed will be limited and concentrates will have to make up a larger proportion.

Burton points out that although the protein requirement increases, the percentage of crude protein does not have to because the total amount being eaten is increasing. For the mature brood mare eleven to twelve per cent crude protein is all that is necessary at this stage.

It is essential that minerals be well-balanced – calcium and phosphorus in particular, but also the micro-minerals that are associated with bone development, skeletal development, etc. – copper, zinc and iron.

For the one thousand to eleven hundred pound mare, Burton suggests the following:
• thirteen to eighteen pounds of hay a day (about two-thirds of the total diet)
• trace-mineralized salt
• four to eight pounds of grain a day (nine to twelve per cent protein)
• ample fresh, clean water.

As well, vitamin A supplementation is normally necessary because the pregnant mare does not metabolize vitamin A as efficiently as the non-pregnant mare. There is about a one hundred per cent increase in the requirement of vitamin A during gestation over the mare at maintenance. The simplest way to supply this need is with a good horse supplement such as 'Something Extra'. If you are buying a manufactured feed such as Gilpa's Microchip feed, the vitamin A will already be added.

Burton stresses the importance of keeping a mare, even at this latter stage of pregnancy, in good condition; that is, not too fat nor too thin. He even suggests that a brood mare that is a riding horse may be lightly worked under saddle until the last week or two of gestation. A certain level of condition makes foaling easier and, as well, is healthier for the fetus.

Mares in Early Lactation: At peak output, an average mare produces somewhere between fifteen and twenty-five pounds of milk per day; therefore, a good, plentiful fresh water supply is essential. In the stall, add an extra bucket for additional water availability and make sure that outside, water is abundant and easily accessible.

A one thousand to eleven hundred pound mare in early lactation should be fed:

- fifteen to twenty-five pounds of hay per day (If hay bellies are not a concern, as much as twenty-two to thirty pounds per day is acceptable.)
- five to six pounds of concentrate mix (Once again, only ten to eleven per cent protein is necessary.)
- a plentiful supply of water.

If you limit feed intake, Burton cautions that protein content must increase.

Creep Feeding: Burton recommends that the creep feed be started at between three to four weeks of age particularly if the mare gives the indication that she's not producing a lot of milk. (Creep feed should be very palatable.) The level of protein must be in the seventeen to eighteen per cent range and the foal should have access to good quality hay or pasture of preferably a fifty to fifty grass / legume mixture. It should be either first or second cut hay of very good quality.

At the University of Guelph Burton uses this mix – corn: twenty-five per cent, oats: thirty per cent, barley: twenty-three per cent, soybean meal: fifteen per cent, molasses: six per cent, vitamin / mineral premix: .05 per cent, and brewers yeast: .025 per cent.

The vitamin / mineral mix should contain calcium and phosphorus as well, otherwise dicalcium phosphate should be added to the creep feed.

Burton cautions that feed should not be left lying around for any length of time so the creep feed should be cleaned out every twenty-four to forty-eight hours.

Creep feeding for the young foal: A few ounces of a mix such as that suggested (give them whatever they will eat up).

By four to eight weeks of age they should be eating two to three pounds of creep feed a day.

A chance for the foal to get away from the aggressive mare is

43

extremely important. Outside pastures could contain a specially fenced off area that the foal can reach but not the mare. Inside a barn, a young foal could be put in a separate stall for a little while to give it a chance to eat.

In Summary: Burton makes the following comments:

• One should be familiar with what is the optimum condition of a mare and feed her to try to keep close to that optimum condition. She should not be too thin, nor too fat.
• Foals should grow on a regular basis. There should be no hitches to a growth curve. Foals who have slowed down for some reason (not enough access to food or insufficient milk from the mare) and who then suddenly receive rich creep feed are likely to run into feed-related problems such as contracted tendons, straight pasterns, etc.
• Burton stresses *quality* of growth rather than quantity. To quote him, 'Everything seems to mesh – the skeleton, the muscle development, the tendons, the ligaments – all should grow together at the same rate.

Feeding the Weanling and Yearling
Nutritional Imbalances Can Cause Problems

QUESTION: I have been breeding and showing horses for three years and am worried by stories of problems that young horses can develop if they are not fed properly. What is a good feeding programme for weanlings and yearlings?

Can you tell me more about the problems that can develop if I feed my young horses the wrong amounts?

EXPERT: A graduate of the Royal Veterinary College in London, England, Dr. Huw Llewellyn spent a few years in a mixed practice before moving to Canada where he completed a Small Animal Surgery Internship at the Ontario Veterinary College followed by a Large Animal Surgery Residency.

44

Llewellyn stayed on at the O.V.C. as an assistant professor for four years before leaving to open the Belwood Equine Clinic in 1980. His specialties are: surgery performed in the field, and reproduction.

A breeder of young horses, himself, Llewellyn became very concerned about correct feeding programmes for young horses when he encountered physical problems developing in his clients' young horses. An enthusiast of nutritionist Dr. Lon D. Lewis and his book *Feeding and Care of the Horse*, Llewellyn highly recommends the text for neophyte horsepersons.

ANSWER: A good nutrition programme should consist of correctly balanced nutrients geared in amount to the age and body weight of the horse.

Each day, a weanling should be fed an amount equal to three per cent of his body weight. This feed should be one-half roughage and one-half concentrate; that is one and one-half pounds per hundred-weight in roughage and one and one-half pounds per hundred-weight in grain. For example: a six hundred pound weanling should be fed nine pounds of roughage (hay and / or pasture) and nine pounds of concentrate (grain).

A yearling should be fed an amount equal to two and one-half per cent of his body weight. This feed should be only one-half to one pound per hundred-weight in grain because the horse's growth rate has slowed considerably; hence, there is a corresponding decrease in his nutritional requirements.

Nutrients: Nutrients for the young horse in order of importance and amount needed are: water, those needed for the production of energy (carbohydrates, proteins or fats), protein, calcium, phosphorus, vitamin A, salt, and selenium.

First, it is important to make sure that there is enough water and feed to satisfy the horse's energy needs. Secondly, ensure that the ration contains sufficient quantities of other nutrients to meet the horse's requirements.

Nutrients Often Fed in Incorrect Amounts: The percentage levels of *protein, calcium* and *phosphorous* are often imbalanced in daily feeding programmes.

What Are the Correct Amounts? The percentage of these nutrients (protein, calcium, phosphorous) that is required in the total air dry ration (hay, grain) is:

Weanlings:		*Yearlings:*	
Protein	14.5%	Protein	12.0%
Calcium	0.65%	Calcium	0.50%
Phosphorous	0.45%	Phosphorous	0.35%

Analysis of Hay is Essential: Contrary to popular belief, it is not possible to tell just how nourishing hay is, by eye alone. Although it does, of course, give some indication, appearance can be deceptive.

It is essential to have the hay that is being fed to the young horses, analysed in order to determine the levels of protein, calcium and phosphorous present.

Hay samples from about ten bales of hay should be taken with the aid of a 'hay borer' which can be purchased from the local office of the provincial department of agriculture and food. Although a 'hay borer' is not essential, its use will result in a more accurate analysis.

The Two Major Problems: Osteochondritis and acquired contracted superficial flexor tendons are the two major problems caused by nutritional imbalances. Llewellyn uses the term, osteochondritis, rather than the word, epiphysitis, which is usually, but not correctly, used. The word, metaphysitis, could also be used as it is the metaphysis (a zone of spongy bone between the epiphysis where growth of the long bone occurs) which actually becomes inflamed, rather than the epiphysis. The use of the term, osteochondritis, avoids both the error and the confusion.

What is Osteochondritis? Bones grow from growth plates which are situated at the ends of the bones (metaphysis). First, cartilage is pro-

46

duced by these growth plates and then this cartilage is converted into bone. Osteochondritis occurs when problems develop in the change over of cartilage to bone causing swelling which in turn results in abnormalities of the bone development.

Examples of Osteochondritis:

• Enlarged Fetlock and Knee Joints
• Open Knees: Open knees occur when swelling just above the carpal joints (knees) gives these joints a 'dished-in' appearance in front.
• Bone Cysts: Bone cysts, most common in the stifle, are actual holes in the bones.
• Osteochondritis Dissecans: Osteochondritis dissecans occurs most commonly in the stifle, shoulder and hock. It is a condition in which a piece of loose cartilage and bone 'lifts off' the underlying bone in a joint and produces lameness and swelling of that joint.
• Wobbler Syndrome: Wobbler syndrome, which involves incoordination of the back legs, may occur as a result of osteochondritis creating problems in the vertebrae and neck. As well, because of the improper growth of bone, a narrowing of the spinal canal may be produced – an abnormality which also results in wobbles.

What Are Acquired Contracted Superficial Flexor Tendons? There is still some discussion as to what causes contracted tendons but the more commonly held belief is that this condition occurs when the bones grow more rapidly than the tendons. The pasterns become more nearly vertical than normal and in severe cases may knuckle forward at the fetlock joint.

Acquired contracted superficial flexor tendons usually result from trying to fatten up a foal that has previously been undernourished.

Warning Sign of Either Major Problem: Any swelling around the joints particularly those of the fetlock and knee indicates a potential problem. 'Hourglass' fetlocks are the most common and 'open' knees the

47

second. Bog spavin is another indication that there is a problem.

Prognosis: If the diet is correctly balanced and the amount the affected youngsters are being given is cut back and if stall rest is given if prescribed, complete recovery may result. In certain instances surgery is necessary. Sometimes, euthanasia is the only answer.

A Final Word of Warning: Correctly balance the nutrients that your horse is receiving and do not feed too much. The calcium to phosphorous ration should be within the acceptable range of one to one, to three to one and the amount of protein should not grossly exceed the minimum requirement.

Do remember that it is possible to kill your horse with 'kindness'.

High Protein May Calm Your Horse

QUESTION: How do you feed a 'hot' show horse so that he looks good but doesn't feel too high?

EXPERT: Dr. John Burton (see Chapter 3, Question 1).

ANSWER: This is a very difficult question to answer because so many factors may influence a horse's behaviour while he is performing in a show – feed, the level of difficulty (is he being over-faced?), training, rider abilities, level of fitness, soundness, and surroundings to mention but a few. You ask, however, about feed ...

Burton suggests that the basis of your feeding programme should be a high forage intake; that is, hay or, if it is available, pasture. Because your horse is a show horse you will not want him to have a distended abdomen or 'hay belly', but *good quality* forage (hay or pasture) should make your horse feel and behave better. (Poor quality hay, with its higher fibre content, may cause a 'hay belly' to develop.)

Burton recommends a forage intake of a *minimum* of one per cent body weight. If your horse weighs twelve hundred pounds, then one per cent of his body weight would be twelve pounds of dry matter or fourteen pounds on an 'as fed' basis. ('As fed' takes into account the amount of moisture in the feed. In hay the percentage of moisture would be somewhere between twelve to fourteen per cent, thus your dry matter figure of twelve pounds should be increased to fourteen pounds to allow for the twelve to fourteen per cent moisture content.)

The *maximum* daily ration can go as high as 1.8 per cent of body weight; that is, about twenty-two pounds of dry matter or, on an 'as fed' basis, twenty-four pounds or approximately one half of a bale of hay.

If the hay is of good quality, it will contain ten to twelve per cent protein and thirty-eight to forty-one per cent fibre. Much higher quality hay may contain fourteen to sixteen per cent protein if it is first cut and as high as sixteen to eighteen per cent protein if it is second cut with a correspondingly lower fibre content.

Because of these protein levels which are found in good quality hay, if it is good quality you are feeding, the protein level of the grain will not *need* to be above ten per cent; however, you may *want* it to be! According to Burton, in other species of animals research indicates that a high level of protein particularly containing the amino acid, *tryptophan*, can actually have a sedative effect. In both pigs and poultry high levels of tryptophan intake have been shown to eliminate some hyperactivity but whether or not tryptophan has the same effect in horses, has not yet been thoroughly researched and documented. There is however, some anecdotal or unpublished evidence that it does indeed have a quietening effect on horses as well.

Burton suggests soybean meal which has a very high protein level of from forty to fifty per cent as being a good choice for a high protein supplement.

For the twelve hundred pound horse that is being *worked regularly* and *pushed reasonably hard*, Burton suggests one of the following feeds. On an 'as fed' basis the maximum intake of feed (forage and concentrates) would be thirty-five pounds which would consist of:

Option One:
• twenty pounds of hay and / or pasture
• thirteen pounds of a low protein concentrate such as straight western oats or a low protein commercial grain mix. Try to keep within a ten to twelve per cent range with ten per cent being better than twelve per cent for this particular diet because of the addition of soybean meal.)
• two pounds of soybean meal (between one and two pounds)

Option Two:
• twenty-five pounds of hay and / or pasture
• eight pounds of a low protein concentrate (as above)
• two pounds of soybean meal (between one and two pounds).

Such a daily diet would exceed the protein requirements of the twelve hundred pound horse but it should limit or lower the energy level.

Burton concludes on this subject, 'I think one would have to "play" with these ratios with the individual horse to see whether or not there was a level that would keep him sharp and looking good but not overactive.'

A Word of Warning: Nitrogen in the protein that is not used will be removed as urea in the urine. When urea combines with the bacteria ever present in a stall, potentially damaging ammonia results. Stable Boy or lime helps eliminate bacteria and *good ventilation* is crucial to protect the horse's respiratory tract.

How Long does Energy Stay in a Horse's System?

QUESTION: How long does the energy supplied by feed stay in a horse's system?

EXPERT: Dr. John Burton (see Chapter 3, Question 1).

ANSWER: Generally the energy that is in feed will last less than twenty-four hours – usually anywhere from a minimum of four to six hours to a maximum of twelve to sixteen hours.

(It is interesting to note that protein, on the other hand, might last for years in the body. When it is consumed in a feed, protein is broken down into its constituent amino acids in the intestines and stomach and absorbed into the body. Some of these amino acids are incorporated into body proteins which might last for years.)

A New Development – Extruded Feed

QUESTION: Martin Feed Mills has been advertising an extruded feed for a long time. Now other feed companies have started to advertise it too. What exactly *is* extruded feed? How is it different from feed pellets? Why are more companies starting to carry it? Is it better for horses?

I know it's important to give horses the best feed possible. Should I be feeding extruded feed?

Your answer will help others besides myself.

EXPERTS: Two experts were called upon to answer these questions about extruded feed – Bill Hatch and Wayne Arndt. Both are employees of Martin Feed Mills Limited of Elmira, Ontario.

Hatch is the company's horse feed specialist. Part of his responsibility involves visiting horse establishments to discuss their horses' feed requirements, introducing them to Martin's extruded feed and the particular types which most suit the age and work load of their horses and returning at a later date to evaluate the horses' progress and answer any questions the customers might have concerning the feed.

Hatch is not new to the feed industry. Prior to joining Martin

Feed Mills in 1983, he had spent twenty-six years at Master Feeds in Guelph.

His experience serves him well. He understands nutrition, has countless contacts in the industry and has developed a reputation for being a personable person and one to whom it is easy to talk.

Hatch himself has a farm background. As well, he is a horse owner and a former breeder. All in all, he has become a well-known personality in almost all segments of the horse industry and is frequently called upon to be a guest speaker at various equine seminars.

Arndt is the plant manager at Martin Feed Mills and is in charge of the machinery known as an 'extruder' and, as well, oversees the actual extrusion process.

ANSWER: You mention that you have seen advertisements for Martin's extruded feed for 'some time' and, indeed, Martin Feed Mills has been developing and improving its extruded feed for the past seven years. It was the first company in North America to develop and carry extruded feed for horses. Now, other companies, recognizing the value of extrusion in equine feeds, have also started to produce extruded feeds.

The story behind Martin Feed Mill's extruded feed is rather interesting. A request for extruded feed came from Armstrong Brothers when Jim Hammond, one of the employees, suggested that the Elmira company be contacted to produce an extruded feed that might help the Standardbred farm in its fight to reduce the incidence of colic fatalities among the young stock who were fed 'free-choice'. The feed mill obliged and for about five years, Martin Feed was making extruded feed exclusively for Armstrong Brothers.

When Hatch joined Martin Feed Mills, he urged the company to pursue the idea of making and developing a whole line of extruded feed for equines rather than just producing another line of 'me-too-type' sweet feeds. Interestingly enough, Hatch had already been enthusiastic about extruded feed before joining Martin.

It was decided by Martin Feed Mills to contact Dr. Harold Hintz, a very respected researcher at New York State's Cornell University.

Coincidentally, Hintz had already considered the idea of extrusion and readily agreed to do a United States study of various feeds, (extruded included) which were to be sent to him by Martin Feeds. The test study Hintz conducted convinced him that the idea of extruded feed should be pursued. Thus Martin Feed Mills' line of extruded feed was 'born'.

The company developed its product based on all of the latest nutritional information supplied by, and in consultation with, Hintz. Even today, Martin Feeds continues to change its formulas periodically to meet the new demands of nutritional requirements as they are discovered by the most recent research. Copper and zinc have been increased to promote stronger bone growth, for example, and biotin has been added to promote better hoof condition.

What Is Extruded Feed and How Is It Made? Extruded feed is the end product of a mash that has been run through an extruder. The mash, of course, is composed of all the necessary ingredients suitable for an equine feed. According to Arndt, a more simple name for an extruder might be 'an industrial-style pressure cooker'.

The extruder is made up of rotating screws and die plates. The screws do two things: they transport the product through the extruder and, depending on the pitch, can increase the shear rate to get more 'cook' on the product as it is travels through. The 'shear rate' is the friction that is built up by allowing the product to move rapidly through the extruder and then confining it into a smaller space. This confinement of a large volume in a small space puts a very high pressure on the product. It is the relationship between the friction which results from compressing the mash and the interjection of steam, that causes the cooking.

As the specially formulated mash moves through the extruder, it suddenly is squeezed through a die plate and released to atmospheric pressure which is, of course, less than the pressure inside the extruder. This decrease of pressure allows the 'bun' or piece of product to rapidly expand, thus entrapping air within, in the process. The end product is referred to as 'extruded kibble', which might be likened in processing method to some of our breakfast cereals.

Because extremely high temperatures can destroy nutrients, control over how long the product stays in the extruder is strictly monitored. Laboratory analysis of both the pre-mix and the finished product is carried on routinely to ensure that the nutritional quality of the feed is as it should be.

How Is It Different From Pellets? Pelleted feed is different in that the mash is heated to a consistent temperature and moisture content and then subjected to pressure which forms it into a pellet. To quote Arndt, 'All that does is eliminate the dust.'

Is Extruded Feed Better for Horses Than Ordinary Feed? You ask why other companies are starting to carry extruded feed and whether it is better for horses. The answer to the second question might answer the first for you.

Studies by nutritionists in the United States have concluded that there are several benefits to extrusion:

• First of all, researchers at Cornell University have discovered that because a horse has to chew 'extruded kibble', he eats it much more slowly than he eats pellets or grain mixtures – a fact which, according to Hintz, may cause fewer digestive problems.
• Secondly, extrusion makes the carbohydrates, proteins and many of the other nutrients more readily available to be digested; thus the enzymes present in a horse's digestive tract need to spend less time breaking the feed down. The results of this increased digestibility are twofold: it is easier *on* the horse's digestive system and thus again reduces the chance of colic; it is much more available *to* his digestive system so that a horse takes in more nutrition with less feed.
• Thirdly, the extremely high temperatures at which extruded feed is cooked destroy the biological activity of enzymes of toxic protein.
• Fourthly, extrusion acts as a product pasturizer and produces a product of excellent bacteriological status; hence, the shelf life of extruded feed is longer than that of other types of feed.
• Fifthly, due to the increased digestive availability of the nutrients,

feed intake of the individual horse may be reduced by twenty percent; in other words, a horse requires less feed because he gets more out of what he is eating.

• The feeding process is made considerably easier because the extruded feed contains all the necessary nutrition; in short, there is no need for supplements.

There are six different rations: Martin Perfect Start Foal Ration / Grass, Martin Classic Horse Cubes, Martin Top Performance Horse Ration, Martin Happy Trails, Martin Twenty-Five Per Cent Supplement and finally, Martin Brood Mare Ration.

(Hatch stresses that the type of ration you buy should be influenced by the quality of hay you are feeding.)

• Lastly, horses who eat extruded feed have cleaner teeth with fewer sharp points. There is therefore less of a need for teeth to be floated.

There are three disadvantages to extruded feed:

• Firstly, extruded feed costs more; however, as you need to feed less, the cost factor becomes negligible.

• Secondly, extruded feed is lighter than sweetfeed and pellets and thus has a greater volume per pound. As a result, storage can sometimes pose a problem.

• Thirdly, at first some horses do not find the extruded kibble palatable as the texture is very different than that to which they are accustomed. According to Hatch this problem is soon overcome as the horse becomes more used to the product. He suggests feeding small quantities at first until the horse has adjusted to the difference.

Extruded Feed and Colic: According to Dr. Terry Morley, the resident veterinarian at Armstrong Brothers, 'Feeding Martin's, has virtually eliminated colic.' Considering that colic is listed as the 'number one' cause of death in horses, that statement carries considerable impact.

Extruded feed has become most popular within the Standardbred industry, but increasingly more and more show and pleasure riding stables are turning towards the feed. Olympic rider, Hugh Graham, and Martin Feed Mills have a sponsorship agreement in which the company provides all of the feed for Graham's Grand Prix horses. It is a great advertisement for the Elmira-based company that Graham has already won a World Cup Qualifier on one of his Martin-fed horses.

Considering the fact that people are often reluctant to change to a new product especially if they are quite happy with what they already have, it is indeed a coup for Martin's that other companies have started to produce extruded feed themselves. If the old adage, 'Imitation is the most sincere form of flattery.' is true, then Martin Feed Mills might well be pleased.

One equine feed specialist in the United States has declared, '... I think that in ten years, extrusion is going to be the main method of processing horse feed.'

4. STABLING / PASTURE / WORK AREA / FENCING / JUMPS

The right setting and facilities can increase your riding pleasure.

Building Your Own Stable

QUESTION: A number of people who have moved out into the country have asked me questions about barns they are in the process of building. Having gone through the process more than once myself, I know there are a great many important decisions that have to be made *before* one even begins.

Some of the questions you need to ask yourself are: What kind of stable do you want? How large do you plan to make each stall? How many stalls will you build? What material will you use? How many windows will you include? Where will the hay and straw be stored?

Factors which won't yet have even entered into your mind will suddenly become 'life and death' issues in importance. To add to the difficulty, is the fact that as with many choices in life, there are pros and cons to each which will have to be weighed carefully.

EXPERT: A graduate of the Ontario Agricultural College in the late sixties, Gary Van Bolderen, Vice President of Agrispan Ltd., has over twenty years of experience in farm building construction. A charter member of the Canadian Farm Builders' Association, Van Bolderen has been President twice and was the first person to be honoured as 'Member of the Year'. He has also won several 'Builder of the Year' awards over the years for different categories of building.

Van Bolderen has served on several committees formed to deal with such pertinent issues as business ethics, structural standards, etc. At present, along with Dr. Russ Willoughby of the Equine Research Centre in Guelph, he is involved with a committee formed to deal with the importance of improving ventilation in stables.

Van Bolderen has helped design and construct barns for such clients as Sam-Son Farms, Armstrong Bros. Company, Moffat Dunlop, Morgan Firestone and Lorraine Stubbs.

Because of the amount of repeat business he is called on to do and the number of customer referrals he receives, for the last ten years Van Bolderen has been able to concentrate on barns for horses exclusively.

ANSWER:
Location of Stable:

• Always take the wind direction into account when you are choosing the location of your stable or you will find that a barn odour is the permanent aroma in your home. In Southern Ontario for example, because the prevailing winds are Westerlies, it is best not to build the barn to the northwest of the house.
• Try to build a fair distance from the house – at least a minimum of one hundred feet and considerably further if possible.
• For drainage purposes, make sure that the barn is six inches to eight inches higher than the surrounding area.
• For the sake of you and your neighbours do try to pile the manure out of sight and some distance from the buildings in order to discourage flies as well as for aesthetic reasons.

Basic Stable Designs:

1) *Two-storey:* This barn has stalls in the lower level and storage space in the second storey. The advantages to the design are obvious:
• Storage is very handy.
• It tends to be tidier looking inside than the one-storey because only the necessary hay and straw is dropped through from above; hence, no large stacks of bales are in sight.
• Generally it is a warmer barn than the one-storey because the hay and straw stored above help to insulate.

There are two basic types of two-storey barns: the *hip roof* and the *gable roof.* The only difference between the two is in the actual shape of the roof.

A two-storey hip roof design stable with a wood frame and coloured steel siding, under construction.

a. *Hip Roof:* The advantages to this design are:
- It has more storage space than the two-storey gable roof.
- It has 'an old country look' about it that many find appealing.

The disadvantages are:
- It is the more complicated to build of the two different types of two-storey barns.
- It is more costly.

b. *Gable Roof:* The advantage to this style is:
- It is less expensive than the hip roof to build.

The disadvantage is:
- Depending on its structure, it has less storage than the hip roof stable.

2) *One-storey:* This stable has no upper level. Usually it has a gable roof design but it may have a one-way sloping roof. Storage must

A one-storey gable roof design stable with a wood frame and wooden siding (cedar board and batten).

either be on the ground floor or in a separate building. The advantages of this design are:

• It is the cheapest of the three designs.
• If storage is separate, there is less danger of fire.
• If there is less of a fire hazard, insurance is less costly.
• The structure does not impede the view to the same extent that a two-storey barn does.

3) *Other:* Any feasible design that a customer has in mind will be erected. Some people like combinations of three designs, perhaps including a garage.

By-laws vary according to the area. Consult the local municipality or deal with a knowledgeable builder for rules concerning: number of exits, strength of building, placement of barn, etc.

Kinds of Materials:

• Steel Frame with Steel Siding: This is the most durable combination and with the exception of concrete block (described below), the least likely to catch on fire. No maintenance is necessary.

• Wood Frame with Steel Siding: This combination is by far the most popular. It is cheaper than steel frame with steel siding, and wood frame with wood siding. If galvanized steel (plain metal colour) is used, it costs even less but it is not as attractive as the coloured steel siding. Maintenance is not necessary.

• Wood Frame with Wood Siding: This combination can be made to look very rustic; however, wooden buildings usually require a fair amount of maintenance.

• Concrete Block: As a building material, concrete blocks are less of a fire hazard. Unfortunately, they tend to be cold and damp, difficult to insulate and more dangerous to horses from an injuries in the stall, point of view.

Building for the Canadian Climate:

• Walls: These should have a minimum of R20 inches of fibreglass or the equivalent insulation. There must also be a vapour barrier for moisture on the warm side (in winter) of the insulation.

• Ceiling: It must have R20 insulation unless it is a two-storey structure. A vapour barrier should be added as with the walls.

• Stable Doors:
   a. *Swinging:* Swinging doors that open inward to the stable are excellent in a Canadian winter because there is no problem with ice and snow. Swinging doors also tend to be more weatherproof than sliding.
   Dutch swinging doors are good for ventilation purposes during our hot Canadian summers.
   b. *Overhead:* Overhead garage doors are impractical in a horse barn as they are a type of door that cannot be insulated well.
   c. *Sliding:* Sliding doors have the advantage that they cannot swing shut on a horse as he passes through the opening. They also may be left partially open to ventilate the barn.

• Windows: A good window size is forty-eight inches by thirty-two inches – a size which allows plenty of light and air. If the windows are

63

too large, too much heat is lost in the winter and too much direct sunlight can add unwanted heat in the summer.

Sliding windows have the advantage over windows that open upwards because sliding windows are easier to open and to be protected.

A window in each stall is a good 'rule of thumb' to add light and ventilation and an interest diversion for the stall's occupant.

• Ventilation: Airborne particles that move around the interior of a stable are cited by researchers as the leading cause of the spreading of equine respiratory diseases. Keeping that thought in mind, it certainly makes sense to consider having a ventilation system installed in your stable when it is being built. (If you wait until your building is completed, installation becomes more difficult and, as a result, more expensive.)

Horses tend to be agriculturally unique in that they are stabled in large areas with few animals per square foot. The problem in horse stable ventilation, therefore, is too much moisture rather than too much heat. Because a low temperature does not carry much moisture, the moisture condenses on the walls and ceilings. If too much air is taken out of the building in order to get rid of the moisture, the barn becomes too cold – again, because there are insufficient animals to naturally replenish the heat. Thus, the general rule in equine barns is to add some kind of supplementary heat, governed by a thermostat which 'kicks in' during the worst parts of winter.

In new buildings, because they tend to be airtight, an inlet system to allow air to enter the building is necessary and this inlet system has to be coupled with exhaust fans to allow the air out. The air within a stable needs to be replaced on an ongoing basis.

Stalls:

• Dimensions: A good sized box stall is twelve feet by twelve feet. Twelve feet by ten feet is also acceptable. Movable partitions are a good idea in case you ever need a foaling stall.

A straight aisle between the stalls with a minimum width of nine feet is practical for mucking out and leading horses in and out of the stable. As well, this width allows room for a tractor to be driven

64

through if that is how you plan to move manure out of the stable.

• Walls: The walls between stalls should be tongue in groove. Some people prefer walls to within one foot of the top because they feel that: horses have less chance to play with each other; germs are less likely to be passed from one horse to another; and bad habits are less likely to be copied when fewer horses can be seen.

Other people prefer walls halfway up with bars or mesh the rest of the way. They feel that: it is friendlier; and the horses are less likely to become bored.

• Bars Versus Wire Mesh: Bars are easier to clean. As well, supposedly horses are less likely to crib because the bars are attached to metal which is fixed to the top of the first board. On the other hand, wire mesh is easier to install. One problem with it however, is that it stretches and thus becomes dangerous.

• Stall Doors: The door openings should be four feet.

a. *Solid Swing Doors:* These are the cheapest to install. One disadvantage is the fact that they take up aisle space when open.

b. *Dutch Swing Doors:* These door are divided into two parts and swing out. If the top half is left open, the horse can put his head out of the stall and look around. Some people like to walk into a stable and see the horses less confined because they feel it is more interesting for the horses and thus more relaxing. It's true. Horses really like to be able to put their heads over a lower door and look around to see what is going on in the stable.

Three disadvantages to this style are: the swinging doors take up aisle space; there are two latches to open; and some horses may reach out and try to bite another horse who is walking down the aisle. If this happens, some horses develop the dangerous habit of rushing down the aisle.

c. *Sliding Doors:* These doors slide on rollers suspended from hangars and because of the quantity of hardware needed are more expensive per door than the Dutch door style.

The advantages of overhead sliding doors are: they do not take up aisle space when open; and horses are less likely to hurt themselves when entering or leaving their stalls.

These doors should never be installed so that they slide on the inside of the stall because if a horse becomes cast against the door it is next to impossible to slide the door open to help the him out of his predicament.

The door should be installed so that it slides on the outside of the stall. Unfortunately, it is then very awkward to hang saddle racks and / or halter hooks on the stall wall.

• Hardware: All hardware should be galvanized or prepainted. Preferably the hardware should be simple to operate but if used on Dutch doors it should be foolproof. Horses are very good escape artists. (I once saw one of my horses calmly walk down my driveway and out onto the road after he let himself out of his stall. Needless to say, I was absolutely horror-stricken!)

Finally, make sure that none of the hardware has sharp edges.

Tack Rooms: One stall may be used as a tack room. The floor may be concrete (washable) or wood (warmer) or asphalt. Windows may be trimmed, lowered for a view and also enlarged, if desired. Base board may be added. Cupboards may be installed and a bulletin board hung.

Wash Areas and Washroom: In a small barn, a wash area is not usually added although it is a very helpful luxury addition. If you install one, avoid a stone dust floor.

A washroom for hired help, for visitors and / or for boarders (should you decide to have any) is a good idea to give you some measure of privacy in your home. It is also more convenient for you, yourself.

Flooring in the Stalls:
• Stone Dust: Often referred to as screenings, stone dust packs like chips so that although the surface is hard it is also rough; hence the horses are not likely to slip. Because it is porous, urine does not remain on the surface, but instead, soaks through. It is very easy and very inexpensive to install. It has two disadvantages:

    a. After some time it packs down and must be levelled out

    b. Any horse that tends to paw in his stall will soon have the screenings and the bedding mixed in together and the surface very uneven.

• Concrete: This substance is easy to keep clean but it has several disadvantages:

a. It does not drain; therefore urine tends to lie on the surface

b. Because it is so hard it can be a problem for the horses' feet and legs. Horses can easily slip on its smooth surface.

The answers to these disadvantages are, of course:

a. To protect the horse by a covering material such as stall mats or, preferably, lots and lots of bedding

b. To texture the surface to lessen its slipperyness.

• Clay: This substance is falling out of favour. It tends to seal up after a while and hence develops some of the disadvantages of stone dust and concrete.

• Wood: Wooden floors are fairly expensive and no longer very popular. Some people install them with gravel underneath for drainage purposes but even so the wood holds moisture and eventually becomes smelly and rotten. Wooden floors should be replaced periodically.

• Asphalt: Although this substance is difficult to install especially after the stalls are in, it does have several advantages over concrete:

a. It is less slippery.

b. It is less hard and thus easier on the horses' feet and legs.

c. It is cheaper.

A coarse asphalt such as HL8 or HL10 is better for a stable than a fine one such as HL4 which is usually used in driveways.

Flooring in the Aisles:

• Stone Dust: It is very difficult to keep the aisle looking neat and tidy.

• Concrete: In the aisle, concrete can be extremely slippery particularly if wet or icy; therefore it should be textured if it is selected.

• Clay: It is very difficult to keep the aisle looking neat and tidy.

• Asphalt: If too finely made, it leaves hoofprints which look untidy and become dirt and dust traps.

• Unilock or 'Pavers': Interlocking stone has become the most popular of all aisle floorings. Although it is the most costly of the alternatives and quite hard to keep clean, it is very safe in that it is not slippery. As well, it is extremely attractive.

Watering Systems:
• Automatic: If you decide to have automatic watering bowls, be aware that there are two different types:
    a. *Float:* Operating on the same principle as a toilet bowl, float bowls refill as the horse lowers the water level.
    b. *Paddle:* When the horse pushes the paddle, water enters the bowl. One disadvantage is that a mischievous horse can flood his stall if he decides to play with the paddle.
• Watering by Hand: Should you decide to water by hand, buy large, smooth-surface buckets. Some of the flexible rubber ones are very hard to clean because the rubber roughens and traps dirt and debris. Avoid cheap metal buckets which will lose their shape and tear because the resulting jagged edges can easily cut the horses' mouths.

Some people prefer automatic watering bowls because they like to know that the horses are never without water. Such a watering system also eliminates a considerable amount of strenuous, time-consuming work.

Others prefer to hand water because it thus becomes possible to keep track of exactly how much water a horse is drinking. (Remember, one of the first things a sick horse does is stop drinking.) As well, buckets are easier to clean than are permanently mounted water bowls.

One way to reduce the lifting and carrying of water buckets should you decide on the hand water method is to run a pipe with a tap into each stall. You can stand and check your horse over visually as you wait for the bucket to fill.

Please note: Whichever system you choose, all water containers should be cleaned thoroughly and regularly both for hygenic reasons and, in the case of the automatic watering system, to prevent blockage of water flow.

68

Arenas: Any horse owners who have endured a Canadian winter will know just how invaluable an indoor riding arena can be. Those who are interested in dressage training should remember that the inside arena width should be a minimum of twenty metres.

Whatever your needs, do not compromise on the basics. If you cannot afford the right building, do not build the wrong one for less money.

Final Helpful Tips:
• Talk to people who are knowledgeable about stable buildings.
• Use common sense in making decisions.
• Don't try to save money by sacrificing certain extras which might well be worth the additional cost.
• Look at other barns and try to learn from the mistakes of others.
• Remember, no matter how good the building is, it is only as good as its manager. Good buildings can be spoilt by poor management.
• Your equine friends probably spend a great deal of time in the stable. Make their surroundings as safe and as comfortable as possible.

How to Stop your Horse from Chewing Wood

QUESTION: I have a Thoroughbred mare who started her life being trained for the racetrack and due to her breeding and early life is, to say the least, highly strung. She is a kind mare but has many bad habits like cribbing and swaying. The worst of these, however, is chewing. Any exposed piece of wood be it a fence post, gate, barn door or wall, vertical or horizontal falls prey to her teeth. A product like Cribbox is not very effective as it is designed to be applied in relatively small areas and needs constant re-application out-of-doors.

She is turned out for twelve hours a day having access to shelter and has hay in front of her twenty-four hours a day. She is worked from two to six hours a week depending on the season and is in relatively good shape. (I ride dressage.)

I do not believe I can cure her of a habit so long and well-established but she is destroying our barn and fencing. We have provided her with her own chewing post and wish to totally discourage her from chewing anything else. Is there any product that can be painted on doorjambs, walls, gates and other large areas of wood that would serve this purpose?

EXPERT: Highly respected horseman, Frank Leach, has been the farm manager at one of Canada's leading racing stables and breeding farms – Sam-Son Farms – since 1976.

Practically 'born in a stall' in Virginia into a family who worked with horses, Leach grew up riding show horses and galloping race horses. He travelled with the United States Olympic Team for eight years at the time when Bill Steinkraus and Frank Chapot were members. For four of those years, Leach was stable foreman. Later, after a sixteen-year-stint with the Firestones, Leach moved to Canada and began his work for the Samuels family.

Frank's wife, Terry, had ridden for the Dick Day Stables for ten years so Leach had known Day's son, Olympic rider and trainer for Sam-Son Farms, Jim Day, for some time. It has been a successful relationship all around. Although Frank originally looked after jumpers, hunters, brood mares, young stock and overflow Sam-Son Farm race horses, Leach presently is responsible for the brood mares only. What a collection of mares they are! When Leach first arrived at Sam-Son, No Class and Loudrangle were two-year-olds. Now Frank has seen them through motherhood.

It is perhaps the term 'motherhood' and the comment, 'You never know everything,' that sums up Leach's attitude to horses.

ANSWER: Chewing wood and even worse, the act of cribbing, can be at best, aggravating and at worst, both destructive and costly. You are certainly not alone in your concern, nor in your attempts to curb such an undesirable habit.

The fundamental concept on which your efforts must be based is that of making it unpleasant for your horse to continue to chew on fence posts, gates, barn doors or walls.

With so many different horses passing through his care at Sam-Son Farms, Frank Leach has encountered problems of all types. Chewing and cribbing are fairly prevalent habits.

Basically, Leach uses three methods to make these habits unpleasant for the offenders:

• The first of these involves a liquid disinfectant known as Creolin. Horses find it very unpalatable and therefore avoid chewing surfaces brushed with it. In the stalls Creolin is used by itself. In the paddocks it is mixed with black paint to give the Sam-Son Farms fencing its own distinctive colour. During the winter when the mares and young horses are kept in smaller paddocks, the fences are repainted frequently as the slightly more confined areas seem to make the horses more inclined to 'attack' the fences.

• The second method employed by Leach to curtail chewing is one suggested several years ago by Sam-Son trainer Jim Day. Some of the fences are topped with one, two or three strands of a clothes-line type wire which is stapled to the top of the planks in each panel. Apparently the horses are reluctant to bite into the wire. Consequently this method is effective.

• A third solution used by Leach is that of mild shock treatment. A wire is connected to a six volt or twelve volt battery and strung out on any surfaces the horses are likely to chew. Outside, in the paddocks where retirees who are cribbers are kept, this wire is laid along the top of the fence. If the horses go to bite or chew, the mild shock they receive is sufficient to keep them away from the fence, but not so strong that it injures them.

For hardened chewers and cribbers, Leach suggests gentle shock treatment in the stalls as well. Wire may be placed along the edge at the bottom of the bars and zigzagged anywhere a horse might be inclined to chew. Leach cautions that the shock must not be strong and again recommends a six or twelve volt battery.

A personal note: For those people with new stables which they are

71

thinking of painting or staining, a product known as Solignum, a stain which contains creosote, is also supposed to be very effective as far as its unpalatability is concerned.

The Perfect Riding Ring
Footing and Appearance

QUESTION: We are considering building a riding ring on our farm. We have a fairly level site picked out with clay / loam soil. We need suggestions for:
- Drainage
- How deep to take off topsoil
- What size
- What type of fill for first level
- How many layers of what type of material
- Does it need packing between layers
- What type of edge – grass – wood, etc.
- Best footing and maintenance for all year round use
- Fencing.

Perhaps you could look into this with *specific* information including typical costs.

It will help a great number of riders who do not have the luxury of an indoor arena.

EXPERT: Known for years as a highly successful international course designer, Robert Jolicoeur has, for some time now, been constructing many of the rings that hold these jumping courses. Outdoor riding areas that stand up exceptionally well in even the most inclement weather are in great demand. Jolicoeur is supplying that demand.

From the ages of nineteen to twenty-one, Jolicoeur worked with horses on the east coast of the United States. On his return to Montreal, he was appalled by the 'terrible courses' he encountered as a rider. After offering to help 'move the jumps around a bit' at numerous shows he eventually began receiving requests to officially design courses.

Involvement with the Olympics brought recognition from the United States as well as Canada and resulted in designing courses for most of the big shows from the Florida circuit to Madison Square Gardens to Sydney, Australia.

This course designer success made him realize that, 'The rings were just terrible!' As a result, he went back to school and studied landscape architecture for four years. His main thought was the footing at show grounds and how to make improvements.

For ten years now, Jolicoeur has operated Sopra Co. which has as one of its main businesses the design and construction of outdoor riding rings. He has become so successful that once again, his work is in demand internationally.

ANSWER: First of all, Jolicoeur cautions that there is no one 'recipe' that works for every ring location. Factors such as area, site, soil, amount of rain and sun, availability of materials – all play an important role in properly developing a riding ring. Jolicoeur's aim is to have a ring in which one can ride in the afternoon even if the ring has been thoroughly rained on in the morning. (Wouldn't that be wonderful?)

His philosophy in ring construction is to go slowly and carefully and make sure every step is done correctly, To quote Jolicoeur, 'You don't build a ring in one week!'

Because each situation is unique, it is impossible for him to give one 'recipe' for everyone, but Jolicoeur does outline principles or guidelines which, if followed, should be tremendously beneficial to the 'do-it-yourselfers' as many of us have to be.

Principles:

• Size: The first principle to consider is *size* of the ring and to make a decision here you have to consider several factors: What use is planned for this ring? What type of horse will be ridden in it? Which type of rider will use it? Are horse shows part of the ring's future?

A ring large enough for two or three groups to work in with

perhaps fences in the middle and hacking on the outside, should be about one hundred and fifty feet by three hundred feet.

On the other hand, if lessons to beginners are going to be given, that open space can be a little intimidating. As well, it is little too difficult for a coach to be heard across such a size; therefore, one of one hundred and twenty-five feet by two hundred and fifty feet might be more appropriate.

Sizes of one hundred feet by two hundred feet or even one hundred feet by two hundred and twenty-five feet are, according to Jolicoeur, just a little too small for a good jumping course to be set up. For dressage, one hundred and fifty feet by three hundred feet is a good size but not big enough for a recognized dressage show which should have a ring width of two hundred feet.

His first advice then is to decide on size requirements before you construct your ring or you might find you can not use it for what you intended.

• Surface: The second principle to consider is *surface*. The ring must have a crown or a slope to it because if it is perfectly flat the water will just sit on it. A one per cent slope would be the maximum desired as more of a slope would show up in the riding. A one per cent slope would only be visible to the naked eye if buildings are nearby to give perspective. Less than a one-half per cent slope will not drain.

A one per cent slope on one hundred feet means there is a gradual descent of one foot. If you crown from the middle of the ring, the one per cent slope would mean a six to nine inch slope from the middle to the sides of the ring.

Ideally the area should have the crown in the middle of the short side so that the water does not have to travel too far in the ring; for example, in a ring one hundred and fifty feet by three hundred feet the crown would be in the middle of the short side and just over three hundred feet long. Thus the water only has to travel seventy-five feet instead of the one hundred and fifty feet it would have to travel if the crown was in the middle of the long side.

74

Remember: Water runs down. The shorter a distance the water has to travel in the ring, the faster the ring will dry.

• Ring Water the Only Water: Another principle to keep in mind is that the *only water the ring should receive is its own*. It should not collect water from any hillsides. Jolicoeur cites Scottsdale as an example of the importance of this principle. With an eleven million dollar expenditure, six rings look like lakes because they are not only collecting water from roofs of adjacent buildings, but also from ground up to half a mile away.

Remember: The ring must be higher than its surroundings. Not recommended by Jolicoeur, but mentioned, are drainage pipes. Many people feel such pipes are a good idea but Jolicoeur explains that if one puts a drainage pipe three to four feet in the ground as farmers sometimes do for agricultural purposes, the drainage is too slow a process for riding purposes. It would take days for such a system to dry a really wet ring. Drainage pipes set in crushed stone at only a two foot depth are better than the aforementioned, but Jolicoeur prefers this method for a grass ring.

• Seal the Surface: The next principle to follow is to *seal the surface*. Clay, if undisturbed, seals by its very nature. Water tends to run off of it if there is a slope but, as soon as clay has been disturbed to any great depth, it takes years before it comes together or seals again. Meanwhile surface water sinks to the depth the clay has been shifted.

Jolicoeur's advice regarding clay is to try to stay with the natural layout of the land. To quote Jolicoeur, 'The less you disturb your clay, the better!' If you have to move clay, do it only six inches at a time, water it and then really pack it with heavy equipment. Make sure there is no air in it because if there is, the clay will hold water too.

The importance of disturbing clay as little as possible is so significant that Jolicoeur even suggests changing the position of the crown in the ring if it means the clay will be moved less; for example,

75

have the crown across one-third instead of across the halfway mark if that suits the natural lay of the land more. Jolicoeur recommends a road grader rather than a bulldozer for grading the ring.

Once the ring has been crowned, wait a little and let the water do its work or roll it to get it perfectly well packed. After that, it is ready for a layer of material.

• Minimal Additional Surface: The surface material should be added sparingly.

a. Jolicoeur suggests that *stone dust* be spread on this clay surface to a depth of one inch. At this point he recommends that you may start to ride on it. The surface will probably come up quite hard. It will be 'harsh' on the horses' feet and it will be dusty as well but the stone dust will mix with the clay and therefore shift less than it would if it remained a separate layer on clay. Less shifting will make for safer footing.

If any corner seems to need it, add a load of stone dust. Sometimes up to two inches overall suits a particular surface, but start with only one inch and add more if needed.

b. After some time has passed, if this surface seems too hard, add about one inch of *coarse sand* that will pack a little. The sand should have no clay mixed in with it. If it has, it will be dusty on a dry day and 'shoe-pulling' on a wet one.

If after six months you decide you would like the footing deeper, add a little more but never add several inches at one time, You are charged by the load, so it does not cost any more to have the truck make a return trip at a later date.

What not to use: Jolicoeur advises against using material such as sawdust. It will either wash away or, because it keeps moisture in, cause a swamp.

• Minimize Dust: Any dirt ring will be a little dusty. To solve this problem there are two possible solutions:

a. Some people put a sprinkler system around their ring but one hundred and fifty feet by three hundred feet is quite a large area.

It would require not only a very good system but also an abundant water supply as it could be a drain on the well.

b. The best dust control, in Jolicoeur's opinion is a *light* coat of oil, but he stresses 'light'. If a thick layer is put down, excess oil will run off and end up in rivers where it creates problems very distressing to environmentalists.

• Ditch: A ditch with a five to ten per cent slope is necessary to carry off drainage, but it should be six to eight feet back from the fence to allow room for maintenance machinery such as lawn mowers. The ditch should be a nice 'gentle' gully as it will be much easier to maintain than a steep-sided one.

Finishing Touches:

• Fences: The type of fencing you will use will depend on what you are going to do with your ring. If you plan to use your outdoor riding area as a paddock, the fencing must be about four and one-half feet high.

Jolicoeur much prefers the area be used only as a riding ring. He favours a fairly low fence of three feet or even less. Such a height will not interfere with spectators and will make the ring look bigger.

He stresses the importance of low maintenance features and for this reason does not recommend that a fence be painted white. A white fence when it peels, has to be scraped before it can be repainted and thus represents a lot of work. He likes a stain or natural preservative.

Fences must be built solidly. If planks are used, two inches by six inches are the best size as they can withstand the weight of spectators.

Again, keeping maintenance in mind, the bottom plank or rail should be high enough that a machine can cut grass under it so that the fence area does not look untidy. As well, that space from the ground to the plank or rail allows equipment to scrape back dirt that gets displaced by horses working close to the fence line.

As a safety factor for riders' knees, etc., put planks or rails on the inside of the posts.

• Landscaping: Proper landscaping really adds to the appearance of a riding ring. Green grass and trees create an attractive setting for the brown of the ring. Because trees take such a long time to grow, it is a good idea to plant them as quickly as possible. Keep in mind the machinery that will be used for grass cutting and make sure that there is room for it to get between the trees and the fence.

Use trees as 'cover-ups'. Hide a busy street and cut down on the noise level at the same time. Camouflage an unattractive building with a tree grouping.

Apart from being attractive, trees can be beneficial in other ways. If a wind blows strongly from one side of the ring, plant trees such as spruce or pine as a buffer or shelter for the ring. Dust will blow around less and coaches will not have to shout as loudly.

A little pavilion built on the long side of the ring and about three feet above the ground will make a pleasant shelter for viewers. As well, if shows are to be held, the pavilion would make a good judges' booth.

If not made professionally, such a pavilion need not be expensive. With a little thought and effort your riding ring can end up looking like a showplace.

Cost: You ask about cost. As you can see, there are so many variables involved such as area, site, availability of materials, and so on, that an accurate price is impossible to give.

Jumps for a Home Schooling Course

QUESTION: I have just moved to a new country place and I want to school my young horse over fences. I don't have any jumping equipment yet, Before I get things set up there are some questions I would like to ask one of your experts. How do I organize a good schooling course? How many jumps do I need? What type of jumps should I build? What kind of wood is best? What are the best standards?

Which cups are best or are steel rods okay? What kind of distance should I put between fences?

EXPERT: Horse shows are a large part of David Ballard's life. They always have been. Son of a former captain of Canada's Equestrian Team, Bob Ballard, David spent much of his childhood at equestrian activities but it was at age fifteen that riding really captured his interest.

Ballard switched from three-day event training when the brilliant Anatol Pieregorodzki died, to Dick Day Hunter / Jumper Stables and really became involved.

He worked in the United States for some time but one very serious head injury which occurred in a riding accident in Boston, followed by a second in Sutton made him retire from riding. The horse world was obviously in his blood, however. After only a three year 'retirement', David teamed up with Torchy Millar and moved to Montreal for five years. There, he became involved with the teaching of riding.

In the mid-seventies he moved back to Ontario and worked for Sam-Son Farms for several years; in fact, he taught the Samuels youngsters until they moved out of the Junior Division and into that of Amateur Owner.

After leaving Sam-Son Farms, Ballard started his own business and for a few years rented facilities in the Hornby area. A few years ago he took the plunge and purchased his own place in a super location on Steeles Avenue near Trafalgar and the 401 Highway. There he is setting about building up his enigmatically named 'Looking Back Stables' into a first rate establishment.

Career-wise he is concentrating in two areas: coaching and course designing. One of his pupils, Heather Speck, rode Escort to the Junior Jumper Zone Championship and in 1986, as well as other courses, he designed the World Cup Class at the Tournament of Champions.

Today, Ballard has his full senior status as an F.E.I. Course Designer; hence he is allowed to design courses for any F.E.I. sanctioned show including the Olympics and World Championships.

A jumper schooling fence at Lynn and Ian Millar's farm.

Thus in 1988 Ballard was the Senior Course Designer for the Spruce Meadows National – the fist time anyone other than Pamela Carruthers had done the course in twelve years or more and in 1989 designed in the United States at West Palm Beach.

Ballard is the Chairman for the C.E.F. Course Designers of Canada.

ANSWER: First of all, Ballard stresses the fact that you need to get the *right kind* of equipment. Although you have not mentioned whether it is the hunter discipline, jumper or three-day that you are interested in, he feels it is most likely hunter-type and so bases his response on that assumption.

What you need to school over, is what you see at horse shows. He strongly recommends buying the jumps already made because he says that by the time labour and supply costs are added up, even homemade jumps become expensive. If, however, you do decide to make them yourself or to have them made, he suggests the following:

- Have them made from spruce or pine as these woods are lighter in weight yet still fairly strong.
- Use pressure-treated wood for your uprights so that they can stay outside. Eventually they should be painted to help preserve them. For hunter fences, white or brown is suitable.
- Consider using ten foot poles and 'fillers' (gates, walls, etc.) as they have several advantages. They are cheaper to buy because they require less lumber and, as well, they are lighter and take up less space if you happen to have your own indoor arena with limited footage. Ten feet is the minimum width you would want and twelve is the maximum. Twelve foot poles and 'fillers' are what you encounter at almost all shows.
- Do not make jumps so heavy that they are impossible to move. Remember, you might have to shift them about on your own.
- Have wing-type standards of the variety seen at shows.
- Keep poles natural in colour or paint them white.
- Include a white or brown gate and a little wall in your set.
- Have at least eight jumps – the number that is the minimum required in the rule book.

On the subject of jump cups Ballard recommends either any of the types available at different tack shops or some custom-made by a welder. Ballard is adamant about *not* using steel rods as they not only are a possible safety hazard regarding puncture wounds but also damage the jumps by breaking down the holes.

Establish a schooling area at your new home. Grass is acceptable but Ballard much prefers a sand ring as the footing is much easier to maintain and good footing is very important when schooling over fences. Ballard stresses the importance of closing the area in. He favours a single board fence about three and one-half feet high but says that even a rope fence backed up with trees is better than no enclosure at all. His experience has been that a young horse concentrates much better in a restricted environment but tends to get 'wide-eyed' in an open field. An outdoor ring about one hundred feet by two hundred feet is a good size.

A good schooling hunter jump with well-constructed wing standards.

You ask about distances between fences. Once again, the course you build at home should resemble what your horse is going to have to jump if you go to a horse show. There are some fairly standard distances when you are cantering from four to seven strides and seven strides would be as long a line as you would want. Four strides on a 'quiet' distance outdoors can be anywhere from sixty to sixty-three feet. (The shorter distance usually suits the green horse, whereas the longer is appropriate for the more experienced horse. Five strides would be a distance of anywhere from seventy-three feet to seventy-seven and six strides anywhere from eighty-four feet to eighty-nine feet. Again, the green horse would do the shorter distance, the more experienced the long.)

Outdoors, the basis worked on is twelve and one-half foot strides to thirteen and one-half foot strides with six feet added to the number of strides for the take-off and six feet for the landing.

For combinations, all hunters should jump from a vertical to an oxer, never the other way around. To jump from an oxer to a vertical is more difficult and in hunter classes the idea is to encourage the horse to go from the progressively easy to the hard in order to encourage him to jump in good form.

The vertical part of the combination can be smaller in height than the oxer and should be well ground-lined in front so that the horse does not try to get too deep to it. A rule of thumb distance for the ground line is two feet in front of the vertical which should be filled in well. The oxer should be rampy; that is, the front pole should be lower than the back pole in order to teach the horse to jump in good form. Such a fence encourages a horse to bascule or round his back and to jerk his knees. The distance for the one-stride combination between fences should be from twenty-four and one-half feet to twenty-five.

David Ballard recommends buying jumps from a professional – possibly one who supplies jumps to all of the big shows in the area. Prices vary tremendously, depending on the intricacy of the jump.

Paddock Fencing
Types and Relative Costs

QUESTION: Recently my husband and I moved from our home in the city to a new house in the country. Right now there is no stable on our property, but we are planning to build one soon and move our three horses from the boarding stable where we presently keep them.

There are no fences on our piece of country land so we are going to have to build at least two paddocks for turn out. Our land is rolling and a bit stony.

We know we have several choices in types of fences that we could build, but we don't know for sure what the advantages and disadvantages are of each kind. Can you also give us some idea of cost because, unfortunately, money has to be a factor.

EXPERT: Ed Kuipery as been in the business of building fences for over thirteen years. He learned the business first hand from Mauna

Martella who started Tree Man Ltd. in the early seventies. Now Kuipery owns the company which he calls 'The Tree Man' and has continued to maintain the excellent reputation that the company earned under the former owner. He takes pride in his work and much of his business is either repeat business or 'word of mouth'.

Because 'The Tree Man' is centred in the Guelph area, Kuipery is used to rolling, stony land.

ANSWER: Before outlining the various types of fencing available, Kuipery points out some general information with which you should be familiar.

Posts should be deep into the ground so that heavy rains and frost do not affect them. The depth of posts is governed by the length of available cedar posts. Since this length is almost always eight feet and horsemen usually like fences to be from four and one-half to five feet in height, posts will be more than adequate three to three and one-half feet deep in the ground. Gate posts and other anchor posts must be more deeply entrenched. Kuipery uses an auger rather than the back-hoe some fence builders use. Although the holes require some hand labour, their narrowness results in much more firmly entrenched posts.

Cost is a factor which heavily influences the size of the posts. Ones six to seven inches in diameter are preferred for strength, but one to four inches are often chosen for their lower cost factor. The number of feet apart that posts should be placed depends in part on the type of fence being built.

Types of Fencing: There is a great variety in the type of fencing which may be chosen. The selection in fences that Kuipery installs includes: plank, post and split rail, post and round rail, wire, wire and board, rubber, chain link and electric wire.

Kuipery describes each, lists some of their advantages and disadvantages and gives a relative idea of the expense of each fence. He does caution that the cost factor varies with the type of land on which the fencing is installed. Very stony areas, for example, represent higher fencing expenses.

Three-board plank fencing is attractive and easily visible to the horse.

• Plank: One popular type of plank fencing with large horse farms is composed of cedar posts eight feet apart with sixteen foot, two inch by six inch 'dressed' spruce (in reality one and one-half by five and one-half inches) used as the planking. Cost influences both the choice of planking and the number of planks used. Spruce is fairly cheap and the cost is further reduced by the use of three planks rather than four.

The advantages of plank fencing are obvious. Not only is it attractive but also it can be stained or painted to match the barn or house. As well, it is highly visible to the horse.

The main disadvantage of plank fencing is the maintenance required to keep the wood properly stained or painted. Not to be forgotten is the fact that if horses chew the planks, the bitten areas are, unfortunately, very easy to see.

Another popular choice in plank fencing is oak which, although referred to as one inch by six inches, is usually one and one-eighth inches thick and a full six inches wide. It is far stronger than the two inch spruce and so hard that horses are unable to chew it – another definite plus factor. Its one disadvantage is that as it is not kiln-dried

Post and split rail fence is very popular.

(it would be too expensive if it were), it will warp a little as it dries.

In either case (spruce or oak), eight feet is not the only distance at which posts can be spaced, but because of the length of the planking of spruce (a standard sixteen foot) or oak (eight foot), such a spacing gives the best price.

• Post and Split Cedar Rail: This type of fencing is often chosen because people already have old split rails on their property. As well, it is frequently selected for aesthetic reasons; that is, it looks attractive on rolling land or in front of an old stone farm house.

Unfortunately, these previously used split rails are not very strong. To help overcome their weakness, Kuipery suggests using six rails with each resting on top of each other and reinforced by being held between two posts at the end of each section of rails.

To try to keep this type of fence as strong as possible, he does not recommend cutting the rails and butting them together, although he will do so if requested and in this case uses four split rails.

Some people add an electric wire along the top to keep the horses at a distance.

Posts and round rails fencing is very strong and attractive.

• **Posts and Round Rails:** This type of fencing has the posts connected by thinner posts; that is, posts of about three to four inches in diameter at the narrow end and five or even six inches are used as round rails. A good recommended spacing for the ground posts is about ten feet.

Such a fence, although very attractive, is surprisingly not very common. It is a good, strong fence with no sharp edges and it requires no maintenance. As well, any chewing which the horses might do is not as visible as on a plank fence.

• **Wire:** If cost is more important than anything else in your decision-making, then galvanized wire fastened to steel stakes is another fence alternative. It is not a very safe selection for horses as there is always the danger that a horse might not only impale himself on a stake, but also put a foot through the six by sixteen inch spaces in the pattern of the wire.

To improve the safety aspect, wooden posts may be used in place of the steel stakes.

Costs vary depending on whether steel stakes or wooden posts are used and whether the distance between posts is increased or decreased. Safety improvements raise the price.

Brace panels must be added in the corners.

• Wire and Board: To the wire fence described above, planking may be added along the top of the wire. This addition makes the fence more visible to the horse and thus safer although there is still the danger that a horse may put his foot through the wire. Because of the planking, wooden posts must be used.

Adding the board along the top of the wire and having to use wooden posts increases the cost of this fence by about fifty per cent over the straight wire.

• Rubber: An extremely safe, strong and very practical fence, it has only two drawbacks. Its appearance its not very pleasant to the eye and it is not easily available.

The posts may be placed anywhere from eight to ten to twelve feet apart but the corner posts function as anchor posts and must be exceptionally strong. Brace panels are necessary because the rubber, stretched tight with a tractor during installation, is under extreme tension.

• Chain Link: The advantages of chain link are obvious. It is very strong. It requires no maintenance and, as well as keeping in the horses, keeps out intruders such as neighbours' dogs. The pattern of the link is far too small for there to be any danger that a horse might put a foot through it; however, a kick from a horse can put a bulge in that will not come out.

It is by far the most expensive of the fences described here.

• Electric: Although not common this type of fence is the cheapest of all. Two or more strands of wire may be used with some of them not grounded in order to make the shock a little more effective. The wire is supported by steel stakes which can be as far apart as thirty feet. Power can be supplied either by a battery or a small transformer.

Wooden posts may be substituted in place of the steel stakes but again they need to be no closer than thirty feet. The wooden posts would increase the price of the fence.

It is not a very popular fence among horse people.

The subject of fencing would not be complete without including information on how to close them off – gates. Kuipery recommends at least a twelve foot width so that there is room to allow a tractor or truck to enter. If the field is a larger one in which you might want to take a combine, etc., he recommends sixteen feet. For those who are positive that they never want to take a vehicle through the gate then a six foot width is sufficient; however, there is always the chance of an emergency in which you need to get a truck and horse trailer into the paddock, so a minimum twelve foot width is a good idea.

The gate posts (a particular kind of anchor post) must be bigger for strength and longer so that they can be put deeper into the ground. Kuipery advises that they should be eight inches thick and nine feet long to allow an extra foot in the ground. He stresses the importance of having the posts in deep enough so that they do not lean from the weight of the gate.

'Pig tails' make good gate closures. Some people like to add a chain around the post as an extra precaution.

Types of Gates:

• The most expensive is known as a 'lifetime gate' which is made of galvanized metal held together by rivets. In Kuipery's opinion it is a very poor gate because if it is hung in such a way that the wind can move it even a little, it cracks and breaks where the hinges are attached due to metal fatigue.
• The cheapest is the wire farm gate which has a galvanized frame with wire. Although adequate, it is not very strong according to Kuipery.
• A little more expensive than the second type of gate but cheaper than the first is the tubular steel welded gate which can be made to order. It is a very strong and light gate.

• Gates may be made out of the same materials as the fence itself. A plank gate, for example, could easily be constructed. Unfortunately, it would be extremely heavy if made the same size as a metal gate and if divided in two and fastened in the middle, would be not only insecure but also awkward to handle for turning out or bringing in more than one horse.

Open-front boots allow the jumper to feel the rails if he hits them and consequently teaches him to be more careful. Ankle protector boots help the horse with interfering gaits.

Leg Protection for Turn Out and for Schooling

QUESTION: Last year I bought a young, very pretty, three-year-old gelding with the idea of showing him next year. He's turned out with other horses (none with shoes on the hind feet) and often has small cuts and swellings on his legs.

I want to know if one of your experts think some kind of leg protection is a good idea. Some people say they cause problems. Also, is it a good idea to put some kind of protection on a horse when schooling? If so, what type? Bandages? Brush boots?

EXPERT: Pat Lang has been involved with the showing of horses for almost thirty years. In the past she owned two conformation-type brood mares and exhibited their offspring on the line. She has sold her young stock both in Canada and in the United States.

In 1980 Lang had the Reserve High Point Filly (two-year-old) and recently a horse which she showed on the line, Yosemite Sam, after placing well in the Conformation Division has gone on to compete successfully in jumper classes.

A George Morris enthusiast, Lang has attended several of his clinics.

All those horsepersons who know Lang are well aware of the extra care and attention which she has always lavished on her horses.

ANSWER: First of all, Lang suggests that your horse be turned out *alone*, if possible, in order to cut down on the risk of injury by other horses.

Secondly Lang recommends protective boots. She admits that while brood mares and quiet pleasure horses may fare very well without boots, a fit, active horse regardless of his age, when turned out or working, can easily take a misplaced step or an out of balance stride, both of which may result in bumps, cuts, splints or worse. One minor injury can be disastrous for the conformation or line horse. It can lay up hunters or jumpers and ruin a carefully planned show schedule. It may impede or prevent a sale or simply put a stop to enjoyable hacks.

Injuries can also be very expensive, not only in terms of veterinarian bills but also in time lost. It is true that most gait-related faults such as cross-firing, brushing and over-reaching can be alleviated by proper shoeing, but booting affords added insurance and protection.

Lang likes to put boots on all young or active horses, both when they are turned out and when they are at work. Most horses, when given a few hours of freedom a day, will take advantage of the time to play. Their legs and hooves may suffer the consequences. (Turn out in this instance, means relatively short daily sessions rather than full time turn out which would definitely make 'booting' detrimental.)

As far as leg protection for the horse when he is being schooled is concerned, Lang points out that horses, when working, are exposed to many hazards and are required to perform exercises with great co-ordination and balance. Different degrees of protection may be used – the degree depending on ground conditions, work being done and personal preference.

Turning out or riding in mud, deep sand, uneven terrain or slippery footing may result in over-reaching and the subsequent possibility of bruised and lacerated heels, separated coronets and pulled shoes. *Rubber bell boots* provide excellent protection for the heels and hoof areas and also help prevent pulled shoes. For these reasons, Lang recommends the use of bell boots for turn out and for riding on the flat and over fences.

Care must be taken to correctly fit bell boots and to check for any chafing. They are available in sizes small, medium and large. Because dirt and sand work up under the boots, they must be kept clean with mild soap and water. 'Pull on' bell boots will probably wear the best, but they are not the easiest to put on. Soaking them in hot water, to soften them, will make the job easier but it is not only time consuming to do so, but also inconvenient if the boots are needed.

Bell boots are also available with buckle or velcro closures. Lang

94

likes the velcro because they can be put on or removed quickly and easily and when one has a number of horses, anything that will make the job easier, certainly counts. As well, the flatness of the velcro helps prevent them from being torn off or chewed off. The velcro does, however, become clogged with dirt and sand and its grip weakens. On the buckle closure bell boots, the leather straps become hard and stiff with mud and water and thus are very difficult to open and close. Cleaning and soaping the leather daily and occasional oiling will help keep the leather soft.

Front leg protection is available in a wide variety of boots. For turn out Lang uses a simple but sturdy vinyl, felt or leather boot. She likes a wrap-a-round for the extra protection it provides against bumps or cuts. Again, the fit must be correct. The boot should not restrict, chafe or 'slop'.

Lang does not like heavily elasticized boots for turn out because she feels they are often improperly fitted and may harm supporting structures in the leg if left on for extended periods.

She stresses that care must be taken to keep boots free from accumulated dirt and sweat and to insure a proper fit to prevent irritation. The use of oil and Lexol on the leather will help to keep it supple.

Front leg protection for the horse under tack varies greatly. Conformation horses need the added protection against blemishes; therefore, in addition to bell boots, a *wrap-a-round leg boot* will protect the front of the leg from rubs over fences, the inside, from brushing injuries and the back, from hind grabs. *A splint support* is advantageous, especially for young horses.

For working hunters and for jumpers for whom minor blemishes are not as important, an *open-front* would be the boot Lang would choose. Such a boot allows the horse to feel the rails if he hits them and consequently to learn to be more careful. Boots with additional support for those horses that might require them are available; for example, heavy leather tendon support at the back or a dropped leather insert on the inside to protect the fetlock joint.

There is a wide range of styles and materials to suit individual needs. The hard plastic provides excellent protection and style but

they are also very expensive. Leather and thick felt produce a functional, less expensive boot but one with perhaps a shorter wear life.
Once again, it is important that the boot fit properly and be cleaned
regularly to prevent irritation.

Hind leg, ankle and hock protector boots are available also for
horses with interfering gaits, weaknesses or individual specific
requirements.

As far as bandages are concerned, Lang's advice is that unless you
have an experienced person helping you to bandage, you would be
wiser to use protective boots. Bandages, if not correctly wrapped,
can do far more harm than good.

How to Keep a Horse's Legs in Good Condition

QUESTION: I have often heard the expression, 'no legs, no horse!'
and I am about to begin schooling my four-year-old horse to jump.
What can I do to keep my horse's legs in good condition?

EXPERT: Liz Ashton of Bolton, Ontario has recently been
appointed the new Chairman of the Canadian Equestrian Team's
Three-Day eventing squad. Ashton holds a PH.D. in Education
Administration and is currently Dean of Hospitality, Tourism and
Leisure Management at Humber College in Toronto. A member of
the C.E.T. from 1969 to 1985 on both the show jumping and eventing
teams, Ashton is eminently qualified for the position.

An 'A' pony clubber, Ashton began her career riding hunters and
jumpers and was ranked the third leading female equestrian in the
world in 1972. Switching to eventing shortly thereafter, she was a
member of the Olympic Three-Day Team at the 1976 Montreal
Olympics, Captain of the gold medal Canadian team at the 1978
World Championships in Lexington, Kentucky and Captain of the
eventing teams for the 1980 Alternate Olympics as well as the 1984
Los Angeles Games.

Ashton has coached junior international and provincial teams, was Director of the Ontario Horse Trials Association and National Director of the Canadian Combined Training Association from 1978 to 1979. She has been an athletic representative for the sport of eventing to the Canadian Olympic Association. She has also been active in the National Coaching Certification Programme in which she has served as a National Examiner since 1979 and as a Master Course Conductor since 1985. Ashton is a Level II Examiner, Coach and Course Conductor and has headed the coaching-readiness course at Humber College.

ANSWER: Ashton gives a detailed reply geared to a young horse with an average rider. Her suggestions cover the following considerations:
- shoeing
- amount of time spent schooling
- footing
- protective gear
- bandaging.

Shoeing: Of initial concern to Ashton is that you make sure your blacksmith trims and shoes your horse's hooves in such a way that any travelling defects such as winging or dishing are minimized. Because flat shoes increase the chances of your horse slipping and injuring itself, she recommends hunter shoes with small corks on all four feet.

Amount of Time Spent Schooling: First and foremost, before any jumping, Ashton stresses the importance of six weeks of 'legging-up' on the horse. The first four weeks should include a lot of walking with intermittent periods of trotting to make sure that the horse's legs are hard; that is, that his bones, tendons and ligaments have tightened up. Keep work periods relatively short, perhaps three-quarters of an hour to an hour as the absolute maximum because your four-year-old is not really mature yet. Even when you begin actual jumping schooling, you should jump only two or three times

97

a week for perhaps ten minutes. A main concern when starting a young horse is not to tire him out. If he does become fatigued, he will start jumping poorly and making mistakes which could lead to injury. A good rule to follow is: based on his accomplishments of the day before, have a realistic objective in mind when you go out and once you reach the objective, stop! As Ashton points out it can be very tempting, especially with a young horse to overjump him if he is going well. Don't do it!

Footing: Footing is a very important consideration in young horses, especially in a four-year-old that has done little work. At this stage, unless he has been on the track, he is basically a soft horse with tendons and ligaments that are not yet strong. Ideally two or three inches of sand footing is great. Alternately, grass with some spongy give to it is very good. Never jump a green horse in heavy mud as doing so is an open invitation for a bowed tendon. Avoid very hard footing as it hurts the horse and turns the horse against jumping.

Protective Gear: Ashton always uses bell boots and in the case of young horses usually front shin boots and hind ankle boots as well. To quote Ashton, 'Young horses particularly, need this kind of protection because they don't know where their legs are going.'

Bandaging: Ashton always bandages a horse's legs after a jumping session. If he has banged himself or if he has the slightest strain, his legs will fill, whereas bandaging will prevent this from happening or at least minimize it. Usually Ashton uses only plain rubbing alcohol under the bandage to help cool the leg.

In Summary: In order to keep your horse's legs in the best possible condition, follow the previous considerations and keep these basic concepts in mind:

• Jumping is not how high your horse can go, but how well he can do it! You should be aiming for developing style. With the development

98

of style will come jumping ability. Ashton stresses that if you push a horse too high, too fast, he will lose his style and stop basculing (arching).

• Have an objective in mind and don't go beyond it! Go slowly and let the horse's mental and physical development determine the speed with which you progress.

A Lower Leg Bandage

QUESTION: Would you please describe how to correctly apply a lower leg bandage.

EXPERT: Intellectual inquisitiveness is the inherent characteristic of Humber Equine Clinic's three-person practice. Headed by senior partner Dr. Darryl Bonder, the practice caters to hunters, jumpers, racing Thoroughbreds, event horses and a growing number of Standardbred referrals.

Much of Humber Equine Clinic's recent fame stems from its advanced work in arthroscopy. Some years ago, Bonder's association with Dr. Jackson, the 'father of arthroscopy in North America,' with Colorado State's Dr. McIlwraith, the world's foremost equine arthroscopist, and with the Ontario Veterinary College's Dr. Hurtig, stimulated Bonder's interest in arthroscopy to the point where he set out to learn all he could about this technique.

Now, Bonder refers to his arthroscopic work as the most rewarding thing he has ever done professionally. From an intellectual standpoint, he feels it has considerably increased his understanding of articular pathology.

The Humber Equine Clinic has spared no expense in purchasing top quality, innovative equipment such as the sector scanning ultrasonography unit which, compared to the more common linear unit, gives a far more accurate picture of what is going on in tendons, ligaments, heart, lungs, liver and kidneys.

Bonder lectures on his field of expertise in continuing education and day courses at Humber College. He also has made several television appearances. His plans for the future involve a continuation of his basic philosophy. 'We want to practice as high a quality of medicine as is humanly possible and economically feasible because we in this practice have a burning desire to know. We want to know. We want to find out and will go to any length to accomplish that.'

ANSWER:

Step 1: Assuming there is no major bleeding, the first step is to cleanse the wound. Bonder recommends a Betadine scrub solution, which may be purchased from a veterinarian or tack shop, a roll of clean cotton and warm water. Take a piece of the cotton, apply the scrub solution directly to the wound and gently bathe and cleanse the wound. If you cleanse the wound well when it first occurs, your chances of negating infection are excellent. Rinse the scrub solution from the wound. Dry the wound with a four by four inch gauze sponge.

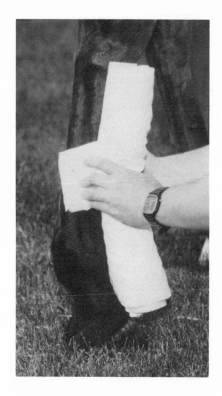

Step 2: Apply a fresh four by four inch gauze sponge directly to the wound.

Step 3: Bonder uses two clean quilted cottons, one at a time, and rolls them around the leg so that the tendon is always pulled to the inside. (In the right leg, you roll in a clockwise direction and on the left, in a counter-clockwise direction.) Bandaging in these directions will take the strain off the tendon. Bonder stresses that adequate padding is absolutely essential under a tension bandage.

Step 4: Roll a four inch wide cling gauze bandage over the quilts. Again, on the right leg, work in a clockwise direction. The cling helps to hold the quilt in place, making it easier to apply pressure with the bandage if necessary. Start the cling at the bottom of the leg and work up to the top.

Step 5: Cover with Vetrap™ Bandaging Tape. Work in a clockwise direction (on the right leg). Start near the bottom of the bandage and wrap downward to just above the edge of the quilts. Then roll the bandage back up the quilt to just below the top edge.

Step 6: The bandage is complete. No taping or pinning is necessary as Vetrap™ Bandaging Tape is self-adhering.

Bonder sums up wound bandaging of the legs with the following suggestions:
• If a veterinarian is called for, cleanse and protect as outlined.
• If a veterinary visit is not needed, cleanse, add V-Sporin or Fura-cin and protect as outlined.

Bonder is not in favour of people using, as he puts it, 'tons of dusting powder'. He stresses the fact that many of these topical dusts are overused by horse owners, and they do tend to act as foreign bodies in the wound. 'If the wound is a stitchable one,' Bonder adds, 'then the first thing a veterinarian has to do is clean all this debris out of the wound.'

Finally, Bonder advises that a person should always consider the tetanus status of the horse and whether or not antibiotics are necessary. If the horse has not had a tetanus vaccination in the last six months, he should have one. If the wound is the full thickness of the skin or a puncture, the horse should be put on antibiotics.

Bonder emphasizes that *puncture* wounds are an extremely dangerous type because, having only a small point of entry with some depth of penetration, they tend to close over at the surface, leaving an anaerobic environment (one without oxygen) in which really 'nasty' bacteria can develop and thrive. In these cases, a veterinarian should always be called, even when the puncture wound looks innocuous.

An Extra Supportive Performance Bandage
The Figure-Eight Splint Bandage

QUESTION: My horse has an old bow (tendon) on his left front leg. I am showing him in the jumper division. Is there any type of strong support bandage I could use on his front legs?

EXPERT: Before beginning his career as a professor of large animal surgery at the University of Wisconsin's School of Veterinary Medicine, Dr. William Crawford was a self-employed racetrack practitioner in British Columbia, Canada.

'I've spent the past twenty-five years in close association with horses,' Crawford said. 'They're my hobby as well as my work.' A previous owner of racehorses, he currently owns cutting horses.

Crawford spent ten years in private practice working closely with racehorses before deciding to return to school to obtain his master's degree in equine medicine and surgery from the University of Saskatchewan, where he also obtained his Doctor of Veterinary Medicine degree. Studying the relationship between racetrack design and lameness in the racehorse has been one of his major areas of interest and research.

While at the University of Saskatchewan, Crawford conducted a major research project on the effects of racetrack design on gait symmetry of the pacer. The results of his study have since been published in professional and lay journals throughout Canada and the United States.

Chiefly interested in orthopaedic diseases of large animals,

Crawford said that his 'primary interest within that area is the prevention of lameness in horses.' He teaches orthopaedic surgery and equine lameness to graduate students and a general surgery course to veterinary medical students.

ANSWER:

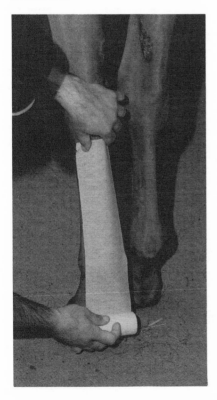

Step 1: Measure and cut two splints. To measure the proper length of the splints, place a piece of Equisport™ Equine Support Bandage down the back of the horse's leg, beginning just below the knee or hock and continuing to well below the ankle. Cut the splint from the roll of Equisport™ Bandage. Then make a second splint.

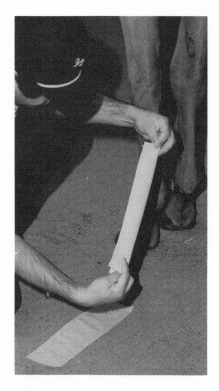

Step 2: Fold the splints in half lengthwise. Press the material firmly together as Equisport™ Bandage is self-adhering. Make sure there are no wrinkles or creases in the splint.

Step 3: Using a fresh roll, begin the bandage directly above the ankle. Wrap once around the leg making sure you wrap the tendons and ligament toward the inside. Figure-eight the ankle once, then bring the Equisport™ Bandage upward in a spiral manner to just below the hock. Be certain to overlap the bandage evenly for consistent support. Avoid wrinkles by straightening the bandage as you apply it. Crawford recommends pulling the bandage firmly across the cannon bone while applying less pressure across the tendons and ligament in the back of the leg. The Equisport™ Bandage should be applied using approximately fifty per cent of its stretch.

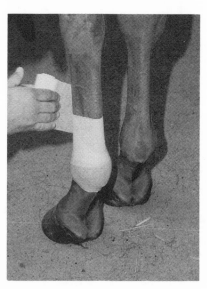

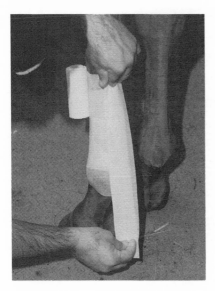

Step 4: When you've reached the point just below the knee or two and one-half to three inches below the hock with the bandage, apply the first splint. Beginning at the top of the wrap, press the splint firmly onto the bandage and down the back of the leg covering the tendons and ligament, stretching the splint slightly, approximately thirty to fifty per cent of the usable stretch, and anchoring it at the bottom of the bandage. The splint will adhere securely to the bandage.

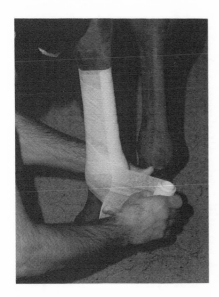

Step 5: Incorporate the splint into the bandage by wrapping over the splint and down the leg in a spiral manner. Apply even pressure across the tendons and ligament. Once again, figure-eight the ankle.

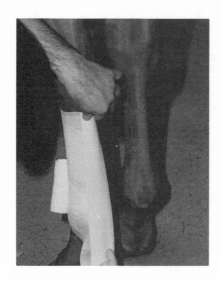

Step 6: Place the second splint down the back of the leg, using the same technique as with the first splint.

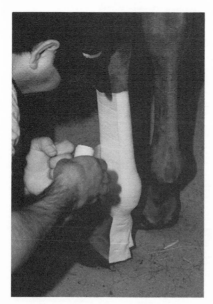

Step 7: Incorporate the second splint into the bandage by figure-eighting the ankle first. Then continue wrapping up the leg in a spiral manner.

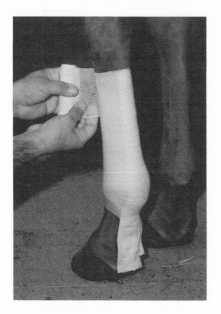

Step 8: Finish the bandage at the top of the leg using the entire roll of Equisport™ Equine Support Bandage. For added safety, strips of Scotch® Vinyl Plastic Tape can be applied to the top of the bandage.

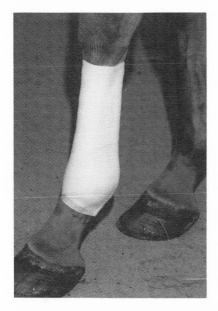

Step 9: Cut off the tails of both splints evenly with the bottom of the bandage.

Trimming and Braiding

QUESTION: This year I want to start entering my horse in recognized shows. So far, I have only had schooling show experience and although I try to turn my horse out well, I never think he looks as good as he could or should. His coat doesn't look as shiny as some of the others do and his braids don't always stay nice and flat on his neck.

What can I do to make him look 'A Number One'?

EXPERT: The four years of experience that Ann Hollings gained while working as a groom for such prestigious stables as Jim Elder's in Canada, and meticulous barns in England, proved invaluable when, in 1976, Hollings started her own grooming business, Professional Horse Services.

The pressures of running a one-woman grooming service for three years convinced Hollings that she should return to school. She has now completed a Masters in Statistics and has achieved her goal which was to become involved in a career in equine research.

It was Hollings who braided my horses when I showed them in conformation classes and her 'swan song' was the braiding of my horse, Dune, when he won the Governor General's Cup at the Royal Agricultural Winter Fair in 1984. Hollings' work always added that extra finishing touch that helped to make the horse look perfectly turned out.

ANSWER: Hollings stresses the fact that a horse must be in perfect condition healthwise in order to look his best. As she puts it, turning a horse out well, begins with attention to the inside of the horse. A well-balanced nutritious feeding programme is essential.

If your horse's coat is not always as shiny as it might be, Hollings suggests that you add one tablespoon of corn oil to his feed on a daily basis. (Vegetable oil, olive oil, wheat germ oil or linseed oil are other alternatives.)

If your horse is on a good feeding programme as well as a good exercise schedule and the addition of oil does not help, Hollings advises you to have your veterinarian examine your horse to try to determine a possible cause. It is possible that your horse needs to be on a more efficient worming programme, for example.

Once all health aspects have been attended to, concentrate on good grooming. 'Lots of elbow grease!' is Hollings' first recommendation. She explains that thorough currying is especially beneficial because it loosens dirt, stimulates oil glands and gets rid of unhealthy hair.

If your horse is at all sweaty when you have finished schooling him, Hollings suggests that you give him a warm bath with nothing added but the mild muscle brace, Vetrolin. She is not in favour of adding oil to the water because she finds it makes the coat sticky. Also she does not like to have shampoo added because she finds it has a drying effect on the hair coat.

It has been Hollings' experience that the action of sweating, itself, seems to improve the coat, perhaps unclogging the pores of impurities.

Caution: Differentiate between a sweat and a lather.

Trimming: How much Hollings trims off of a horse depends on the conditions under which the horse lives. If your horse spends a great deal of time outside, Hollings recommends trimming a little less than if his turn out time is limited. Her general rule of thumb is to take off all the hair that detracts from the outline of the horse. This would include:

- All the whiskers underneath and around the nose.
- The hair around the edges of the ears and the longer hair inside the ears. Although many people clip the ears out completely, Hollings is not in favour of doing so, especially in the summer or when the insect problem is bad.
- A bridle path only wide enough to allow space for the bridle. Hollings feels that too wide a bridle path shortens the appearance of the neck.

• Any feathers on the leg and the hair above the pastern area. Hollings cautions against taking away too much protective hair as problems such as mud fever can arise.

• A line around the coronary bands.

Unlike some grooms who trim horses, Hollings does not like to remove either a horse's eyelashes or the whiskers around his eyes. Her reasoning is based on the fact that the location of the eyes in a horse's head makes it extremely difficult for the horse to see anything up close to his head. Because of this eye location, a horse needs eyelashes as well as the 'eye whiskers' for sensory perception. Horses do not usually mind their whiskers being clipped so Hollings trims them off first. If a horse is really badly behaved, Hollings has the animal twitched and then works as quickly as possible to finish. She only tranquilizes a horse in extreme cases as a last resort.

Mane Braiding:

• Number of Braids: Hollings does not like to see a tremendous number of braids. She gives several reasons. Not only is it harder to make the crowded braids lay down properly, but also it means that the horse has to stand still longer. Hollings is of the opinion that a large number of braids does not, as many people argue, make the horse's neck look longer but instead probably makes the judge wonder if you think the neck is a bit short. (Something you would worry about in conformation classes). Hollings averages twenty-two braids a mane and never worries about odd or even numbers for mares or geldings. She does suggest that you braid as far down the neck as possible, including the hairs on the withers. By doing so, she feels you are increasing the appearance of length in the neck. If your saddle rests on these lower braids, do not braid down so far or your horse will be uncomfortable.

• Mane Length: For sausage-type braids Hollings recommends a mane pulled to a length of four inches. For button-type braids (her preference) she recommends a mane from two and one-half to three inches in length.

• Mane Thickness: Hollings points out that it is easier to put nice braids in a thick mane. If you plan to show all season, you might be wise to scissor-cut or razor-cut what is left in your hand. Such a cutting action does not give the mane the appearance of having been cut.

• To Wash or Not to Wash: Hollings' answer is not to wash the mane or the tail before braiding. The natural oil, if left in the hair, will lend some stickiness which will help to make the braids stay in better and longer. Of course if your horse is a grey or a palomino you have little choice.

• Tangles: Thoroughly comb the mane so that there are not any tangles. Hollings stresses that this is an essential step in good braiding.

• Thread or Yarn: Hollings uses braiding thread rather than yarn because she likes the braids to blend in with the horse rather than to be a focal point.

She never uses rubber bands because she finds that braids just do not lie flat if fastened with elastics.

• Size: Hollings does the first braid, making sure the part is straight and then uses a human comb to measure that braid's width so that the remainder of the braids will be exactly the same size.

Down or Out: Pull the braid down as close to the neck as possible as you work so that the braid will tuck under and lay flat when completed.

• Begin at the Top: Hollings begins with the forelock when braiding because, as she puts it, 'That's the fussiest part.' If you are working on a horse that will soon fidget, you are wise to get the top of his head done right away. She then does four or five braids right at the top of the mane and turns these under before continuing down the neck. This way she has the most difficult section done first and can move with the horse if he fidgets later on.

• Hairs Sticking Up: If you find little hairs sticking up out of the braids, Hollings suggests that you wait until you finish braiding before doing anything about them. When you stand back and take an overall look they will probably not be as obvious as you had thought they would be. If you must get rid of them, do not cut, pull! Do try to avoid touching them if possible. They will never get to be long hairs that can be braided in, if you continually cut them.

• Grease: Do not use, 'Dippety Do', vaseline or hair spray to help hold hairs in place. If you do, the result will be a greasy or sticky mess.

• Braid Removal: When removing braids use a seam ripper. The use of scissors makes it very difficult to avoid inadvertently cutting the hair.

Tail Braiding:

• Try to braid the tail only a short time before your class. Not only is a braided tail uncomfortable for the horse but also an insecure braiding job might not hold as long as it will need to otherwise.

• Thoroughly comb out any tangles before braiding.

• Use only small bunches of hair. If you take too much hair each time, the braid will be far too fat by the time you have finished.

• Pull the hair right from the back. If you do not, strands of hair will hang down behind the tail.

• Pull each braid segment tightly to hold the braid in a straight line.

• Tuck the finished braid under rather than up or in a pinwheel. Again, Hollings' reasoning is that she does not like to detract from the clean lines of the horse.

• Wrap the tail in a wet elastic bandage (not too tightly) and leave the bandage on until just before your class.

• Hollings likes to bang the tail to get rid of ragged ends. She finds that usually about one inch is enough to remove. Because of the fact that when a horse moves he naturally carries his tail out slightly from his body, Hollings places a brush under the tail or asks someone to place an arm under it before she makes the cut. Such a precaution avoids having an angle at the bottom of the tail when the horse moves and his tail position changes.

• Take the tail braid out as soon as possible after your class. As has been said, a horse finds a tail braid very uncomfortable and, as well, the braiding may cause some tail hairs to fall out. Your horse could finish the show season with a very thin tail, if you are not careful.

• Hollings never twitches a horse for braiding unless it is absolutely necessary. She prefers to move with the horse rather than make braiding sessions unpleasant for the animal.

A personal comment: One enterprising exhibitor, faced with a very agitated horse, stood behind the closed ramp of her trailer (on a bale) to braid the tail. The ramp, or lower door, protected her from any possible kicking that her horse might have done.

Hollings uses ear clippers for all of her trimming work because they are not only practically noiseless but also, due to their size, far more precise.

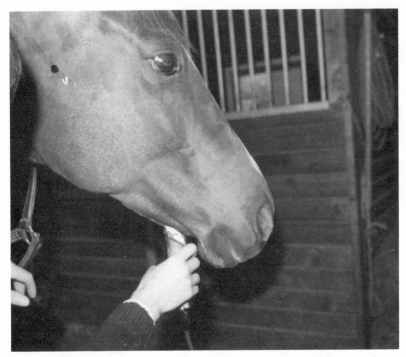

Step 1: Using ear clippers, the longer hairs are trimmed from underneath the horse's head. All whiskers around the nose have been removed.

Note that the halter has been moved back around the neck to get it out of the way of the clippers, but yet still afford some control of the horse.

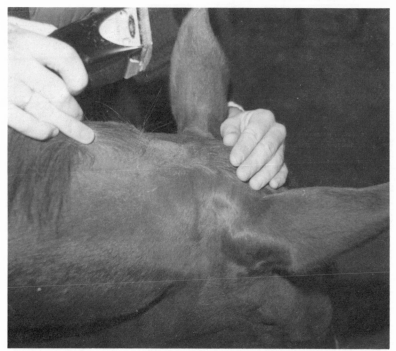

Step 2: An area wide enough to allow room for the bridle has been trimmed behind the ears.

Caution: If the bridle path is made too wide, it may possibly shorten the appearance of the neck.

Not Shown: Excess hairs on the legs and just above the hoof are also removed.

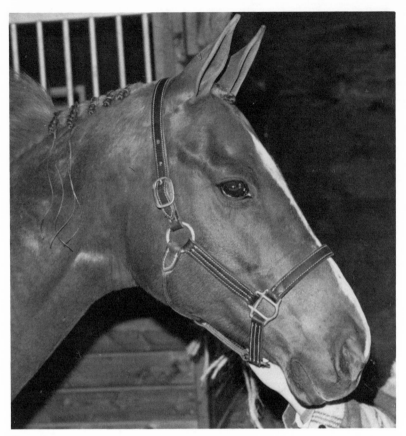

Step 3:
• Note the ears. All of the hair around the edges of the ears has been trimmed. As well, the longer hairs from inside the ears have been removed.

Using Hollings' basic rule of thumb: all hair which detracts from the outline of the horse's head has been removed. The eyelashes remain.

• Hollings braids the forelock first, then works from the top of the mane down, because, if the horse begins to get restless after standing for some time, it is more difficult to braid near the head than it is lower down.

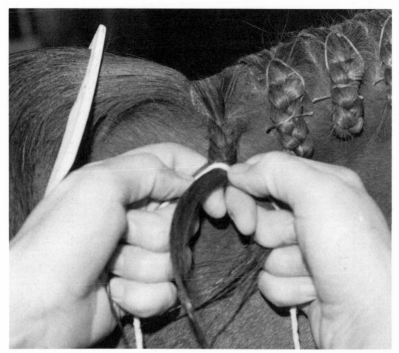

Step 4: Hollings braids by pulling the hair *down* against the neck.
Halfway down the braid, using white yarn for visibility, she places
the yarn across the braid and then plaits it in. Note the use of the
human comb for holding the next part of the mane out of the way.
Hollings also uses the comb to measure the width of each braid.

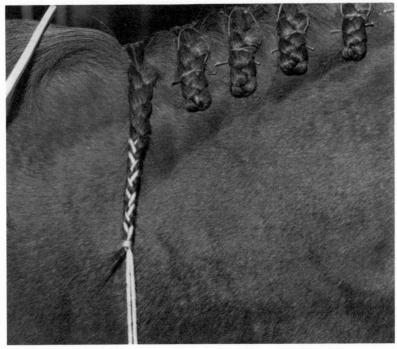

Step 5: At the end of the braid, Hollings ties a half hitch knot.

Hollings always braids as close to the end of each bunch of hair as she possibly can. She uses a fairly lengthy piece of thread – about sixteen inches long.

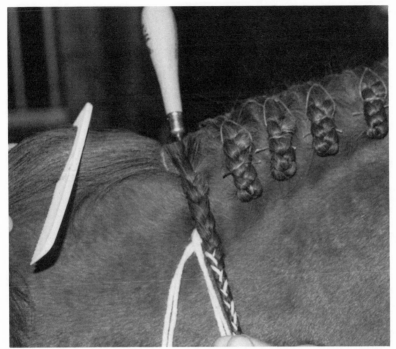

Step 6: A rug hook is inserted into the top of the braid and the yarn at the end of the braid is pulled up and through, tucking the lower part of the braid under.

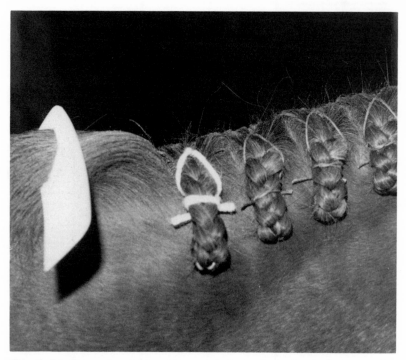

Step 7: Hollings ties the braid up and always knots *under* because she feels, as mentioned previously, that a good braiding job is one that does not call attention to itself but rather 'takes the hair out of the way' so that the lines of the horse are uncluttered. If using yarn, knot on *top* so that the yarn shows. Its colour may be coordinated with part of the handler's or rider's outfit.

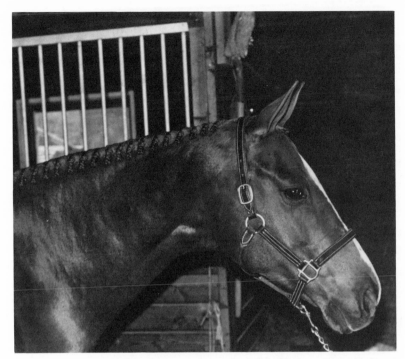

Step 8: A well-braided mane: the braids are neat, evenly spaced and uniform in size. As well, they are lying flat on the horse's neck.

Note that the mane is braided as far down the withers as is possible. If the saddle interferes with these last braids, either leave the hair unbraided or cut it off.

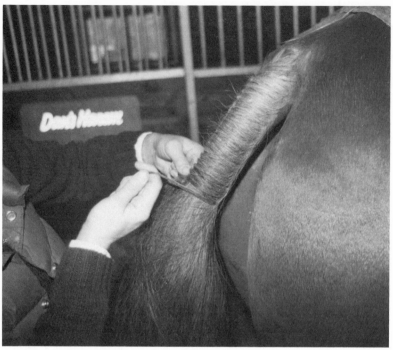

Step 9:

• A five foot piece of thread is laid against the tail with about a foot of thread left over at the top (up on the rump), and a foot or more past the end of the tail bone.

• Hair is pulled from the very *back* of the tail in order to avoid having bits of hair dangling when the horse lifts his or her tail.

• The hair must be pulled *tight* to keep the braid both straight and neat.

• Very *small* bunches of hair must be used so that the braid does not become too fat.

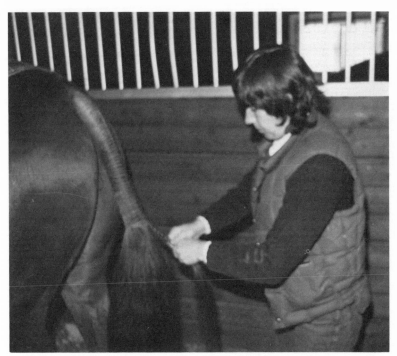

Step 10: Hollings braids as far down the tail bone as suits the conformation of the horse *and* the length of his or her tail. Usually this most suitable spot is the end of the tail bone. She then finishes braiding the sections of hair in hand, making sure that the long thread is worked in as well.

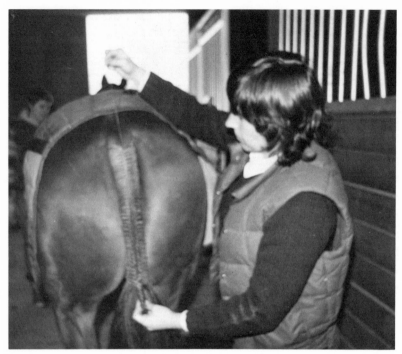

Step 11: The long thread is pulled from the top, gathering the braid under in a loop and holding it securely in place. This thread is then cut off at the top. The rug hook is put through the braid at the top and two pieces of thread are knotted in to help hold the braids in.

General comments: When braiding a mane, dampen it in segments with a wet brush or sponge. Wipe off any moisture. Dampen the top part of the tail when braiding and wipe off moisture.

Finishing Touches:

• Hair Coat: Hollings uses 'Show Sheen' to put that last special touch on the appearance of the horse. She finds that as well as adding a shine to the horse, it appears to repel dust.
• White Markings: Corn starch may be rubbed well in over any white on the horse (blaze, socks, etc.)
• Eyes and Muzzle: Vaseline may be added lightly around the eyes and muzzle of a horse to add lustre. (It is used in the showing of line horses rather than of performance horses.)
• Hooves: Scrub hooves clean. The use of hoof black, etc. is optional.

A Final Note: Make sure that *your* appearance does justice to that of the horse.

Blanketing

QUESTION: I am the owner of a horse that refuses to keep his blanket on in the stall. He has ripped several blankets and getting them repaired is pretty costly. I'm not sure just how he manages to wriggle out of the blanket but sometimes the owner of the stable where I board my horse finds the blanket still done up but lying in the straw. Other times he has found my blanket in pieces.

I do a lot of riding in the winter and I like to keep my horse's coat from becoming too thick.

If any of your experts know anything I can do to stop my horse from this annoying and costly habit, I would appreciate hearing about it. Thank you in advance for any help you can give.

EXPERT: Diana Gill has been a major driving force behind the organization and development of line class shows across Ontario. She has given unstintingly of both her time and abilities to help make these shows a success. Gill, herself, has bred several line class champions and as a co-owner has won the highly coveted Governor General's Cup. Obviously she is very used to keeping horses in show condition.

ANSWER: Gill uses a 'bib' on horses who are escape artists when it comes to getting out of their blankets. A 'bib' is constructed of leather or hard plastic and is attached by straps and buckles to the lower rings of the halter. The 'bib' hangs down under the chin of the horse and prevents him from being able to get his teeth in contact with the blanket.

Gill favours blankets with leg straps which encircle the hind legs. These leg straps prevent the blanket from sliding forward or to one side if the horse grabs at it with his teeth. Her preference in make of blankets is the Baker. She feels that although they are initially more expensive, their price, in number of years used, is quite reasonable.

To introduce a horse to wearing a blanket, Gill keeps a special 'training' blanket. On it, she smears melted Cribbox in big patches. On top of the unpleasant-smelling and foul-tasting Cribbox she sprinkles liberal dashes of curry powder. The 'finished product' smells rather awful but is effective in stopping the horse from chewing on the blanket.

Underneath the winter blankets which Gill uses on her horses, she places a summer sheet. This sheet is much easier to wash than a heavy blanket and because it is clean, it is less irritating to the horse's hair coat.

A personal note: Horses kept well-groomed are less likely to play with their blankets. Often it is simply itchy skin which starts them grabbing hold of the blanket and finding they can pull it off. As well, boredom plays a part. Horses standing in for twenty-four hours a day are more likely to get into mischief than ones who are turned out regularly.

6. CARING FOR YOUR HORSE'S FEET

A well-trimmed, correctly-shod foot.

Hoof, Heel and Foot Problems

QUESTION: Why are my horse's feet cracking?

How can I get rid of weepy sores on my horse's heels?

What is causing that unpleasant smell I notice when I pick out my horse's feet?

These are but a few of the questions I have been asked by anxious horse owners who are concerned about the condition of their horses' feet.

Some of the most common problems which might be encountered in the feet of a horse, the treatment and, more importantly, the best way to prevent the problems from occurring in the first place.

The old adage, 'No foot, no horse!' is a very valid one, for without good feet a show horse's career can be not only disrupted but also terminated.

EXPERT: Dr. Darryl Bonder (see Chapter 5, Question 3).

ANSWER: First of all, it is important to have a clear understanding of the function and design of the hoof.

The horse is a uniquely designed animal for running and, through evolution, has become a uni-digital animal that exerts tremendous pressure on its hooves, especially when in full gallop and in landing after fences.

The wall of the hoof is thicker and harder at the front with less water content because it is a more rigid surface. In the heel, it is thinner and more flexible with a greater water content. The hoof is designed to absorb shock. To quote Bonder, 'Within the horse's foot is a hydraulic mechanism.' To explain, 'The foot has a tremendous blood supply spread over a great surface area – the laminae, which diffuse shock. When the horse's hoof hits the ground, the blood is squeezed up and out of the foot and then returns in the non-weight bearing phase of running.'

131

What Are Cracks in the Hoof Wall? Cracks in the hoof wall are given different names depending on where they are located but, basically, they are all the same. These cracks usually extend up from the weight-bearing surface (the ground surface) towards the coronary band. They may extend right into the coronet itself and become a very painful lesion.

• Why do they happen? Cracks are a reflection of the stress on the hoof and the hoof, not being able to cope with that stress, cracks.
   Inability to cope can be caused by:
   a. Improper shoeing.
   b. Too long a hoof that has been trimmed incorrectly.
   c. A defect in, or injury to, the coronary band so that the germinal cells that produce new horn are not capable of producing proper horn and thus the horn is not as strong as it should be.
   d. Excessive drying out of the hoof so that the water content is not there and therefore the hoof is not as flexible as it should be.
• Dangers: The depth of the crack, that is, whether or not it enters into the sensitive laminae and sensitive structures will determine the degree of lameness. If the crack is superficial, the horse may not be lame at all. A deep crack can result in a 'three-legged' lameness.
   As Bonder points out, the most serious aspect of quarter crack is that if it occurs, there is an open doorway for infection to enter into those deeper, sensitive structures and because the horse is walking in manure and urine, it is very easy for bacterial infection to take hold.
• Treatment: Treatment varies from corrective shoeing, to rather traumatic blacksmith surgery which involves cutting out the damaged portion of the hoof wall.
   Another often used method is wiring the crack shut by putting two screws on either side of the crack and a tension band across it.
   Bonder routinely covers cracks in the initial stages before they dry out. He suggests Vetrap™ as an ideal covering in that it not only adheres closely to the hoof wall but also is waterproof. As well, other materials may be added underneath. Time to allow the crack to grow

out properly is extremely important. Also necessary are proper nutrition, a clean environment and good lubrication of the hoof. The risk of infection suggests it is a good idea to flush out the crack with antibiotics and to give a toxic injection.

• Prevention: Competent blacksmith work is crucial. Improper work may cause cracks to occur. Some types of hooves are more prone to cracks than others. If a horse has very dry, 'chippy' feet, lubrication will help to encourage new growth.

What Are Cracked Heel, Grease Heel, Scratches, Mud-Fever? Each of the above names refers to the same problem. Cracked heel is a condition that occurs between the fetlock and the coronary band of the heel; that is, on the back of the pastern area.

Similar in appearance to the eczema that some humans experience, it is an inflamed reddening – a weeping type of lesion which might start off superficially but proceed deeper. For the working animal it is a very painful condition.

• Why does it happen? The causes or possible causes of cracked heel are tremendously varied. Some are:

a. Improper grooming of the area.

b. Standing in a wet stall.

c. Salts and chemicals that are put on arena footing, driveways and roads.

d. An almost allergic reaction to various things in the environment.

e. A predisposition to eczema in some horses.

• Dangers: Cracked heel may lend itself to a secondary infection either fungal or bacterial in type. The raw area provides an ideal environment for infection to develop – a situation which is compounded by the fact that a horse stands in manure and urine.

• Treatment: A combination of a good cleaning regimen plus the application of a suitable ointment is the best way of clearing up cracked heel. Bonder suggests the use of a good surgical scrub such as Bridine or Betadine to cleanse the area thoroughly. After drying the location properly, the application of an antibiotic-corticosteroid ointment plus one with antifungal properties should dramatically reduce the inflammation within two or three days.

• Prevention: Prevention of cracked heel is very difficult as some horses seem very sensitive and predisposed towards the condition. Obviously, good hygiene in the barn is very important. The heel area should be properly cleansed of any arena, paddock or road residue, and if the area is washed clean, it should be dried thoroughly.

What is Thrush? Thrush is a disease which affects the sulci – the grooves on either side of the frog and in the frog's middle. The odour of thrush, overwhelmingly strong and foul, is usually noticed first. If the point of a hoof pick is stuck into the sulci, it usually will go in quite deeply and can practically be turned around in the space. The material there is soft and 'gooey' and ranges in colour from blackish, through greyish to almost white.

• Why does thrush occur? Thrush is related to cleanliness and the shape of the hoof. Possible causes are:
    a. Improperly cleaned stalls.
    b. A naturally deep sulcus.
    c. An inadequate amount of frog contact with the ground.
    d. A boxy or club-shaped foot.
• Dangers: The greatest problem with thrush is that various bacteria can penetrate deep into the sulci, especially the anaerobic-type bacteria that can live without oxygen. The frog, a spongy material that self-seals, is a perfect environment in which these organisms can multiply and, if sealed in, create an abscess. A really deep-seated infection can become so bad that it affects the coffin bone. If such a condition occurs, it is known as osteomyelitis and, to quote Bonder, 'By this time you're in deep trouble!' A deteriorated coffin bone with actual holes can result.
• Treatment: In the initial stages of a deep-seated thrush infection, Bonder likes to clean the area out thoroughly and flush it with a medication that includes hydrogen peroxide which liberates oxygen and thus makes an unsuitable environment for anaerobic bac-

teria. If mixed with Bridine or some other type of soap or solution containing iodine or perhaps an antibiotic such as Furasone, it can be carried into the infected area. Bonder suggests the twice daily use of a fifty-fifty mix which will dry the problem area and keep it clean.

Not recommended in the initial stages of a deep-seated thrush infection which makes the area very sensitive, are such medications as the caustic copper sulphates like Kopertox. After some healing has taken place and only the more superficial layers are involved, the astringent properties of these products are beneficial.

• Prevention: Clean bedding is important, as is proper hoof care. A hoof should be washed with water and disinfectant, perhaps every other day and picked out once a day.

A good blacksmith will make the hoof a self-cleaning mechanism in that the bars will be open and material can work its way back from the point of the frog towards the base of the frog.

Remember: Early detection is crucial. The more deep-seated the disease becomes, the more serious it is and the more difficult to eradicate.

A personal note: In each of these three conditions, good stable management plays an important role in preventing them from occurring as well as being crucial in their treatment. Clean stalls and thorough grooming, as well as being aesthetically pleasing, are downright essential to the well-being of the horse.

If the Shoe Fits ... How to Recognize Good Shoeing
Beware: Bad Shoeing Can Cause Problems

QUESTION: Can you explain to me how to know when the blacksmith has done a good job? What do you watch for when he's working on a horse's feet?

Is there any reason why one horse in particular will lose his shoes? Why do some horses develop cracks in their hooves? What can be done so this doesn't happen?

EXPERT: With forty years of experience shoeing horses in the Toronto area alone, Ernie Jay is one of Canada's best known and most highly-regarded farriers. With clients like Mac Cone, Doug Henry, Tom Gayford and John Weir, who all have been with Jay for a long time, he shoes some of Canada's top horses.

Jay has always had a reputation of being a hard worker. These days, now that he is 'letting up a little', his first clients of the day don't see him until about seven o'clock in the morning. In the summer, when things get a little bit more hectic, Jay is usually on the job at 6:30.

He has brought along four apprentices so far and takes pride in the fact that they are all successful farriers in Ontario's horse industry.

'There are no miracles in this business, but a lot of problems that you see are caused by bad shoeing,' says Jay.

ANSWER:
Characteristics of a Good Shoeing Job:

• A good farrier, especially when working on a horse for the first time, will pull off both front shoes and examine the feet carefully. He does the same with the hind feet. If necessary, he will move the horse forward and backwards a few steps to determine the horse's lower limb conformation. A horse with a problem such as 'winging' or' toeing in' will be watched jogging out.

• If the front feet are approximately the same size and shape, a good blacksmith will trim them naturally, but if they are not, then he will try to even them up as much as he can. Sometimes a smaller foot looks contracted – the heel is higher. Jay takes the heel down a little and he lets the toe extend out. If the horse is a show horse, he extends the shoe out around the foot a marginal amount. If the horse is a runner, he does not extend the shoe because the horse might interfere; that is, hit his other leg with the protruding shoe. The larger foot usually has a splayed appearance. Jay narrows it a little. The hind feet should also be treated as a pair to be matched as perfectly as possible.

136

It is important that all four feet be shod as *evenly* as possible, but Jay cautions that 'You can't do it all at once.'
• Check the angle of the front feet. It should not be less than forty-five degrees but can be fifty degrees or more depending on the conformation of the horse. Hind feet are, of course, steeper.
• The wall of each foot must be made perfectly level and so should the shoe. If both are level, the shoe will meet the hoof evenly all the way around. According to Jay, quite a few farriers have a tendency to take the foot lower to the outside and this one-sidedness leads to distortion in the growth of the foot and to lameness. If the foot is not levelled correctly, too much pressure will be brought to bear on one part of the foot while the other part will not be carrying any weight. As a result, one area takes all the strain and the horse mill move badly. Of course, if part of the hoof has broken away, it is not possible to have the foot and the shoe touch all the way around and all a farrier can do in such a case is hope that no problems will result.

If you are fortunate enough to have a horse that has good straight legs in front and discover after shoeing that he begins to toe in or to toe out, you can suspect that although the feet and shoes appear to be level, they are not.
• Make sure that the shoe is nicely rounded and fits the outline of the hoof. On front feet, no hoof should project over the toe of the shoe but, in the case of the hind feet of hunters and jumpers, many farriers set the shoe back from the toe about one-quarter of an inch so that if the horse overreaches or forges, he is less likely to hurt himself.

On both front and hind feet, the shoe should not be too short. If it is, it will be 'buried under the horse's heel'. It is important, in Jay's opinion, to extend the heel of the shoe a fractional distance beyond the foot; in other words, on looking down from the outside, you should be able to see the heel of the shoe slightly protruding. Such an extension of the shoe helps to take some of the weight strain off the heel.
• Watch that the shoe is not riding on the sole of the foot. The outside rim must be longer in order to bear the weight of the horse.

There should be no excessive paring of the foot. Any ragged

edges should be trimmed from the frog but the sole should not be cut unless the foot is long overdue for a reshoe and an extra sole has developed.

• Although it will be difficult for you to spot, it is imperative that the bar of the foot *never* be cut. The area where the bar of the foot turns round to form the wall is known as the seat of corn. Often farriers cut away that angle to give the horse the appearance of a nice widely-spread foot. This 'opening of the bars' is the worst thing they can do because they are taking away one of the main supports of weight and such an action leads to contracted heels.

• Check the foot to make sure that the nails have been driven in as evenly as possible. Some farriers drive nails higher than others do. Jay, himself, is in favour of driving nails fairly high in order to get into the stronger foot area.

• Make a point of checking the area that has been rasped. The only places allowable are just under the bed for clenches and a recessing of the horn to bed the toe clip. Rasping opens tiny tubes in the horn tissue which then loses moisture and becomes dry and brittle. Oiling will not help.

• Watch for cold or hot shoeing. According to Jay, at the track cold shoeing is done because a farrier can easily change the shape of light racing shoes. In the case of heavier shoes for hunting, jumping, or roadwork, etc., hot shoeing is *mandatory* with a new pair of shoes because no standard shoe size is exactly correct without some change having to be made. In order to change the shape of a heavy shoe, a farrier must heat the shoe.

Problem Feet Are Not All That Common: Jay stresses that problem feet are not as common as horse owners seem to think. Many difficulties can be avoided by making sure that you have a good blacksmith.

As far as losing shoes is concerned, correctly fitted ones, on properly trimmed hooves, should not come off unless they are pulled off in deep mud or improperly nailed on in the first place.

Cracks in hooves are either caused by neglect or result from hooves being 'shelly' or thin-walled. Obviously the former problem can be corrected by more frequent trimmings. The latter, 'shelly' hooves, can be improved by making the walls of the hooves tougher. This toughening process can be started by the application of ointments or oils to the coronet from which the new hoof growth develops. The sole of the foot and the frog may also be well-oiled. Jay cautions against putting oil on the lower exterior part of the hoof as he feels that such an action only softens an area that needs to be very strong. Some suggested oils or ointments are: Hooflex, pine tar, castor oil or lard.

If a horse does happen to have real problem feet then they should be packed every day or every other day, particularly the front feet. Jay is in favour of natural materials such as mud or blue clay and water. There are various store-bought hoof packs which are also effective. The choice is up to the owner of the horse.

How Often Should Horses Be Re-Shod? Horses that are on a very strenuous show circuit sometimes need to be shod as often as every fourth week, whereas horses ridden for pleasure only, can go as long as eight weeks between shoeing.

7. CONDITIONING AND FITNESS
YOUR HORSE AND YOURSELF

Fitness is important for both the horse *and* the rider.

Preparing for the Training Level in Eventing

QUESTION: Much attention is given to conditioning for Preliminary Eventing and up, but little is given to the Training level. I would like your help in developing a training schedule for a horse in his first year of competition at the Training level in eventing.

We went Pre-training last year with no problems as far as endurance was concerned. But in order to prepare for the next level I'd like to know how many hours per week we should be spending on road work – what type – how much walking, trotting, cantering, etc.

We live in a relatively flat area. My horse is an eight-year-old, three-quarter-bred hunter with no past problems with respect to legs or general health. Of course I realize that our roadwork should be combined with dressage work now and fences as he becomes more conditioned. We did not do very much this winter apart from weekend hacking. We started up again in February riding three to four times per week. With the roads free of ice, we would like to start getting ready for the coming season.

EXPERT: Liz Ashton (see Chapter 5, Question 2).

ANSWER: Ashton outlines a *three month* programme which will help to condition your horse for competition at the Training level.

1) *First month:* Ashton suggests that you spend the first month 'legging-up' your horse. Begin the month with daily walks twenty minutes in length. As the month progresses, slowly increase these sessions to an hour. During the latter half of the month, introduce short periods of trot. Each trotting session should last no longer than three minutes at any one time.

2) *Second month:* As you go into the second month, you can begin to do a little bit of actual schooling work in the form of gymnastic jumping and dressage work. When doing your dressage work, make sure

that you keep your horse in a relatively long frame as it is too soon to ask your horse to work too much on the bit.

The second month should also include roadwork, preferably in the country rather than, literally, on the road. On days when you are not doing any gymnastic or dressage work, hack your horse for the full hour. Let the type of terrain over which you are travelling, determine the speed at which you go. Where the footing is good, trot. If the footing is hard or stony, make sure you walk. *Don't* exceed five minutes of trotting at any one time. Let your horse's respiration or breathing be your guide. If the horse at any time is blowing, slow down to a walk.

3) *Third month:* At this stage Ashton emphasizes the importance of a fairly systematic type of schedule. A suggested typical programme is outlined as follows:

Monday: Do dressage and roadwork for a total of one hour. Start with the dressage so that if you encounter problems in this phase, you can spend longer on it by shortening the roadwork. For example:
• dressage – twenty minutes; roadwork – forty minutes.
• dressage – thirty-five minutes; roadwork – twenty-five minutes.

Tuesday: Do conditioning work #1, which is:
• Warm up at a walk and trot for about fifteen to twenty minutes.
• Gallop for a half a mile at four hundred meters per minute.
• Rest until the horse is no longer blowing.
• Gallop for a half a mile at four hundred meters per minute.

Wednesday: Do jumping and roadwork for a total of one hour.
As with Monday's dressage, start with the jumping so that if you encounter problems in this phase you can spend longer on it by shortening the roadwork.

Thursday: Do dressage and roadwork as on Monday.

Friday: Do conditioning work #2, which is:
• Follow Tuesday's outline but substitute two-thirds of a mile for one-half of a mile.

Saturday: Do *either* dressage and roadwork *or* jumping and road-work. (Let the horse's needs decide which of the two you work on.)

Sunday: Rest.

Repeat this schedule weekly until the end of the month with the exception of the *conditioning days* which will have these changes:

Conditioning #3: (on the second Thursday), which is:
• Warm up at a walk and trot for about fifteen to twenty minutes.
• Gallop for three-quarters of a mile at four hundred meters per minute.
• Rest by walking until your horse is no longer blowing.
• Gallop for three-quarters of a mile at four hundred meters per minute.

Conditioning #4: (on the second Friday), which is:
• As for Conditioning #3 but substitute one mile for three-quarters of a mile.

Conditioning #5: (on the third Thursday), which is:
• Warm up at a walk and trot for about fifteen to twenty minutes.
• Gallop for one-half a mile *but at* four hundred and fifty meters per minute.
• Rest until your horse is no longer blowing.
• Gallop for one mile at four hundred and fifty meters per minute.

Conditioning #6: (on the third Friday), which is:
• As for Conditioning #5 but substitute two-thirds of a mile for one-half of a mile.

Conditioning #7: (on the fourth Thursday), which is:
• As for Conditioning #5 but substitute three-quarters of a mile for one-half of a mile.

Conditioning #8: (on the fourth Friday), which is:
• As for Conditioning #5 but substitute one mile for one-half of a mile.

Ashton stresses the fact that conditioning work should *never* be done closer than every third day.

General Comments:

• When galloping her horses, Ashton uses brush boots, hind boots and bell boots on her horses for their added protection. She does not use pads on her horses' feet unless they are horses with flat feet.
• If you are not sure of just how great a distance four hundred and fifty metres is, then Ashton advises that you mark the distances off and get the speed firmly fixed in your mind.
• Your horse must be ridden *six* times a week, not just two or three. If you are short of time, then get a friend to work your horse. It is very important that he work regularly and not stand in his stall.

Exercises for the Rider

QUESTION: I have not ridden very much since last summer and, although I've tried to keep in shape with other sports like skiing and volleyball, when I finally did have a chance to ride last week, my legs were 'killing' me.

Now I at last have a horse of my own again, and, with show season coming up, want to get in shape as quickly as possible. What exercises can I do to strengthen the muscles I will need for riding?

EXPERT: Allan Scott has recently become the Fitness Director for the Toronto's Skydome. A well-known fitness columnist for publications such as the *Toronto Star*, Scott has also been the Director of two highly-respected fitness clubs – the Cambridge Club and the Adelaide Club. Scott has had an impressive track record in the field of fitness including the title of Director of Testing and Research at the Fitness Institute.

Not only does Scott have a knowledge of the physical requirements of the sport of riding but also he has, in the past, developed a fitness programme for some of Canada's leading equestrian competitors.

ANSWER: Following is a list of exercises that Scott recommends for getting riders into shape quickly and efficiently:

• The Ball Squeeze.
Props: a tennis or racquet ball.

Hold the ball in your hand and squeeze as hard as you can once a second until you can't squeeze any more.

Change hands and repeat the exercise.

Build up until you can do this twice on each hand.

This exercise will strengthen not only the fingers and forearms but also back up through the shoulders.

• The Shoulder Shrug.
Props: two equal weights or, substitute two soup cans or two books, etc.

This exercise is just like it sounds. From a standing position with your arms at your sides and weights in your hands, shrug your shoulders up towards your ears as far as you can.

Repeat thirty times.

This exercise will help to strengthen the arms and shoulders.

• The Chair Step Up Exercise.
Props: a strong kitchen chair.

First step up onto the chair with your left foot and then step up with your right foot. Stand straight up on the chair. Then step down with the right foot and down with the left foot. This total action would be one count.

Repeat thirty times.

Rest fifteen or twenty seconds.

Repeat this exercise totally, three times.

It will develop strength in your leg muscles. (One of the many benefits derived will be more ease in mounting from the ground.)

• The Ball Squeeze – sitting.

Props: a beach ball or perhaps a volleyball or basketball.

Put the ball between your legs at your knees and squeeze the ball by trying to push your knees together. Squeeze as hard as you can. Squeeze for a second, relax, squeeze, relax for a total of thirty seconds.

Rest for fifteen or twenty seconds.

Repeat.

This exercise will help to strengthen the thigh muscles and to give thigh grip.

• The Squatting Exercise.

Props: a chair, preferably kitchen-type.

Stand facing the back of the chair with one hand resting on it. Squat down until your thighs are parallel to the floor and then slowly stand.

Repeat and build up until you can do sixty without stopping.

This exercise will help to strengthen the legs.

• The Triceps Press or Back of the Arms Exercise.

Props: two kitchen chairs.

Get on the floor between the two chairs and place your hands on the seats of the chairs. Try to lift yourself up off of the floor using your hands and arms only. (Whether or not you can do it doesn't matter but the important factor is the effort.)

Try to do this exercise fifteen times.

If you can do it successfully, fine, but if not, you're still going to be working the right muscles.

- Abdominal Area Exercise One: Sit Ups.
Lie on your back with knees bent and feet flat on the floor. The important factor is not how you get up into sitting position but how you go down. Uncurl slowly as you lie back down.
Work up to twenty-five of these sit ups.

- Abdominal Area Exercise Two: Leg Raises.
Sit on the floor with your legs straight out in front of you and with your upper body resting on your elbows at your sides. Lift your legs three or four inches off the floor, spread them apart, put them together and lower them slowly.
Work up to thirty times.

The last two help to strengthen the abdomen and in so doing, strengthen the back. (Although often a neglected area in riding, the back needs to be kept strong, supple and very flexible!)
Scott states that in two weeks you should begin to feel that your riding muscles are far more fit and capable.

An aside: For beginning riders who have trouble keeping their heels down when riding, I asked Scott what exercise he would recommend. He suggests the following:

- The Calf Raise.
Stand with toes on a stair and the heels off. Raise your heels off the stair and then lower them as much as possible – the lower the better.
Such an action will help to stretch the Achilles tendon which in turn will help you to lower your heels further.

A personal note: Good luck with your exercises and remember ... physical fitness is always a good investment. The time spent is never wasted.

149

8. TRAINING YOUR HORSE

Winning performances such as this by Mac Cone are the culmination of years of training for both horse and rider.

Longeing – The Proper Way

QUESTION: My horse is a very excitable three-year-old gelding. He is very green. Is it a good idea to spend a lot of time longeing a green horse? Some people have told me that longeing is a strain on a horse's legs. Is this true? How long a period of time should you longe a horse in each work session? How many times a week should you work a young horse? Can you longe a horse with just a halter on its head or should he be wearing a bridle?

EXPERT: Christopher Todd and his wife, Mai-Liis run Equinox Training Centre in Stirling, Ontario.

Todd's experience as a rider and trainer spans twenty years and four countries. He gained the prestigious British Horse Society's Instructor Certificate (BHSI) in 1973 while working as chief Instructor at the Wirral Riding Centre in England. At that time the Wirral was ranked among the top three training centres in Britain. His then competition horse won several Prix St. Georges classes and was placed in the British National Championships in 1974.

More recently, in Canada in 1984 and 1985 he rode in recognized competition at Medium I and II Levels on a grade horse trained by himself. The combination was never unplaced and at the Genn Farms Show they won both classes and the Medium Championship against national and international riders.

In the United States as Senior Instructor at the Potomac Horse Centre he coached staff members to win their sections in One and Two Events. Todd has also taken time from his teaching and training duties to study Haute Ecole with an instructor of the Spanish Riding School at a private stable near Vienna, Austria.

Perhaps Todd's forte in horsemanship is his ability to include psychology as an integral part of a horse's training.

ANSWER: Todd takes note of the fact that you say your horse is 'an excitable three-year-old' and points out that no training method, if divorced from sensible stable management, is going to be of any help. He suggests that one of the first things to look at is WHY the horse is so excitable and whether the feeding of grain, the daily turn out and the every day handling, etc. is appropriate for the horse's age, size, breed, etc. Any necessary changes should be made as soon as possible.

You do not mention whether or not you have actually ridden your green horse yet. Horses as young as three may very often get excited because they suffer discomfort caused by trying to carry the weight of a rider while their muscular structure is underdeveloped. Todd is of the firm opinion that no real ridden work should begin until the horse has turned four.

As well, he points out that if your knowledge of longeing is limited, you might be wise to initially work under the guidance of a more experienced person. A positive beginning is of paramount importance when working with green horses.

If a horse is sufficiently grown, *if* a horse is sufficiently developed both mentally and physically and *if* a horse is a suitable age, *then*, ten to fifteen minutes of longe work twice a day is recommended on a six-day-a-week basis. A horse should be given one day off a week.

It is not so much the longeing itself but *how it is done* that can put a strain on a young horse's bones and ligaments. Obviously, if the horse is allowed to work at a panic pace, in a too tight circle for long periods of time, physical damage to the legs is very likely to occur. Todd points out, however, that longeing is a basic method of training horses before they are ridden that has been used in the Spanish Riding School upwards of five hundred years, and, to use his words, 'The horses last forever.'

As far as the size of a longe circle is concerned, the rule of thumb is that it should be determined by the trainer's control of the horse. Remember, the farther away the horse is from the trainer, the less control the trainer has, but all other things being equal, the less stress on the horse's legs. Todd suggests that you start out on a twelve to fifteen meter circle and try to increase the size to twenty meters within the first few days when the horse has an understanding of what he is doing.

Yes, you can longe in a halter (a leather one) as long as it fits snugly; in fact, Todd much prefers longeing on a halter to lunging on a bridle with the line attached to the bit. He stresses the fact that inevitably there is going to be some occasion when the horse shies or leaps about and the horse with the longe line attached to the bit gets a jerk in the mouth. Even longeing in a strong wind can cause a horse discomfort if the line is attached to the bit.

Suitable Longeing Equipment:
Todd suggests the following equipment:
• a well-designed cavesson or a leather halter (either should fit properly)
• a longe line preferably web with no large, heavy snap, only an ordinary size one and with no chain
• a longe whip
• a lightweight surcingle (Initially this should be fastened not too tightly; therefore, a breastplate to prevent it slipping backwards is a handy extra.)
• a saddle
• a bridle (a straight rubber snaffle bit is best at first)
• side reins (leather with no elastic insets are best in Todd's opinion).

In the early stages only the first items are necessary. As the training progresses, introduce him to the saddle and, later, the bridle. Side reins are best used only by experienced trainers or under experienced guidance.

You mention that 'any information' would be helpful so Todd outlines the method he uses:

> The first thing the horse has to learn is to lead properly from each side. Initially the trainer walks level with the horse's shoulder and if necessary encourages him to walk on with

the long whip behind the girth so that, in fact, the horse slightly leads the way and the trainer has a loose rein on the cavesson. If you can do this, then you can longe the horse, because all you have to do is get a little bit farther away from him.

After awhile you will probably have to walk a circle staying slightly behind the horse to start with. Eventually your aim must be to get so that you can stand still while the horse performs a perfect circle around you with a light but consistent connection to the longe line. The rhythm of the horse's movement should be regular – not hurried but reasonably active. The longe line should be *in contact* – not loose.

Helpful Hints:
- Keep the longe line smooth and untwisted.
- Do not wrap the longe line around your hand.
- Keep the whip still. People often thoughtlessly wave it around, thus upsetting the horse.
- Be consistent. Keep the same tone of voice for whatever instruction you give.
- Remember the two basic whip signs:
  a. Move the lash from behind the horse to send him on.
  b. Swing the lash out towards the shoulder to move the horse out on a circle.

In Summary: To quote Todd, 'Basically when you're longeing, you're riding the horse from twenty feet away with the longe rein, longe whip and voice instead of the legs and hands. These aids must be handled properly in order to get good results from the horse.'

How to Make a Horse Stand Still While Being Mounted

QUESTION: Help! What do you do to stop a horse from walking just when you try to mount?

EXPERT: Andrew Dalnoki, Chief Instructor at the Eglinton Pony Club where he has taught for the last two decades, provided the answer to this question. With previous experience at the McGuiness Farm at a time when dressage was studied there, at the Crang Farm when hunters were prepared for the field and for the show ring and at the late Lou Mikucki's at the time when he was importing horses from Poland and training them for show and re-sale, Dalnoki took with him to Eglinton a solid background in all phases of horsemanship.

Now, at Eglinton, he specializes in teaching hunter seat equitation to advanced and show riders. As well, he breeds and develops Canadian Sport Horses for the equine market.

ANSWER: A partially mounted rider with one foot in the stirrup can easily be dragged and stepped on if his horse bolts; thus, for safety reasons alone, Dalnoki feels that it is very important to *train* a horse thoroughly to stand still when it is being mounted. He stresses the need for consistency, patience and attention to details in the handling of the horse.

Here are the steps he advocates:

1) Decide firstly where you plan to mount and lead the horse to that spot. *(A personal note:* Use some psychology as to where you make your choice.)

2) Hold your reins taut in your left hand, on fairly strong contact in order to give yourself more control of the horse.

The outside rein should be especially tight but not to the degree that the horse's head turns to the outside. As well as both reins, hold the mane, not, Dalnoki stresses, the saddle.

Hanging onto the pommel of the saddle when you mount often results in a twisted saddle. This in turn frightens the horse and makes him more likely to move on next time you mount.

3) Face the back of the horse, hold the left stirrup at right angles with your right hand and place your left foot in the stirrup. Be careful to avoid digging your toe into the horse's stomach. As Dalnoki points out, such a dig could be responsible for making the horse move on.

If at this point the horse does move on, take your foot out of the

157

stirrup and make the horse back up to his original position. If the horse has backed up rather than moved forward, Dalnoki walks alongside him to his original position. It is psychologically important to mount where *you* decide to, not where the horse chooses to let you.

4) Swing your right leg over the saddle, into the right stirrup and lower yourself *gently* into the saddle. Some people drop into the saddle 'like a ton of bricks' and it is little wonder that the horse moves off; in fact, some horses tend to walk on because they are expecting that jarring sensation in their back at any moment. Dalnoki stresses the fact that if the rider is large and the horse particularly sensitive it is even more important to be careful that you sit gently in the saddle.

5) If your horse still moves on when you follow this procedure for mounting, Dalnoki suggests asking someone to assist you by holding the horse. Make sure your assistant is quiet and firm but not rough.

6) Once your horse gets used to standing still, try mounting on your own again, without help. If you are successful, make a point of never letting the horse move on until you have asked him.

Some horses become very skittish when you go to mount. If this is the case make sure first of all that you are not the cause of his distress. If he associates you with the saddle slipping (because you have not tightened the girth properly and have tried to pull yourself up with the saddle) or with a bang on his kidneys (because you come down hard in the saddle) he naturally will be reluctant to have you mount.

Dalnoki stresses the futility of losing your temper, jerking the reins and / or yelling at the horse. Such action will only upset the horse more. If he is really frightened, use tidbits such as a piece of carrot or a lump of sugar and try to win his confidence.

Take your time and follow each of the suggested steps with the aid of an assistant, if necessary. Remember, your patience will be rewarded with a more obedient horse and an increased safety situation.

Seats, Styles and Stirrup Length

QUESTION: What are the theoretical differences among the following forms of equitation: basic seat, balanced seat, dressage seat, and hunt seat?

Also, what variations in style and stirrup length would a rider employ in going from dressage to jumper to hunter class to the cross country phase of an event?

EXPERT: In 1988, event rider, Peter Gray, represented his native country, Bermuda, in the Olympic Games at Seoul, Korea. With his classic style, his obvious talent, his ever increasing experience and his dedication to self-improvement, he is fast becoming a real contender.

Seoul was his third Olympics. In the 1980 alternate Olympics, the then, inexperienced Gray managed to place thirty-second out of ninety riders. In 1984 at Los Angeles, before an injury to his horse forced him to withdraw at the end of the cross country phase, Gray was in thirteenth place.

In 1987, Gray accomplished the highlight of his career to date when he won a bronze medal in the Pan American Games. At the end of the year he was the Ontario Horse Trials Association's leading rider.

Gray is an articulate horseperson who enjoys training horses and riders as well as competing. He, in turn, works in close conjunction with his coach, the well-known rider and trainer, Colonel Michael Gutowski.

At Gray's ninety-eight-acre Stone Hill Farm northwest of Erin, he has developed cross-country courses for future events.

Meanwhile, with the future success of his farm and training operation hinged on his riding successes in international competition, Gray is presently training and competing in England and competing in Europe as well.

His future goal, of course, is to compete successfully in the 1992 Olympics. Obviously, Gray has every intention of continuing to move onwards and upwards in Olympic endeavours.

ANSWER: Gray defines each of the seats:

• Basic Seat: A basic seat is the fundamental style of equitation. It enables the rider to have a comfortable hack through the country, to school a young horse, to go trail riding or to go fox hunting. It is a seat which allows versatility to ride both on the flat and over fences. It is a seat suitable for exercising or for schooling and for young or old horses alike.

Its function is to afford comfort for the rider (through a range of stirrup lengths) and to offer a secure position.

• Hunt Seat: A hunt seat is a style designed to allow the horse's unrestricted natural forward motion. It is suitable for the exercising of young horses, for galloping across country, for jumping or for showing a hunter. 'The balance point is shifted forward in this style, as the upper body leans slightly forward transferring weight from the rider's seat (and thus from the horse's back) down through the lower legs to the heels and stirrups.'

• Dressage Seat: A dressage seat allows the distribution of the rider's weight mostly through the seat by maintaining a vertical upper body position.

The legs become limbs whose function is to indicate aids for executing various movements and creating impulsion. They are no longer an 'anchor' for balancing the upper body. As already mentioned, the majority of the rider's weight is in his seat which remains very deep, thus influencing impulsion and engagement.

• Balanced Seat: Gray's definition of a balanced seat is one which describes the centre of gravity rather than one which indicates a style of equitation. The rider's centre of gravity must always co-ordinate with the horse's centre of gravity no matter in what sphere of equestrian discipline one is involved. It must encourage absolute harmony between horse and rider and is applicable and desirable in the basic seat, hunt seat and dressage seat.

Stirrup Lengths: From a dressage position where the stirrup length is comparatively long, the seat deep and the upper body vertical, to a jumper position, obviously the stirrup length must be shortened, so that the rider can comfortably remove the weight from the horse's back as his upper body tilts forward. This distribution of weight to the lower leg allows the rider to maintain his 'balanced seat' as the centre of gravity is moved forward.

The position in the jumper rider varies from anything from a forward seat to a more upright position depending on the situation of the jumping course and the type of animal. Gray prefers a more upright upper body position through the 'balancing zone'; that is, between fences where rhythm, balance and impulsion are key factors. On the approach to the fence a more forward seat is adopted. The weight off of the horse's back and the very light rein contact allow maximum freedom of the horse's head and neck and relaxation of the muscles through his back. The style, however, may also vary according to the type of riding a specific breed of horse may require.

Showing a hunter, in Gray's mind, requires a continuity of style and balance and rhythm from the moment the horse enters the ring. For this reason the hunt seat is maintained throughout the jumping round and the upper body never comes vertical enough to encourage contact of the seat with the saddle.

The style for riding cross-country has a wide range of positions depending on whether the terrain approaching the fence is uphill or downhill, on the speed of the approach and on the nature of the terrain on the landing. The stirrup length is considerably shorter than required for the other disciplines in order to maintain that 'balanced seat' previously discussed whether approaching a steeplechase fence at six hundred and ninety metres per minute or jumping an obstacle with a six foot drop into water. For these two extremes of types of fences one goes from a very low, forward, tight, highly energized position for the speed of steeplechase to a manoeuvrable, supple and independent upper body which moves in an ever increasing upright position to adjust to the continually changing centre of gravity as the horse is in flight over the fence, through to the descending drop into the water.

Between cross-country obstacles, speed is the essence and the tremendous forward motion of the galloping stride must be completely unrestricted by the rider who adopts a sympathetic forward position, with weight completely out of the saddle and distributed to the lower leg allowing a strong 'anchor' to maintain perfect balance as the horse negotiates the ever changing terrain of a cross-country course.

Saddles: For dressage, because of the importance of the rider's weight being distributed into his seat, a saddle has been adapted with a very deep seat which has support through a high pommel and a high cantle.

In cross-country work, especially the steeplechase phase, the saddle must have a much bigger seat and the knee rolls must be very, very much more forward to allow the quite short stirrup lengths.

For hunter and jumper work, a flat saddle has been very popular until recently when the pendulum of preference seems to be swinging back towards a slightly deeper seat and slight knee rolls.

How to Use Your Own Fences Effectively

QUESTION: Now that I have my own fences at home, how should I use them to get the most out of them? I want to do everything as correctly as I can.

I also would like to know what kind of fences help certain kinds of problems. For example, my horse gets sloppy over his fences sometimes and he stops in front of anything that looks really different.

EXPERT: David Ballard (See Chapter 4, Question 4).

ANSWER: Ballard makes some suggestions for riding your young horse over this new hunter course. He comments:

> Once you get the material, obviously you don't start over a whole course, Start with one pole on the ground. Trot over it. Maybe canter over it and then put it between wings. Do gymnastics. Set out a grid with maybe four or five poles on the ground approximately four feet apart. Trot those. Then just using poles, build an x. Trot the x and then canter. Make a little oxer and trot and canter it. Then, still using this single fence, let him trot it and then canter it. Put in your wall. Let him trot and canter it. Then extend it to a line. Trot one and canter on down to an x. Progressively build your course up that way. Start with *one* jump and then substitute as time goes on. That way you can get your horse used to different kinds of material.

You ask what kind of fence helps certain types of problems. If your horse is getting sloppy over fences even though they are filled in properly and have good ground lines, there are, according to Ballard, two possibilities: either he wants to be sloppy or he is being jumped over too small a fence all the time. Try him over something a little bigger. If he seems to have lost interest in the jumps, try him over a tight gymnastic. If he hits it when he jumps, possibly his interest will have been awakened. If he does not hit it, you have still accomplished your purpose.

In this thinking, Ballard is a believer in what he refers to as 'Jim Elder's philosophy' and that is, 'Try to present the fence to your horse, but don't try to find a good distance. If he bangs the fence, he has gained some experience. If he does not bang the fence then he has learned something. *A horse has to be able to take care of himself!'*

Schooling with this philosophy in mind, working over combinations at a canter, twenty-four feet apart or less with a square oxer rather than a 'rampy' one, will give you the tight gymnastic you need.

If fences that look different are a problem, Ballard recommends riding or shipping your horse to neighbouring stables for schooling. Enough exposure to different-looking fences will usually calm your horse when he encounters something new.

In regard to all at-home schooling, Ballard has one very important piece of advice. 'So many of these things we're discussing are variable and a lot of times inexperienced people take them as absolute. Maybe one distance is encouraging a horse to jump poorly and yet they don't have the flexibility in their knowledge to say, 'Oh I should lengthen it or I should shorten it.' No matter what they do, I don't think they outgrow the need for someone to supervise. They should try to find a professional within the neighbourhood or easy commuting distance to help in the schooling.'

Jumping for the Inexperienced Rider and Green Horse

QUESTION: I have a five-year-old mare, slightly over fifteen hands. She is a halfbred – Clydesdale and Morgan. I want to teach her how to jump. Is it possible? Is she too old? If so, where do I start? My parents said they would like another horse. Should I forget about training my halfbred to jump? Or should I train her and the new horse? Or should I just train the new horse and leave the half-bred for western? What sex is best for jumping and what breed? What age is ideal?

EXPERT: Jen Hamilton is a first-rate instructress. She is that ideal combination of teacher and rider – a graduate in education with experience in teaching school and a longtime student of George Morris with impressive experience in showing horses both in Canada and the United States.

Hamilton grew up in upstate New York and started riding with Russell Stewart, but changed instructors in 1962 when an advertisement for riding lessons from George Morris caught her eye in *The Chronicle*. Thus Hamilton became one of Morris's very first students, even before he had his own riding establishment.

As a junior, Hamilton competed for years in the hunter, jumper and equitation divisions at many of the most prestigious outdoor and indoor shows in North America.

Later, Morris, in his book, *Hunter Seat Equitation*, was to include a picture of Hamilton, then Marsden, with the following:

> Good classic form. Short in height, Miss Jen Marsden has to situation herself quite behind a horse at all times to use what length she has to best advantage. This, however, in no way hinders her definite approach to riding and with her terrific 'eye for distance' she may be an inspiration to those who think they're not built to ride.

This was glowing praise indeed from someone who has the reputation of being a perfectionist.

Hamilton took lessons from Morris on a regular basis for three years and even now, twenty-five years later, frequently attends his clinics.

In the last sixties, Hamilton came to Canada to attend Dalhousie University in Nova Scotia and has lived in that province ever since.

A freelance instructress, Hamilton not only coaches in her area, but also travels across Canada and the United States to give clinics. 'I love clinics ... I really like teaching!' admits Hamilton and it is that enthusiasm coupled with her knowledge and teaching skills that make her clinics so informative and enjoyable.

In 1975, a career highlight for Hamilton was to be the first winner of the Martini and Rossi Award as Horsewoman of the Year. Certainly another highlight has to be the fact that she was called on by the Canadian Equestrian to write the Level III Manual for Coaching. With no format to follow, Hamilton chose to write it in outline form so that, as she puts it, 'The reader can pick it up and put it down but still get something out of it quickly.' That 'down to earth' practical approach to teaching enables Hamilton to help those with little experience as well as those far more advanced.

ANSWER: First of all, to answer your specific questions....

'Is it possible to teach her how to jump?' To quote Hamilton, 'I think *any* horse *can* be taught to jump, but will every horse make a Grand Prix horse? No, very few do! Also is every horse *safe* to jump? You need help to teach them safely. Will it be a show horse? I don't think so. The size and breeding probably mean that it is not a very good mover. It won't be able to make the distances, but that doesn't mean it will not be a useful animal. It could be a good 'learning' horse. The main thing is its attitude and we haven't been told what it's like.'

'Is she too old?' No, she is a very good age to start.

'Should I forget about teaching her to jump?' No.

'What sex is best for jumping?' Either a mare or a gelding is fine.

'What breed is best for jumping?' Hamilton feels that at your stage of riding, the most important consideration is a good attitude and a certain amount of experience. There is no *one* breed that is best.

'What age is ideal?' Hamilton explains, 'If you are thinking of a new horse, what I like for kids starting is an *older* horse that has a marvellous teaching attitude. It won't mind any of the unintentional mistakes you may make. It knows its role. It will be more than happy to jump up to a three foot course.'

Now, you ask, 'Where do I start?' It sounds as if you have no jumping experience and because your horse has none either, Hamilton stresses that it is very important you have a ground person or coach to help you. An inexperienced rider cannot and should not (for safety's sake) teach a green horse.

The foundation of all good jumping lies in having good, basic skills on the flat. If you do not have these skills, then you should take riding lessons to learn them. You need the following:

• a functional position (You must learn body control.)
• coordination of aids (You must learn to keep the horse between your hand and leg and teach her how to go forward and how to come back.)

- the feeling of, and how to establish, *balance, rhythm* and *straightness*
- independent leg and hands
- the knowledge of how things should feel and how to make the correction if things do not feel right.

Your horse has to be taught:
- acceptance of your aids
- the ability to go forward with balance, rhythm and straightness.

Once the flat work has been developed to the point that you have control over your body and a positive effect on your horse, with help from your ground person, you can start the jumping process. We will be working on skill progression; that is, slowly developing skills, one upon the other.

Step by Step:

1) Start with an *individual* pole on the ground. Put a standard on either side so that you can funnel the horse in towards the pole. If you have no standards, put the pole perpendicular to the fence and another pole parallel to the fence so that you have formed wings for the pole.

Trot over the pole and then canter until the horse can trot and canter over the pole in a balanced and straight trot and canter.

2) Next, add a second pole nine feet apart from the first pole. Trot the horse over both poles. Make sure that your horse is straight and that she keeps a very quiet but forward rhythm. (When the horse trots over these nine foot poles, she must put one complete stride in, in other words, just put one front foot in, then the other front foot and then out.)

Once you can do that, you can start cantering the poles. Again, rhythm, straightness and balance are very important. Keep the right contact so that you are actually supporting the horse.

3) Start setting up courses with the poles still nine feet apart so that you can do a course of side / diagonal / side / side.

167

Trot this course but make sure you maintain that rhythm, balance and straightness. Then canter the course. Use a two-point or half seat.

4) Start changing the distance between each of the poles; for example, keep side A at nine feet, change the diagonal to a shorter distance so that your horse will learn to compress the stride and one side B open up the distance to teach the horse to lengthen her stride and then finish on side A that remained normal at nine feet apart.

Over the shorter distance or 'closed' poles be more in a three point or full seat because that will help in balance.

Do side / diagonal / side / side at a trot and then at a canter. Make sure you have contact in the reins with your horse's mouth.

Caution: It is very important that you never shorten the poles to closer than six feet nor open them up to more than twelve feet and always make any changes gradual ones of not more than one foot at a time.

5) Go back to poles at just the nine foot distance apart and practise with a *softening* hand as you come into the poles and a *releasing* hand over the poles. You must be able to maintain your balance without hanging on to the horse's mouth.

These exercises are helpful in several ways. They teach you the feel of a round, balanced stride. They teach you to ride to a specific place – the centre of the poles. They teach you to go around the turns to the next poles in a straight approach and because of all these things, they are teaching you accuracy and discipline.

These exercises also help your horse. They teach her to accept your aids and to be ridden in a balanced state, at a correct rhythm, in a straight line.

Says Hamilton, 'It's only a three inch course, but we are jumping. We are establishing all the skills. We've established that the rider has position, that he can ride with contact and he can ride with a soft and releasing hand.

6) When both your horse and you can maintain balance and position in a controlled forward motion over poles, you are ready to raise them.

Place *three* poles nine feet apart. Once again have standards next to them and run out poles as wings. Trot over these poles with a releasing hand until you and your horse are really comfortable.

Then you can make a little cross rail where the middle pole is with the centre of the cross about one foot high. Come in with soft hands, releasing over the first pole while supporting the horse with the leg. The horse will jump the cross rail and then canter away from it.

Caution: It is possible that your horse will need a shorter distance than nine feet because of her breeding. The ground person or coach will be able to tell you if she does.

7) When you feel comfortable over this one foot cross rail, you can raise it up a little. You can change the cross rail to a vertical, but make sure that you make each change gradual and that you raise it no higher than three feet.

You now can canter this little gymnastic but remember, you may have to adjust the placing poles.

Throughout all of these exercises, you must still be thinking about *balance, rhythm* and *straightness.*

Hamilton stresses, 'You're never to progress to new or more difficult exercises or raise the jump until you and your horse are *totally confident* with the present exercise.' She adds, 'You're never going to progress until everything is calm, quiet and confident.' Hamilton cautions, 'Don't be afraid to drop back if you have a problem.'

8) At this point Hamilton moves on to gymnastics, particularly a three-element gymnastic. Start with poles on the ground with standards and run out poles. Think of the three poles as A element, B element and C element. There must be eighteen feet between A and B and nineteen to twenty-one feet between B and C. Trot through the gymnastic and canter through it, always very quietly, with rhythm and straightness, with contact and with the softening, releasing hand.

Then raise the B element to just a low cross rail. Trot in. Raise the C element to a cross rail. Trot in. Put the A element up as a cross rail and trot through the three elements.

Remember, make sure you are confident with each step before you proceed to the next one.

Later you can raise B to a vertical and go through several times. When you are ready, raise C to a vertical. Eventually make it an oxer. This gymnastic exercise teaches the horse confidence. As well it teaches the rider position.

The next natural skill progression is to do lines but you really should progress no further without a coach on the ground during your schooling sessions.

Good luck in your riding and do remember to wear a hard hat at all times when you are jumping!

Lines and Distances or 'Making Strides'

QUESTION: I have trouble finding my distances when I ride my pony over fences. What can I do?

EXPERT: Enthusiastic and vivacious, yet keenly critical and demanding, Bobbie Reber is the epitome of the attitudes which she expects and encourages in her students – positive and professional.

Formerly of Reber Ridge, Reber is now in partnership with Stephanie and Mike Grinyer at Round the Bend Stables northwest of Toronto. The partnership is an ideal combination of interests and talent. Reber admits she loves teaching and she loves hunters and that is exactly her involvement. She trains children, juniors and amateurs for the Hunter 'A' Circuit. Grinyer is a well-known and successful rider who competes on the Jumper 'A' Circuit up to the Grand Prix level.

Round the Bend is expanding. A recent lengthening of the arena and additional stabling has increased its capacity to forty-seven horses. There are new paddocks for the horses and a viewing room for boarders and spectators, respectively.

An early background in eventing, experience as a young girl in riding difficult horses on the hunter show circuit and a year's training in an instructor's course in England have combined to make

Reber a knowledgeable horseperson who stresses the importance of consistency in training both horses and riders.

Reber is perhaps best known for her ability to match the right horse with the right rider. She strongly believes that the temperament and personality of the rider should be considered as significant factors in the selection of a suitable horse.

That she is successful both in her horse and rider combinations and in her teaching is obvious. To date, she has produced about forty-six Zone Champions and Reserve Champions on the 'A' Circuit.

ANSWER: Reber stresses that there can be a number of different reasons as to why your pony is having trouble making the correct number of strides while on course. She outlines them briefly.

• Soundness: If the pony is an older one, the problem may be a gradually shortening stride due to ageing. There is also the possibility that the pony has had some laminitis or navicular activity. You would be wise to discuss this type of problem with your veterinarian.

• The Smaller Size in his Division: A thirteen hand or slightly over twelve hand pony who has to show in the medium division against ponies over thirteen hands, or a fourteen hand or slightly over thirteen hand pony who competes with ponies over fourteen hands often has trouble making the distances.

Says Reber, 'It is amazing how much bigger a fourteen hand, two inch pony is compared to a fourteen hand pony when it comes to size of stride!' Of course, as Reber is quick to point out, 'There are certainly exceptions in all sizes. Some ponies have very large strides no matter what their size.'

The breed of the pony or the type of cross-breed that he is will have a significant bearing on the length of his stride. It is Reber's experience that ponies who seem to have Thoroughbred in them compared to those with Quarter Horse blood are more likely to have a longer stride.

She concludes, 'Again there are always exceptions and a good striding pony can be of any breed.' You will know if being the smaller size in his division is the cause of his problem.

• Lack of Education: If the pony is young or green, he might not be balanced nor able to learn how to lengthen his stride without becoming strong or running away. Reber outlines simple exercises which will help you to educate your pony.

First of all she cautions that it is very important that the pony's stride be developed the correct way. On the flat he must learn to canter in a balanced frame and as well he must learn how to lengthen and shorten his stride.

Reber recommends this exercise: In an arena or outdoor ring gallop the pony down the long side and shorten his strides around the ends. Later, canter across the diagonal (hopefully incorporating the flying change) and shorten his strides in the corner. Be careful to keep the impulsion. Next put two poles down on the ground on the long side and place them sixty feet apart. Canter down what in a jump setting would be a four stride line but in poles on the ground is a five stride line (five strides within the poles). Make sure that you do it in five. Next, shorten up the pony's stride to a six stride (six strides within the poles) line. If you and your pony feel really comfortable, gallop down in a four stride (four strides within the poles).

Such an exercise will teach you to start to increase the pace to a five line or shorten your pony's stride for a six line. Learning to be more aware of strides will make you a more technical rider. The exercise will teach your pony a versatile canter – shortening and lengthening his stride.

Eventually Reber encourages 'a steady six, a steady seven, a flowing five and a forward four' so that you will be aware of the range of stride and the adjustability of your pony. Your pony will understand that a softening hand and a forward seat mean lengthening the stride, whereas a little deeper seat and a little 'take-back' hand means shortening (with his hocks underneath him rather than with his weight on the forehand).

Reber refers to this 'two poles in varying stride numbers' as being 'a simple exercise that not too many people can get into trouble with.' It is one that you should be able to do without a professional being there with you.

An extension of this exercise is recommended with a little x and a vertical. For trotting in, if your pony is a medium pony, set these two fences fifty-eight feet apart for a steady five but if he is a large pony, set them sixty feet apart for a quiet five. Trot the x and canter on to the vertical. (It is very important that you ask your pony to approach in a straight line. Any spooking or drifting will add footage and thus throw the distances off.) The first few times you trot the x and canter on to the vertical, ask your pony to do the five strides in six. This approach will make him comfortable with the line and will eliminate any possible feeling he might have of being rushed. Then, with this established comfort because of the extra stride and because he has already been taught to lengthen and to move forward in response to your leg on the flat, he will be ready to do the line in the correct number of strides. Once you and your pony can trot the x and canter on to the vertical in the correct five strides comfortably, canter to the x and on to the vertical. Increase the distance between the x and the vertical to sixty feet for a medium pony, the same distance as for the large pony. Once again, add an extra stride to the correct number of strides which is five steady strides if your pony is a medium pony and four strides if he is a large pony. When he is comfortable cantering the x to the vertical with the extra stride, do the exercise with the correct number of strides.

In Summary: Reber stresses an important point which reveals her feeling that the proper training of the pony is more important than early ribbons at the shows – 'At shows repeat the exercise of adding strides in all lines until he has more mileage and is comfortable in all types of conditions.' (What a great attitude!) Once he is comfortable and is not green about the jumps he should be able to do the lines easily. A note to remember: Most courses are set on an eleven to a twelve foot stride for large ponies and a ten foot stride for medium ponies.

Training the Three-Year-Old Potential Show Hunter

QUESTION: I have a nice three-year-old gelding which I want to show as a hunter on the 'A' Circuit one day in the future. Right now, the only things I've done with him are some walking and trotting on the longe and some riding at a walk and at a trot. I want to make sure I don't do anything wrong and that's why I'm asking for help.

Here are some things I'd like to know about:

• How much should I try to do this year? When should I canter him? Should I do any work over poles? Should I do any work over low jumps?

• Am I using the right tack? I have a jointed snaffle that I use but someone told me a straight rubber bit would be better. What about a martingale? Is it a good idea to use draw reins?

• How much should I try to keep him together? How can I get him off the forehand?

• If he's three now, how long should I spend schooling him before I think about schooling shows? I'd like to have some kind of a timetable.

I know I'm asking a lot, but I want to organize some kind of long range plan to best get him ready.

I have been riding for over twelve years.

EXPERT: 'Torchy' Millar is a Canadian equestrian who needs little introduction to the horse world. He first became a member of the Canadian Team in 1967 and has represented Canada at two Olympic Games – Mexico and Munich. In 1982 he won the Quebec City World Cup Grand Prix and was a member of the Nation's Cup Team at Spruce Meadows.

One of Millar's specialties has been developing young horses up through the hunter ranks and on to international jumping. Edenvale was one such horse that Millar purchased as a three-year-old and on whom he won the Rothmans Grand Prix at the Royal Winter Fair. Another was Phoenix Park whom Millar purchased in Ireland and later sold to the British Team. A third was Passage West another Irish horse whom Millar recently sold to a purchaser from the United States. Passage West was second in the trials for the World Championship team in 1986 and in 1988 as well as having a lot of Grand Prix placings, was sixth in World Cup standings.

ANSWER: Millar agrees that you are correct in wanting a goal plan but stresses the fact that a *timetable should be tailored to suit your horse* and his mental and physical capabilities rather than that your horse be regimented to a possibly unsuitable schedule.

Depending on your horse's talents, and based on the fact that you are already walking and trotting him under saddle as well as on the longe, it is not unrealistic to plan to be jumping two and one-half to three foot fences, including some lines and simple changes around the ends of the ring by the end of the year.

At your present stage, the first thing Millar suggests that you do is introduce your horse to cantering on the longe. He recommends a longeing cavesson as his personal preference but says that a snaffle bridle would also be acceptable. He advises against using a surcingle and side reins at first, unless your horse tends to 'throw' his head high and needs more control. If such is the case, the side reins should be the type with elastic insets and should be adjusted very loosely. Make sure you do not try to 'set the head down'.

Millar favours teaching a horse to canter on the longe first, because he finds that the circle work encourages a horse to start to balance himself and to develop some cadence to his canter.

At this point in your horse's schooling you could begin to ride him at the canter. Most young horses tend to work on their forehand, but, as time goes by, you should find that he will gradually start to come together; that is, become more balanced and learn to adjust to the weight of a rider on his back. Meanwhile, you can help to get him off of the forehand by using plenty of leg to push him up into your

175

hands. As he lightens in front, he will become more comfortable. Millar cautions against cantering in too tight a circle at first as a really green horse will have great difficulty maintaining balance; however, as you feel your horse improving, you can make your requests more sophisticated by doing both more circle work and increasingly smaller circle work (within reason).

During the same time phase that you are working at the canter, you could introduce your horse to jumping while on the longe line. Millar stresses the fact that for this step the tack used should be either a longeing cavesson or a halter. He advises against using a bridle as it is easy to snatch the horse inadvertently in the mouth when the animal jumps. As well, of course, he points out that side reins must definitely *not* be used.

Millar likes to start off the jumping with the obstacle being simply composed of two or three rails in a pile. Work at a trot only and keep the atmosphere low-key and relaxed. From this simple mound of rails, you can progress to an x. To make it easier for your horse at first, put a rail about six feet out from the x. This rail will help set your horse in the right position for the jump. Gradually build up a little two foot high vertical and then perhaps introduce him to a little oxer.

Millar stresses the importance of doing as much work to the right as to the left. 'Most people,' says Millar, 'do eighty per cent of their work on the left and you must watch out for that and balance it.' Perhaps the first two jumping sessions you could work to the left, but if you do that, make sure that the third and fourth times you work to the right.

Besides trotting single jumps on the longe, you can also introduce little gymnastics such as jumping from one x to another x. Start your horse simply and then graduate to an x to a little vertical and to an x to a little oxer. Later introduce a third element, so that your horse jumps an x to a little vertical to an oxer, etc. The distance between the first two obstacles should be a comfortable one for the horse. With an average horse, start off at about seventeen feet because at first the horse is a little spooky and often backs off. Later, increase the distance to eighteen feet and when a third is added, the distance between the second and third should be about twenty-one feet. Use trial and error to adjust the distance to your horse's comfort.

If your horse has shown an easy, relaxed attitude in your longe work over fences you could try building up a single fence to three and one-half or even four feet when longeing. By so doing, you will get some kind of indication of his ability and scope – knowledge which might help you to assess his future potential.

Once your horse has become comfortable jumping out of a trot on the longe you could begin to ride him over small obstacles but out of a trot. Begin with the same type of fence as on the longe and gradually work up. Again, as you work over an x or a vertical or an oxer, a rail six feet out from the jump will help.

So far, you have worked on longeing and on riding at the canter, on longeing over fences at the trot and on riding over fences from a trot. Millar suggests working on these aspects of training for a couple of months but suggests that you intermingle the schooling sessions. In other words, he feels that you do not have to master your horse being ridden at the canter before you start trotting jumps. He recommends varying your schooling. One day longe on the flat. Another day ride him at the canter. A third day longe over fences. A fourth, ride him at a trot over fences.

One cautionary note from Millar, 'I wouldn't attempt to start jumping at a canter until the horse is very comfortable at a ridden canter.' Only when he canters well on the flat 'with a semblance of balance, impulsion and cadence' should you try to canter over any jumps. As well, he points out that 'an inexperienced rider can do a lot with trotting over jumps without getting into any trouble but when you get into cantering you start to have to find good distances to the jumps to make the horse comfortable.' Experience is therefore an important factor as to when to canter over jumps.

When you do begin to canter over jumps, jump small fences. Progress to two in a row and then try three in a line.

Millar's next step is one often omitted but an excellent one for a green horse. He recommends taking your horse out to another place, perhaps a friend's stable and working him over new obstacles in a different setting. Millar has found this step really helps and is far less traumatic than making the horse's first outing one at a busy schooling show with all the accompanying noise and confusion.

When your horse is jumping a few fences in a line, doing simple changes around the ends and working over courses at another stable, you could enter a few winter schooling shows *but*, as Millar cautions, a lot depends on the individual horse. As for recognized showing, 'These days' to quote Millar, 'it takes a reasonably well-adjusted, precocious individual to come out and show First Year as a four-year-old.' Possibly the answer might be to show in the Low Hunter Division for the summer.

Bits: 'I think in terms of a bit, unless a horse had a real problem, I wouldn't necessarily be that keen on just a straight rubber snaffle. If he's extremely sensitive, I'd consider it, but a lot of young horses just learn to lean too much. A jointed snaffle would be my preference.'

Martingales: 'I generally tend to put a standing martingale on practically everything to start with, but I usually leave it fairly loosely adjusted on a young horse. It's more or less just to have it there so they can't throw their heads up very high and maybe hit you in the face.

'I wouldn't have a martingale in a situation where it interfered with the horse such as jumping where it might grab their noses when they tried to arc over a jump.

'A young horse will gawk and look at something and there's nothing wrong with having a well-adjusted, reasonably loose standing martingale on a young horse so that he can't get himself in too much trouble.

'If a horse is in a situation where he's continually got his head in the air right at the end of the martingale, then obviously there's a problem that you'd want to correct and not have the martingale as the correction.

'Later on down the line if a horse is excellent and does everything very well, you can go without a martingale, but some horses tend to look a little better with the martingale. They don't look as naked!'

Draw Reins: 'I'm hesitant to recommend draw reins on a three-year-old without a pretty experienced rider but I'm not saying that they should not be used. I think there are cases where they could. If you did have an extremely difficult head problem where a horse carried its head high in the air or poked its nose a long way up, you could consider putting draw reins on, but again, not hauling them in too tightly and one always has to remember that you have to use more leg to compensate. If you just pull their head down, they just get worse on their forehand. To make sure you're not accelerating the problem of them on their forehand, you have to use your leg and keep them (the horses) up in the bridle.'

Schooling the Young Horse

The atmosphere when Millar schools a youngster is relaxed and low key. When longeing, he keeps his voice soft and calm. When riding, his reward to a horse is a quiet pat or stroke.

Part of his equipment when riding young horses or older ones too for that matter, are spurs which he feels help to keep the horse from becoming 'dull-sided', the way so many are if they are continually being 'banged against' with a rider's legs. Needless to say, good leg control and balance are essential when using spurs. As well, Millar carries a crop.

Well Adjusted Tack: Typical tack when schooling a young horse under a rider. Note the standing martingale and its adjustment.

Under a Rider ... At a Walk: As this horse has already had some limited show experience, he is ready to be asked for a little more collection.

Millar allows very green horses to be more on the forehand.

Notice Millar's leg position. His spurs are not digging into the horse but his 'quiet' leg is on the horse, encouraging forward impulsion.

Under a Rider ... At a Trot: Initially Millar posts when schooling at a trot. With this slightly more experienced horse, he does occasional sitting trots, increasing the contact between hand and mouth and asking for more collection, while keeping a firm leg on the horse in order to maintain his cadence and impulsion. The rider's leg plays an important part, because a young horse will often 'back off' (lose his steady forward impulsion) when he first feels an increased contact on his mouth.

Under a Rider ... At a Canter: Millar's upper body remains very quiet. Note, however, that he does not drop his shoulders forward as many riders tend to do. He keeps his circles very large with very green horses. As a horse becomes more balanced, he reduces the size of the circle, again using his legs to maintain impulsion and keep the horse 'tracking' on the circle.

Jumping on the Longe: During the same time phase that Millar works on a green horse's canter under saddle, he begins him jumping on the longe at a trot. His preferred tack is a longeing cavesson.

At the beginning, Millar uses three or four rails laid in a pile as a first obstacle. Later he progresses to a small x. This particular jump can be graded at about the third stage of difficulty. Note the use of barrels as standards. Millar uses them because they do not interfere with the longe line.

As well, note the rail about six feet out from the obstacle. It helps to guide the horse to the right take-off spot for the jump. An angled rail resting on the inside barrel acts as a wing to channel the horse towards the jump. When longeing over jumps, it is very important to give the horse his head in the air. Be ready to move your arm and let out the longe line to avoid jerking his mouth.

Jumping under a Rider ... First Stage: This pile of poles is the first type of obstacle a young horse encounters under Millar's training. The horse trots over the obstacle with Millar doing a posting trot. Wing standards are used to avoid run-outs and to guide the green horse over the obstacle.

Jumping under a Rider ... Second Stage: A low cross pole acting as a ground line on either side of the x is the type of jump used at the horse's second stage of development. Later, as in this picture, a second x is set up. The horse is still jumping at a trot. It is important to teach your horse to go straight! Use your legs to keep him from zigzagging and make sure you get a square approach to the jump. The distance between the two obstacles should be one that is comfortable for the horse. With an average youngster, Millar starts off at about seventeen feet, because at first the horse will be a little spooky and will back off. Later, Millar increases the distance to eighteen feet.

Millar suggests that you use trial and error and adjust the distance to your horse's comfort.

Jumping under a Rider … Third Stage: A slightly more difficult type of second obstacle is next. The spread of this small oxer invites the horse to use his back over the fence. Note the ground lines on either side of the pole.

A Three-Part Gymnastic: A third obstacle is added. The distance between the second and third should be about twenty-one feet. Once again, adjust the distance to your horse's comfort. If the horse runs out between jumps, Millar is quick to hit him sharply with the crop to teach him that such behaviour is not allowed. To help avoid this problem, keep your upper body angle open in between the jumps and steer your horse. Many riders tend to drop their hands towards the horse's mouth and lean forward too soon, in anticipation of the jump. This will encourage your horse to run out.

Jumping at a Canter: A more challenging jump, such as the one shown, needs to be approached at a canter.

Millar cautions against jumping at a canter until the horse is very comfortable at the canter. Only when the horse canters well on the flat with a semblance of balance, impulsion and cadence should you try to canter him over a jump.

Training the Jumper

QUESTION ONE: Why does flat work help Grand Prix jumpers?

EXPERT: Ian Millar and Grand Prix success go hand in hand. With a total of Grand Prix wins that is always increasing, he is undisputedly Canada's winningest rider.

From an individual gold in the 1987 Pan American Games, to his victory in the DuMaurier Invitational (the first Canadian to win that event) a short time later, to his first World Cup win in 1988, Millar is constantly gaining international claim for Canada. Now, his latest coup is to be the first rider to ever win the World Cup in two consecutive years.

Millar attributes much of his success to lessons learned from former teachers, associates and friends:

From his first instructress, Rita Gardiner, he was given the gift 'that it is never the horse's fault.'

From his second teacher, Dr. Bode, a German dressage rider, he learned to train through repetition rather than to escalate the strength and impact of his riding aids.

From an Ottawa instructress, Nancy Woods, he learned jumping, training and showing. He learned the business end of the horse industry. He learned how to choose a horse. Together they came up with Millar's first Grand Prix horse, War Machine.

From Toronto-based Doug Cudney who bought War Machine and who owned Shoeman and Beefeater, he was given the opportunity to gain international experience – to ride those horses on the Fall Circuit in 1971 and to qualify for the Munich Olympic Team in 1972.

From Jackie Morold of Dwyer Hill Farms where Millar spent eight years, he learned why a person would involve himself or herself in the sport as a backer and a sponsor and what a person who makes such a generous commitment requires in return.

From Randy Roy whom Millar declares 'even thinks like a horse,' he learned a lot about being a horseman.

From George Morris, he learned the importance of the word 'system'. He learned to take his natural instincts and techniques and everything he knew and had learned how to do, and package, label and categorize them into a system that encouraged efficiency.

From his wife Lynn who like Randy Roy is an outstanding horseperson who knows a horse, its heart, its mind, and its anatomy, he has received an ongoing check and balance to his competitive drive.

As the teaching of each of these people came together, a total picture of the horseman and the horse industry was painted – a picture that as it was composed, Millar stepped into and thus, became.

In 1980 Millar and Lynn bought, renovated, added onto, and generally established the lovely Millar Brooke Farm in Perth Ontario. There in an atmosphere of peace and tranquillity, Millar schools his Grand Prix horses and other rising stars in the barn.

Millar works hard! At home he schools numerous horses each day. At shows he has the reputation of being at the barns at 5 A.M

It is virtually impossible to think of Millar without thinking of the horse who has carried him to so many victories – Big Ben. The two have become one of the most popular combinations ever on the International Circuit.

Through intelligence, stamina, natural ability and sensitivity and with the help of friends such as Big Ben, he has established himself at the top – a superb rider and an all-round horseman.

ANSWER: Good flat work is the foundation of the pyramid of the Grand Prix horse. Without it, the proper results are impossible to achieve. Flat work takes raw talent and refines it by teaching a horse how to use every part of his body in the most efficient way possible. It teaches a horse to operate from every pace, every distance and every balance. As well, it gives the rider control and that control is essential for success in the jumper ring.

Significant Characteristics of the Grand Prix Horse: Not necessarily in order of importance, Millar describes what he looks for in a Grand Prix horse:

• Such a horse has to have the right basic instincts about what to do with his legs and his body when he faces a jump.
• He has to have the raw power and the strength to hoist himself off of the ground.
• He has to be careful; that is, he has to have an innate instinctive desire to jump free of rubs.
• He has to be sound or sound enough to compete in the sport.
• He has to have the range of stride – the natural ability to shorten and lengthen his stride – to go from an eight foot stride to a fourteen foot stride.
• He has to have the mind to allow all of these things to happen. The mind Millar likes is aggressive.
• He has to be independent, but not so aggressive, independent and brave that he can't be harnessed and controlled.

Millar describes the essence of such a horse:

> In the end I want to be sitting on a horse who thinks he can jump the moon and who would jump through a ring of fire without a second thought. I want a horse who if I make a drastic error and the thing looks like it is all going to fall apart, is an independent enough horse to say, 'Well, I'll just take over and solve this problem.'

Millar's Basic Training Philosophy:

• Control and the 'Yes' Response: The very characteristics of the Grand Prix horse, make him a potentially very difficult animal to train. Part of Millar's basic training philosophy is *not* to dominate such a horse in an obvious 'head-on' approach. As he puts it, 'I try to control him and train him the way a smart wife trains her husband. She gets him to do things by having him believe that it was all his idea in the first place. He is therefore quite happy to go ahead and do whatever it is she wants because she has positioned the situation so beautifully and so subtly. I gain control of a horse in the same way.'

The 'yes' response plays an important role in Millar's training. He compares himself to the 'old' Fuller Brush salesman who led a potential customer through a series of easy, positive-type questions to establish a 'yes' response and hence close a sale.

Thus does Millar develop each training session.

The 'yes' response begins in the Millar Brooke barn. By the time a horse has been taken out of his stall, has had his feet picked out, has been groomed and tacked up, he has already said 'yes' many times. When he travels forward at a walk from a halt and trots around the field or arena on a long contact, he is saying 'yes' and 'yes' again.

Gradually the questions asked of the horse start to become a little more difficult, but as Millar stresses, 'Knowing *when*, is just as important as knowing *how.*' He tries never to ask a question that a horse is not ready to say 'yes' to because a 'no' response probably means a fight – a fight which Millar knows he will most likely win, but one which the chances are will leave 'a chip on the horse's shoulder' and an unpleasant memory that he will ever after associate with Millar and remember every time he sees or hears him. To quote Millar, 'Horses don't reason all that well. They learn through repetition and if you put the wrong data in them, it will haunt you forever because horses don't forget.'

It is through the education of flat work that Millar controls his horse. He controls the mind by getting the horse to do things with his body. He decides what flat work to do by analyzing the horse's natural desires, instincts and abilities and he warms up using these natural aspects because they are easy for that particular horse to do.

• Control and Specific Training: Once the warm up phase is over, he starts to probe the areas of the horse's weakness:

a. If it is a lethargic, slow-moving horse with a great, long, powerful stride, Millar concentrates on shortening the stride and making it very active.

b. If it is a horse who is stiff and rigid through his back, Millar

A shoulder-in.

A half pass.

does a lot of shoulder-ins, half passes, turns on the forehand and pirouettes at the walk and even the trot.

c. If it is a horse with a natural instinct to get strong and run away with Millar, he does a lot of half halts.

d. If it is a little bit of a lazy horse who does not want to come forward, Millar makes a number of sharp, strong forward transitions and extensions.

• Control and the Counter Canter: According to Millar, most horses do not like the counter canter. They find it difficult to do. As a result, the counter canter becomes a very valuable exercise because the rider is getting the horse to say 'yes' to something he did not want to say 'yes'. It becomes a wonderful intellectual training exercise. As well, he explains that it stretches muscles and ligaments in the back, the neck and the hindquarters thus giving more range and strength to the horse It also teaches him to balance and to slow down in the corners, because he finds that the easiest way for him to do the counter canter is to slow down and shorten his stride. Millar finds it a wonderful exercise for one of those horses that has been running through the corner with his head turned to the outside, but he emphasizes the importance of waiting until the counter canter is a realistic expectation, because it is an extremely difficult exercise for a horse to do.

• Control and Training – The Essence: What Millar is doing, in actual fact, is finding the things that the horse does not like to do. Logically enough, usually his dislikes mentally are related to his abilities physically. Millar works on these problem areas until the horse can do them more easily. Eventually the horse becomes very good at them. Thus Millar has extended the range of the horse's physical ability to that of a complete horse – a complete athlete.

He continues using this basic training philosophy throughout the horse's career. (His purist attitude is very much in evidence when he admits to never having trained a horse one hundred per cent.)

195

An extended trot.

The difficult counter canter is a very valuable exercise for 'getting the horse to say "yes" to something he did not want to say "yes."'

196

• The Importance of Friendship: Once a horse has reached an international level, Millar likes to think of him as his friend, but he stresses the importance of controlling and training him *first*. As he puts it, 'I can win with a horse who is not my friend as long as he is controlled and trained. I can't win with a horse who is my friend but out of control and untrained. To get the very best effort – the outstanding effort – he has to be controlled, trained *and* my friend. That x factor – that personal relationship – has to be in place.'

Further thoughts: Millar considers the horse to be just as big a friend to man as the dog and he feels that the potential for friendship should be appreciated by any rider or trainer. Those who treat a horse as they would a machine are losing out on what the sport is all about and it is only the generosity and willing spirit of the horse that enables them to get away with it. ('Amen' to that!)

Millar takes that consideration of the horse and lets it guide him in his selection of a working environment. He chooses a quiet, peaceful, large green field surrounded by trees. He chooses comfortable, safe, footing. He knows that in such a setting, the horse will feel happy, relaxed and at home because such an environment is one that is natural to him.

Always, Millar tries to gear his mind to that of the horse. He knows the horse does not relate to all of the time and emotional pressures that man faces. The horse cares about his comforts – his feed, his stall and his safety.

Perhaps what sets Millar apart from the average rider is that he is not 'just a rider' but rather a *total* horseman who understands the importance of caring for the *total* horse. That particular attention to detail seems to be the key to his success as a Grand Prix rider.

QUESTION TWO: How would you train a potential jumper over beginning fences?

EXPERT: Ian Millar (see previous question).

Three or four cavaletti spaced three and one-half to four feet apart teach the horse to compress his stride.

A jump about nine feet (sometimes less) after the trot poles is another exercise which makes the horse work at fitting his stride to the distances.

ANSWER:

• The Importance of Control: It is essential to have control of the horse before a useful, productive, personal relationship can be established. Only with control, can the rider become the teacher and the horse, the student.

• The Importance of a Training Philosophy: A long-term plan is essential as is working out its implementation. All the exercises that are selected to be worked on should be geared to expand the horse's abilities, both mentally and physically so that he is in a position to be able to deal with the problems which he will face when he enters the show ring.

Says Millar, 'Just about everything I do with a horse, I have the end objective of it being useful or having an application in the show ring.'

• Training by Challenge: Millar's philosophy of training over obstacles is an extension of that which he applies when working on the flat. He likes a training exercise to have a challenge to it. An example of his 'training by challenge' approach can be found in the way he teaches one of his big, powerful movers to compress his stride yet keep its power. Millar puts three or four trot poles fairly close together and trots the horse through. Although such a mover would find it very easy to float through over poles farther apart, he finds it difficult at the shorter distances. This is where the effectiveness of such an exercise lies.

It is definitely not easy and the horse learns from the challenge. As Millar explains, 'It doesn't matter what the horse does well or what he likes or doesn't like, because the course designer is going to set up a certain exercise and the horse had better understand that he must conform to the exercise.'

Cavaletti: Millar begins with three or four rails on the ground at the fairly short distance of from three and one-half to four feet apart. He starts out by riding the powerful, 'long-geared' horse slightly *under*

Bounce jumps after the trot poles are set eleven feet apart.

An oxer at the end of a gymnastic teaches a horse to use himself effectively.

the pace to make it easy for him. Once the horse understands the principle of the exercise, Millar gradually starts to add a leg and seat and back and pace so that what the horse has to do is keep the activity but not let that activity translate into length.

When the horse understands that exercise, Millar raises the cavaletti off of the ground six inches and goes through the same procedure.

Once the horse has mastered that exercise, Millar puts the rails back down on the ground and introduces a jump.

Cavaletti, Jumps and Distances at a Trot: Millar makes the distance from the last cavaletti to the jump only about nine feet and sometimes a little less. Once again, his reason for not having a greater distance is that he does not want to make it too easy for the horse. As he puts it, 'I regulate pace or whatever to help him do it, but he'd better figure out how to *conform to the exercise.'*

If Millar sets up a bounce jump, the distance is eleven feet. For a one-stride jump he uses a distance of eighteen feet and for a two-stride jump, twenty-seven to twenty-eight feet.

Jumps and Distances at a Canter (no trot poles): Further into the exercise when the horse is working out of a canter, a bounce jump is eleven and one-half feet or perhaps twelve. For a one-stride jump he uses a distance of twenty feet or possibly twenty-one feet and for a two-stride jump, twenty-eight feet to thirty feet.

Jumps and Ground Lines: Millar uses ground lines a lot with a young horse to help him understand the jumps, but, once the horse does comprehend, Millar usually takes the ground lines away. Because today's course designers tend not to use such lines, it is important that the horse learn to assess a jump in the ways that will work for him once he is in the show ring.

As Millar explains, 'The sport has become so sophisticated today that a horse has to be just as sophisticated to solve the problem; therefore, his training has to be sophisticated.'

Once a horse understands the jumps, Millar takes the ground lines away.

A typical Millar gymnastic – some fences without ground lines.

Jumps and Becoming Familiar with the Unfamiliar: At Millar Brooke Farm where Millar does all of his actual training, there are a tremendous number of jumps in all shapes and sizes. Many of them are natural-type obstacles such as graves, dry ditches, a liverpool, a water jump, and so on.

Millar knows that course designers are aware that this type of fence is probably going to cause a problem and so they usually make these obstacles less high and less wide than other jumps. As a result it is not normally the jump itself that is the difficulty, but what is underneath.

Says Millar, 'To lose a class over something like that is just unnecessary. It means you just didn't do your homework. It's pretty basic, easy homework to take care of, but it has to be done.'

Millar practises regularly over such fences so that when he goes to a show even though the obstacles might look a little different, the horse is familiar with the type and thus goes ahead with little or no apprehension.

Further thoughts: Millar feels very strongly that a very common error in approach made by many riders is that they try to transpose their wishes, their pressures and their methods of thinking on their horses. Explains Millar, 'A horse does not relate to the pressures of traffic on the highway, of appointments or of winning a class.'

He finds it amazing that people end up creating a fight with their horses during last minute cram sessions to teach something before a big show. It is not that he does not think they will eventually teach whatever it is they are working on, but more that it is not the way Millar likes to train.

He tries to slow his whole way of thinking down to that of the horse. He finds that if he ever makes the mistake of thinking he has to wind a lesson up in a few minutes, he never accomplishes very much because he has let his mind slip into a 'human gear' and the horse is not in that gear. The minute this happens, he and the horse are no longer on the same wavelength. They are no longer communicating effectively.

Millar describes his approach: 'I am a repetition-type trainer.

I am not keen on escalating the strength and the impact of my aids. I would much prefer to repeat until I get the desired result. It is slower and less dramatic, but for me it is more permanent and more lasting and gives me a happier, more generous horse when the job is finished.'

That Millar considers the type of approach, just as important as the results, is clearly revealed when he concludes, 'I really think it is important for people to understand that the horse is a generous and giving and willing animal.

'What makes riding so special is really understanding and relating to another living being.'

His 'friends', as he refers to his international horses, seem to reciprocate that feeling. They seem to want to respond to him. It is perhaps this rapport that has helped to make Millar not only Canada's leading rider, but the world's number one equestrian. After all, generosity is a two-way street!

Riding Your Horse 'In a Frame'

QUESTION: One of the current expressions that judges and trainers frequently use in describing the movement of horses is that they trot or canter 'in a frame'. Can you explain exactly what that means and how it is achieved?

EXPERT: Tom Gayford is a man who needs little introduction to the equestrian world. A rider all his life, Gayford has won so many awards they are too numerous to mention. He cites the winning of the Olympic Gold Medal by the team he captained in Mexico as the highlight of his riding career and places the winning of the 'Alternate Gold' in Rotterdam where he was Chef d'Equipe as a close second. Rocket, his champion hunter, and Big Dee, his talented and successful jumper, have been but two in a long list of his well-known mounts.

ANSWER: Trotting or cantering 'in a frame' refers to the visual picture that a well-balanced horse forms as he moves forward in those gaits. Gayford explains, 'If you visualize a picture frame with a horse centred squarely in it, there should be nothing "hanging" out in front, nor trailing out behind.'

Keeping this 'framed horse' in mind it is easy to understand why this visually descriptive phrase is currently in use. Even a non-rider is able to pick out those horses who are moving 'in a frame' and those who are not.

There is nothing new about the idea. Only the terminology is different. In past times the word 'balanced' was used to describe this same way of going. As Gayford puts it, 'A horse moving in a frame is a horse that's balanced on his hocks.' and enlarges on this description by adding, 'He's not all sprawled out, but "together", moving in a light rhythm.'

In your question you ask how moving 'in a frame' is achieved. As Gayford points out, to answer such a question in detail would cover a long and involved set of lessons, but he does outline some basic concepts which will give you an idea.

Ideally, working towards achieving balance in your horse should begin as far back as the early 'breaking' stage. Gayford himself, only does a limited amount of longe work as he tends more towards driving and riding. He cautions against the improper use of side reins in longeing because he feels that their incorrect application can bring about the very aspects you must try to avoid – a 'dead-mouthed' horse which leans on the rider's hands, thus being either 'sprawled out in front' or 'over-bent'.

Gayford puts a great amount of emphasis on the relationship between the use of the hands and of the legs in achieving a balanced horse.

To use his words, 'To balance a horse you always get his attention first, with the leg. Before you take him with your hands, you take a stronger contact with your leg – never the other way around. It's a very fine split-second movement, but you always use your leg first.'

Movements to work on, to help achieve balance are increasing and decreasing of pace, half-turns, neck bending, leg yielding, quarters in, quarters out and very minor two track work. Your horse must be on the bit or, to quote Gayford, 'accepting the bridle' before you begin to jump.

A horse who is properly accepting the bit will have a rounded back, neck and head but his nose should never be at an angle of more than eighty degrees; that is, never perpendicular nor behind the vertical.

Also, learning to flex and bend laterally in the neck and back is important to your horse's basic schooling. Make sure that in turns his head is bent in the direction in which he is going and not pulled to the outside. You should be able to see at least the 'inside' eye of the horse and possibly more, depending on the degree of the turn.

A number of people are guilty of incorrectly using draw reins to force a horse's head, neck and back into a rigid position. Unfortunately, such an error makes it impossible for the horse to use himself at all as he is far too stiff. Such a horse is not moving in a balanced fashion.

Once a horse has accepted the bit and Gayford has started schooling him to jump, he sets up a simple fence at both sides of the ring, and, in a nice even pace, canters the whole circle, steadying the horse from running after each jump and maintaining a good rhythm. He finds this exercise really helps a horse to move in a balanced way.

Gayford stresses the importance of being gentle and taking your time when schooling. To be able to train a horse to work 'in a frame' is a skill which take a great deal of knowledge and practice to accomplish. There are no artificial short cuts.

How does it feel to ride a horse who is moving 'in a frame'? To quote Gayford, 'You feel that the horse is underneath you. The horse isn't heavy in your hands – he's almost a little lighter in front than he is behind. His hind legs are underneath him almost like a spring and his front end is just flowing on in front.'

The Flying Change

QUESTION: How do you teach a young hunter to do a flying change?

EXPERT: Teacher, rider and trainer Wayne McLellan acknowledges: 'To me there's nothing more thrilling than putting together a round whether it be hunter or jumper and doing it with the clearest, easiest messages to my horse and having a happy understanding horse in the end.'

That he accomplishes this may be seen in the smooth and flowing hunter rounds for which he is well known.

McLellan approaches riding as an art. He is self-taught. As he puts it, 'I've watched the world do their thing and I've taken a little from everyone but *always*, from *day one*, I knew there had to be a system and a formula and I have been struggling to put it together for myself over the years – to make it the easiest, shortest way of producing an end – by conserving time and energy.'

He has put almost twenty years into developing and perfecting his system. He credits Edna Arrow whom he refers to as 'a fabulous horsewoman' with inspiring him to learn to do things right, from the beginning. It was Arrow who encouraged the then teenager, McLellan, to work for the Elliot Cottrelle family during his summer holidays for four years and it was at their quality establishment that he feels he started 'on the right train of thought'.

With riding and teaching experience gained at two or three different professional stables, about nine years ago he became associated with Robert Meilsoe. The two, now in partnership at Gimcrack, have developed a successful teaching, training and showing establishment where things are done in a first-rate manner.

McLellan has won many championships. He rode Bare Fax, for example, to the Conformation Division Championship twice at the Royal Winter Fair. As well, he has coached his students to many successes. One of his pupils, Anne Auty, won the C.E.F. Medal Final two years in a row.

Meanwhile, McLellan describes another kind of highlight: 'Just teaching or educating horses *and* riders – giving them a sound knowledge – that gives me as much of a kick as anything – absolutely!'

ANSWER: Before attempting to educate a horse to execute a flying change, a rider must have a sound knowledge of good, basic flat work. That flat work should include an understanding of lateral aids which play a major role in McLellan's approach to the flying change.

Lateral Aids: 'Basically the lateral aids will control the shoulder and the haunch,' says McLellan.
• The Shoulder: The horse should be able to move from a shoulder left to a shoulder right. In a shoulder left a left indirect rein or a left bend will move the shoulder to the right; that is, distribute the horse's balance to the right. In a shoulder right, the opposite is the case. A right indirect rein or a right bend will move the horse's shoulder or distribute his balance to the left.
  Caution: McLellan points out that these 'shoulder bends' are more like neck bends and *not* to be confused with shoulder-in movements.
• The Haunch or Hindquarter: The horse should be able to move his hindquarter from right to left in response to the displacement of either leg *behind* the girth, pushing the weight from one side to the other.

McLellan works on the shoulder exercises first. These exercises should be done at a walk first and only when the horse clearly understands the aid and the correct response should they be done at a trot, eventually the canter and finally the gallop. Once the horse comprehends these through circles, serpentines, changes of direction, etc., then McLellan adds the displacement of the hindquarters.
  Cautions: It is very important to teach the horse to comprehend the *degrees* of the correct aids. A horse should understand, for example, a little leg and how to react, a medium leg and the correct reaction and a lot of leg and the right response. At first, because the horse is only beginning to learn, the movement of the shoulder or of the hindquarter is greatly exaggerated. McLellan explains, 'On the rider's part the resistance might be very strong and demanding but it should never be erratic.' Once the horse attains a clear understanding, then the degree of straightness becomes greater.
  McLellan stresses the importance of trying to keep the horse as

soft and relaxed as possible through each degree of response to the rider's hands or legs. As well, a consistent pace must be kept up at each gait and the same rhythm must be maintained whenever a line or direction is changed. Cautions McLellan, 'If the horse gets quick or misunderstands, the rider should go back to a review of the basics.'

McLellan stresses that it takes a long time and a lot of consistent work to strengthen the horse's back and neck muscles to prepare him to be physically ready to go on to the flying change. As he points out, 'In the sophisticated dressage field, the flying change is a very advanced movement, yet we expect it from our pre-green hunter.'

Basic Aids for a Canter Depart: When discussing how to teach a flying change it is essential to review the basic aids for a canter depart which can be accomplished from a halt, walk or trot.

McLellan reviews the aids for a canter when on the left rein:

I would be asking my horse with a left indirect rein to slightly bend to the left and slightly displace the shoulder out to the right. My right rein will prevent the shoulder from going too far out and it will also control him if he gets a little too quick. The strength of that left bend or that right rein depends on the degree I need to maintain and again, when I first teach it, it is exaggerated. As they learn and become more under-standing and more supple, it will be a straighter line.

My left leg will be used at the girth to keep the shoulder out (so my inside aids – my left rein and left leg are keeping the shoulder *out* slightly so he doesn't lean as he starts the canter depart) (my right rein is controlling pace *and* keeping the right shoulder from moving too far out) and my right leg is slightly displaced behind the girth pushing the horse's haunch to the left so it favours the left lead (and that right leg's degree depends on the horse's education and how much I need to push the horse into the canter).

The Counter Canter: McLellan refers to the counter canter as a wonderful exercise for understanding the positioning of the horse's body or 'where the different parts are' in order to maintain the lead whether it be left or right. As well, the horse reveals whether or not he is aware of the aids and the correct response to them.

Basic Aids for a Counter Canter Depart:

> I would use a right indirect rein so that the shoulder is *in* off the track slightly with the left rein preventing it from going in too much. The left leg is behind the girth, pushing the haunch to the right to favour the right lead. I'll have to be stronger and a little more clear because it's more common they would favour to move *off* the rail than towards and my right leg is also controlling the shoulder.
>
> I'm sitting deep in the saddle, my shoulder, my body, my hip angle are slightly relaxed to follow the motion of the horse, but my hand, my seat and my leg are doing most of the influencing as required.

McLellan teaches the counter canter from the walk, the trot and the canter through transitions and changes of direction.

Basic Exercises: Some basic exercises would be to canter for ten strides on one lead, make a transition to a walk or a trot and then canter on the opposite lead. The pace must be even, with the horse on the bit and the aids very clear.

If the horse starts to get hollow or tense in his back and his head comes up and the jaw is rigid, the horse is *not* ready to execute a flying change. Review the basics for however many schooling sessions it takes to get the horse soft, supple and relaxed.

Work on straight lines, changes of rein through a half turn on the centre line not always using the track but the one-quarter or three-quarter line or centre line.

When the horse stays soft and on the bit and he goes through the motions of his transitions into a counter canter, he is ready to do the flying change.

The Flying Change:

If I am counter cantering on the left rein, the ideal is my left leg slightly displaced behind the girth to keep its haunch out, to keep him influenced – to keep his balance on his right lead and my right rein would be the dominating rein so I'm pushing him from the left leg laterally up to my right rein – leg before rein – so it's the drive forward and then he sits in my hand. (The flying change is in forward movement. The horse has to jump. He has to step forward into it.) Of course, my right leg and left rein are still up at the wither giving and taking as much as I need to keep the shoulder bent, but my two constants are my right leg and my left rein which are controlling the shoulder. So, I'm counter cantering on the right lead. Now if I were to want to do my switch to the left, then I would *slowly straighten* my horse and then change everything. My right leg would push the haunch in to the left rein, thus my flying change.

For the first few changes McLellan will generally work at a little more of an extended canter as the horse is stepping up from behind and he is assured of the forward motion.

Remember, at first he exaggerates the displacements of the shoulder and of the haunch, but by the time the horse has been working on it for a year, he will look almost straight. (The more educated, the straighter the movements.)

On a more sensitive horse McLellan might be a little more forward and if the horse is a little sluggish, he might use his back a little more to encourage the forward drive.

Caution: The flying change is a change of the *horse's* physical position. It should *not* be a change in the rider's body position. If McLellan finds that he is beginning to be guilty of a lot of 'jumping up and down' or excessive body motion, he drops his stirrups to encourage a deeper seat.

McLellan stresses that there is a systematic approach to teaching the flying change and he keeps the horse's frame of mind comfortable with the situation. For some horses it is a very natural movement for their balance. For others, ones who are long and strung out, for example, it is a little more demanding. It is essential that you understand the physical and mental being of your horse before you pursue any of this and make sure that your analysis is incorporated into your training situation.

Unwinding the Stiff Horse

QUESTION: I have a seven-year-old gelding, Quarter Horse / Thoroughbred cross that has shown a good deal of progress in the two years that I have had him. He has excellent conformation, good stamina for cross country, and a super temperament. However, in his dressage tests the recurring judges' remarks are that he is stiff and lacks impulsion and engagement of the hindquarters. I have been trying to 'loosen' him up by longeing him once a week with side reins, and encouraging him to bend and flex. I also do a lot of work on the flat (transitions etc.) and suppling exercises such as circles and serpentines. I have heard that the shoulder-in movement is good for encouraging a horse to use his hindquarters, but my horse seem even too stiff to do this. He appears determined not to bend and stubbornly resists all my attempts to the contrary.

I have done a good deal of reading on training as well as sought out the opinion of others at the farm where I ride. However, I feel that I have done enough 'experimenting' and I am in need of some truly professional advice. Do you have any suggestions on how I might 'unwind' an unusually stiff horse. He may be determined not to loosen up but I am just as determined to correct him of this unflattering hindrance to his movement.

EXPERT: Christilot Hanson Boylen needs little in the way of introduction to equestrian readers across Canada. For many years she has been successfully showing in international dressage competition including representing Canada in the Olympic Games four times.

Much of her early training and theory lessons came from the late General von Oppein-Bronikowski, a member of Germany's 1936 Olympic Gold Medal winning team.

In later years Boylen studied with Egon von Neindorff and Willi Schultheis, and since 1974 with Georg Theodorescu.

An author, her manual, *Basic Dressage for North America*, is an easy-to-read guide on how to train a horse up to the lower level dressage tests.

ANSWER: In a sense, working on shoulder-in at this point is a little like running before you can walk properly. According to Boylen, the first and most basic two-track movement that should be taught is *leg yielding* and she cannot over-emphasize the importance of this exercise in suppling horses.

Boylen stresses the fact that work on two-tracks should begin with the *easiest* exercise and that is *leg yielding* with the horse's head to the wall. Both horse and rider will benefit from practising this exercise because it not only teaches the horse to yield away from the sideways driving aid but also it teaches the rider that she must keep the horse straight in front and that she must use the outside rein.

In her manual, *Basic Dressage in North America*, Boylen describes the proper execution of leg yielding:

> The horse has little head positioning and stands at approximately a forty degree angle to the wall. The body is straight. The inside legs step forward and over the outside legs. Leg yielding can be started when the horse has learned to do the turn on the forehand and circles easily at the trot and canter. Leg yielding should not be ridden through corners.
>
> The aids are applied as follows: The inside leg goes behind the girth, pushing the horse sideways. The outside leg controls the amount of angle that the horse takes (never more than forty-five degrees) and also pushes the horse forward. The inside rein places the horse's head slightly to the inside, the outside rein keeps the horse's neck straight.
>
> It can be done at the walk and later at the walking trot. The horse and rider will find it easier to do if the horse's head is facing the wall first. Later, it can also be done with the horse's head facing inwards.

Other variations of the same exercise include increasing and decreasing a square. According to Boylen, common faults include:

• The exercise is started before the horse is on the bit. *Correction:* Ride the horse straight forward, put him on the bit before beginning the exercise.

• The horse falls over his outside shoulder. *Correction:* More use of the outside leg and rein aids, reinforced with a whip if necessary.

• The horse refuses to step sideways. *Correction:* Stronger use of the inside leg and rein aids, reinforced with a whip if necessary. In the case of the whip, it should be used behind the firth along with the rider's inside leg.

• The horse rushes away from the sideways driving inside leg. *Correction:* Use lighter aids and stronger contact with the outside rein and leg to contain the horse.

• The gain becomes uneven and the horse loses his balance (off the bit). *Correction:* Ride straight, put him back on the bit regulate the tempo, and start the leg yielding exercise over again.

• The horse becomes nervous and twitchy, swishes his tail constantly. *Correction:* Try working without spurs, perhaps using a whip as an added aid.

Boylen suggests that you and your horse become proficient at leg yielding and summarizes the importance of the exercise with the words, 'It's amazing the progress that can be made by just that one exercise – leg yielding – being done correctly.'

Important Use of the Term 'Inside or Outside' Leg: The term inside or outside leg, does not necessarily always correspond with the inside or outside leg depending on the direction in which the rider is going; for example, when on the left hand, normally circling to the left, the rider's inside leg would be the right one. If the horse was on the left hand and was going to execute a turn on the forehand, however, the inside leg is always the leg from which the horse is yielding. Therefore, the right leg would be called the inside leg, and the left leg becomes the outside leg.

A final suggestion: If you are unsure about the correct use of the required aids you might be well advised to take a few lessons from a *qualified* dressage instructor.

Resisting Forward Motion

QUESTION: I have a four-year-old, seventeen hand gelding which I have owned for three years.

Problem: I have been riding him on the flat since he was two-and-a-half-years-old and I have not experienced any problems that could not be overcome, until the past two to three months. He has developed the very frustrating habit of lifting his head up and down and swinging it from side to side, as well as sticking his tongue out the side of his mouth.

When I longe him I use a surcingle and side reins and he does not seem to bother with his head or tongue; this only occurs when I am riding him.

I have tried different tactics with him, thinking I may be pulling too hard on his mouth. I give him a loose rein, yet this does not help. He only pulls the rein more and therefore causes me to lose all contact and control.

I originally had him on a snaffle but changed to a rubber snaffle thinking that the other one may be pinching his mouth. Still there is no change. It has been suggested to me that I use a martingale or side reins when I ride him, but I am not fully aware of the proper use of these and I would not want to do harm or cause any more problems, especially since he is still a young horse.

I have his teeth floated on a regular basis and there don't seem to be any problems with his teeth or mouth. He had a wolf tooth growing in in the fall but it was level with the gum and the vet was unable to remove it, and didn't think it should cause him any problems.

I have reached the point that it is not enjoyable to ride him because it turns into a battle. I would hate to think this problem can't be solved. I would eventually like to compete with him and I feel he would do well if this problem could be overcome.

EXPERT: An articulate perfectionist, Lorraine Stubbs epitomizes the very philosophy of the Introduction to her Canadian Equestrian Federation book, *Winning Dressage* – 'Dare to Try!'

Stubbs has 'dared' in many fields of endeavour in the horse world. As a dressage rider, she has represented Canada in the Munich Olympics and is currently competing successfully onwards and upwards on two young horses which she has brought along herself – Firmus and Gregor. As a dressage coach and F.E.I. judge, she travels extensively to give ever-popular clinics and to judge at high-calibre shows. As a breeder of Canadian Sport Horses, she has frequently shown her home-breds on the line and now as a breeder of Thoroughbreds, has sold yearlings at the select sales. As a racehorse owner, she has raced one of her home-breds, Bravest Shot to stakes victory. As well, Stubbs is a member of numerous organizations such as Cadora, the Canadian Thoroughbred Horse Society and the Canadian Sport Horse.

At her scenic Rock Eden Farm, Stubbs continues not only to 'dare to try' but also to dare to be successful.

ANSWER: Stubbs zeroes in on the fact that this behaviour (of lifting his head up and down and swinging it from side to side as well as sticking his tongue out the side of his mouth) is a form of resistance. Because he does not act this way when you longe him, it would appear that he is resisting you as the rider rather than you as the trainer. Despite this fact, Stubbs still feels that you should check other possible factors as well, namely his teeth once again, and the tack you use and adjust.

Firstly, although your veterinarian was unable to remove a wolf tooth last fall, it is now possible that it could / should be taken out. As well, it is possible that other teeth could be bothering him.

Next, make sure the fit and adjustment of the tack is correct. Stubbs suggests that you revert to the regular jointed snaffle as she sees no advantage to a rubber one. Width-wise, a seventeen hand horse with a head of a proportionate size would need a bit at least five and three-quarters inches in size and most probably even larger. (A too wide bit is better than a too narrow one.)

Stubbs stresses that the bit be adjusted high enough in your horse's mouth so that he cannot get his tongue over it. When the bit is adjusted correctly, there should be slight wrinkles in the corner of his mouth. Possibly, if he is managing to put his tongue over the bit, it should be adjusted just a little higher than it normally would be. Stubbs recommends a drop noseband or a flash noseband rather than a plain cavesson so that the horse's desire to open his mouth can be controlled. Such a noseband will also help to keep the bit a little higher up in his mouth. The fact that a flash noseband 'has a little more strength' makes it the preferential choice in this instance. Make sure that either the drop or the flash is adjusted *firmly*. To quote Stubbs, 'You'd be surprised at just how tight that can be.'

Stubbs is totally against your riding with side reins or draw reins because in the hands of a novice such aids can cause problems. Instead Stubbs suggests a running martingale not only to help keep the reins together if he moves from side to side with his head but also to give some control if he tries to lift his head too high. (A running martingale, by the way, is allowed in dressage shows in the C.E.F. rule book for warm ups although not for classes.)

Now, back to the problem which Stubbs feels lies between you, the rider, and your horse. Essentially the problem is one of communication. The horse needs to 'get the message' that he *must move forward*, rather than up and down or from side to side. You must therefore *drive* your horse forward using seat and legs to keep the horse in front of you rather than let him be behind your aids.

Stubbs suggests that you longe the horse in side reins in each direction for a total of ten minutes before you ride him. *Make him move on.* That will help to enforce in his mind that he must go forward. Thus, hopefully, he will stay in the proper form when you ride him.

Given your horse's present age and considering how long you have been riding him, Stubbs stresses that you should be riding him 'on the bit' rather than just 'on contact'. For a clarification of these terms, she quotes from her book, *Winning Dressage:*

When a horse in *on the bit* the poll is the highest point of a slightly arched neck; the horse's nose will be slightly ahead of the vertical line; the horse will carry more of his body weight with his hindquarters and thus use his back more efficiently. This suppleness will be carried through into the horse's mouth making him more submissive to the rider's hands.

You mention that you have tried to 'give him a loose rein ...' Inconsistent contact with the horse's mouth is most aggravating to him. It certainly confuses communication. Remember you should be working towards riding him *on the bit.*

Finally, Stubbs suggests that when your horse 'starts to fool around', you should ask yourself what you have been doing for the last five to ten minutes. Often riders fail to give their horses variety to keep them interested. Try to vary your programme.

Include a change of tempo in your forward movements from time to time. If he starts to stick out his tongue, an increase in the tempo will most probably stop him from so doing.

In Summary: Stubbs strongly recommends that you have a knowledgeable ground person check your seat and aids. The Canadian Equestrian Federation book lists certified coaches and Stubbs suggests that you seek a Level II or Level III person to help you with your aids at this awkward stage in your horse's training development. Cautions Stubbs, 'Although the problem you describe is not a serious one, it should be "nipped in the bud" as soon as possible.'

Rein Backs

QUESTION: I have a problem which seriously affects my showing. My problem is my horse gets very upset and nervous when she is asked to rein back. There are some times when she simply refuses to go back at all. The proper aids are being used on her. She just tosses her head sideways and keeps it up in the air and won't lower it until she is asked to move forward.

This is very disturbing even in our schooling because every time we halt she thinks we're going to rein back and she fools with her head. It was probably due to her early training which was before I owned her. She is now six. She was always ridden in draw reins and she was backed into walls, boards, etc. as a punishment unfortunately, once too often. We have tried to assure her that nothing like that was going to happen to her again, but she seems to have developed a mental block which prevents her from understanding this.

EXPERT: Colonel Frederick Graffi, a former Hungarian cavalry officer, taught riding in Argentina before arriving in Canada in the fifties.

A dressage enthusiast, Graffi was a well-known rider and instructor. He was noted not only for his expertise in training horses, but also for his very sympathetic and kind approach. His horses were truly his friends.

Graffi, almost a centenarian, has been retired for quite some time.

ANSWER: People differ as to their ideas of what the 'proper aids' are, so first of all, Graffi explains how to execute a rein back on a green or nervous horse. The rider should lean a little forward in order to free the horse's hindquarters from the weight of the rider and make it easier for the animal to step back. Squeeze both legs lightly against the horse's sides and, as she lifts her leg to step forward, use the reins in a slight restraining motion until the horse takes one step back. Immediately stop and pet the horse as a reward. Try a second step using the same method. Again reward the horse. Make sure that you do not use more than two or three steps back.

In really difficult cases Graffi suggests having a helper on the ground. He stresses the importance of choosing an assistant who is quiet, kind and patient with horses. With the rider giving the correct aids, the helper on the ground should lightly tap the horse on both of its knees to encourage it to move its legs a step backwards. When the horse has reined one step, immediately stop and pet the horse. Try a second step.

Another suggestion which Graffi makes for a difficult case is for the assistant on the ground to face in the same direction as the horse and hold a treat such as a piece of carrot or a lump of sugar behind and slightly below the horse's nose. While the rider lightly applies the correct aids, the helper moves the treat slowly backwards enough to encourage the horse to rein back a step. Graffi stresses the importance of keeping the horse's neck straight. In other words, move the treat back towards the horse's body not over to one side or the other or the horse will twist its head and not keep straight.

Please note: Smooth contact and light hands will help to keep your horse's head quiet. Make sure that you avoid sharp or jerky movements.

If you follow Graffi's suggestions, you should meet with success. Take your time and build slowly on each successful attempt.

A personal note: Never try to get your mare to rein back until you have spent sometime riding her forward smoothly and rhythmically. You are more likely to achieve a good rein back when your horse is relaxed and supple.

How to Prevent Run Outs and Refusals

QUESTION: My new horse has a big jump but he rushes towards his fences badly. What should I do to try to calm him down?

EXPERT: A former Olympic contender and member of the Polish Cavalry, Lieutenant Colonel Michael Gutowski is an expert rider and trainer as well as a well-known instructor and judge. A list of his former pupils reads like a 'who's who' list in Canada's equestrian community. Riders such as Liz Ashton, Jim Day, Jim Elder, Peter Gray, Jim and Doug Henry and Torchy Millar have all benefitted from 'The Colonel's' expertise.

In January 1989, in celebration of the 'Year of the Coach', Gutowski was awarded an Honourary Level III Event Coaching Certificate.

ANSWER: Gutowski points out that rushing is a form of disobedience as is refusing or running out. A horse who rushes his jumps lacks emotional and mental stability either because of his temperament or because of too-hurried training. Because of this instability, quiet, calm schooling is essential. The psychological atmosphere of such schooling helps to produce favourable results.

In order to correct rushing, several steps are necessary and Gutowski stresses the importance of not going on to the next step until the horse is relaxed and moving quietly and rhythmically.

First you should go back to basic work over poles spaced from four and one-half feet to five feet apart, depending on the size of the horse. Continue to walk and to trot over these ground poles until the horse is moving calmly.

The second step is to place a low jump at the end of the poles about nine to ten feet after the last pole. The distance of nine to ten feet depends once again on the size of the horse. Trot over the poles and jump the obstacle. Work at this if the horse moves quietly. If he begins to rush, work at the first step again.

Next, work out of a trot over a low combination jump. Normal distance between two obstacles in a combination when approached at a trot is twenty-one feet and for a smaller horse, less. For a rushing horse the distance can be shortened to nineteen feet.

Later, add a pole on the ground in the exact middle of the two jumps so that the horse has to shorten his stride. This middle pole can later be changed to a very low jump. This triple combination will encourage the horse to concentrate and his looking down at the obstacles will result in arching.

Attempt the fourth step when the horse, approaching in a trot and jumping calmly continues at a quiet canter after clearing the obstacles. Slowly circle in a large arc to the left or right depending on which lead the horse is cantering and go over a low jump which has previously been placed there. If the horse becomes excited, quietly turn out in a circle away from the jump and do not attempt to go over the obstacle.

When these four steps have been completed successfully, the horse is ready for the final phase. Canter quietly among the jumps in the ring. If the horse is not rushing, select a fence and go over it. Canter until he is quiet, select another obstacle and jump it. If at any time the horse rushes, be prepared to retrace your work and begin again.

Please note: Never deliberately change to a faster gait as you approach a fence. Doing so only encourages rushing.

Why a Horse Might Refuse a Fence

QUESTION: I recently purchased a very 'pricey' horse that had been doing exceptionally well in open jumping classes. He had shown both indoors and outdoors and had a reputation as being a good honest jumper. Now, under a professional rider, he has suddenly started quitting. What do you think the problem could be? Some people have said he's just gone sour. Others say it's the change of rider. What approach would be best in dealing with this difficulty?

EXPERT: For expert advice on this question involving jumping, I turned to one of Canada's own greats in the sport of riding – Jim Elder. For over thirty years he has been a competitor in the Olympics, in Pan American Games and in top calibre shows, from coast to coast and from country to country. A gold and a bronze medalist, Elder frequently captained Canada's equestrian team, lending a very important depth of experience and a very competitive spirit to the other members.

Although a rider of international level horses, Elder has never lost his interest in 'making' a green horse. His enjoyment of the fun and the challenge involved is indicative of his whole approach to the sport.

Elder's answer covers all aspects of the problem and yet is so concisely phrased, I use his words....

ANSWER: 'The problem of becoming an habitual stopper could develop for many reasons. Since I have not ridden your horse, nor seen him perform to feel and watch his reactions to jumping, it is impossible for me to pinpoint the exact cause of the problem. I assume the horse is not dead green and has been jumping in at least the preliminary division of the 'A' Circuit shows. It must be remembered that a horse is not a mechanical object but an animated being with his own thoughts and feelings.

'My first reaction would be that he's hurting somewhere. He may need reshoeing. It could be that his tack is poorly fitted and bothering him. Perhaps the bit is too severe. Possibly he's physically sore or mentally run down. There is also a chance his blood level could be low. Some of these factors, if they are the case, would be enough to put the horse off the desire to jump.

'For horses to jump around the courses we're asking them to, it is extremely important that the horse has confidence in his rider and vice versa. As top show jumpers are normally sensitive animals, just a change to a rider who has a different riding and training technique may be enough to throw the horse off. It is therefore important after buying a horse, especially if it has been going successfully, to try and adapt to the horse's best way of going or at least meet him halfway. It takes time to change a horse and if he becomes confused, he loses confidence, so allow the horse time to adjust before attempting any big courses.

'The result of a bad crash or fall at an obstacle can also have serious consequences. A young horse especially, can be completely ruined with such a traumatic experience. When this happens I am afraid all you can do is start over again. To build the horse's confidence, the following will help. Jump *small* obstacles. Work over cavalletti. Give him a change of scenery as a ring full of jumps will tend to keep him tense. Go hacking. Ride him out across country (perhaps jumping small, natural obstacles en route). Also, vary his programme by turning him out in the paddock for a few hours or by longeing him over small obstacles.

'When you show him again, drop him down a division, even if it means putting him in some hunter classes for a school. The important thing is to get him back again jumping willingly and easily.

'Probably the best advice of all would be to have an experienced and reliable horseman either ride him, or watch him school, in order to give you a sound appraisal of what is bothering him and how you can deal with it.'

Why a Jumper (or Hunter) Might Have his Head and Neck Flexed to the Outside Around a Course

QUESTION: Why do riders bend their horses to the outside when going round the corner of a jumper course?

EXPERT: Ian Millar (see Chapter 8, Section 2, Question 2).

ANSWER: Although a purist in his training sessions at home, Millar finds that at horse shows, the long term goal of perfecting the horse's way of going sometimes comes into conflict with the short term goal of winning. Says Millar, 'What happens, is a compromise.'

Millar describes the situation well: 'Obviously coming through the corner you'd like a horse bent around your inside leg, a little more solid contact on the inside rein as being the guiding rein and your horse bending around the corner. That is, of course, the way I would teach them at home and that is how I would train them when I am in the warm up area preparing for a class. As I canter through the corner I would definitely want him bent that way and if he wasn't bent that way, I'd take a moment and review it.

'But, once they get in the show ring these horses know the sport and they anticipate where they are going. They anticipate the corner and they know very well that as they go into a corner they are soon coming out of a it and facing another jump and there is anticipation in that. All of a sudden they override and ignore these good basic aids that they have learned at home and reviewed in the warm up area and cut in to go to the jump.

'What most riders would then do is apply the inside leg and say, "No! No! Stay in this corner and bend around my inside leg." But this thousand pounds or more of eager animal says, "No! No! Never mind your inside leg. I'm going with the jump right now."

'As a little bit of a desperation measure the outside rein is used far

225

more and hence the horse is held into the corner but out of shape and out of form.

'Most riders *want* their horses to canter through the corner with their spines prescribing the bend or the curve of the corner and bent beautifully round the inside leg, but the reality of an anticipating, aggressive, keen horse in the show ring isn't necessarily going to obey those aids and therefore there is a compromise to keep him in the corner and an unpleasant-looking bend is the result.'

How to Control Behavioural Changes At a Show

QUESTION: I have been using a full cheek snaffle on my six-year-old hunter. At home it seems to be an adequate bit and I have no problems controlling him. At shows he can be very strong, even to the point of being out of control sometimes. I would like to know what is the next bit I should consider or series of bits I may want to consider so that I can control him more effectively.

For your information I am showing in hunter classes over fences. I plan to show in jumper classes in the future.

EXPERT: Originally from Memphis, Tennessee, Mac Cone trains horses, coaches riders and buys and sells horses at his aptly-named 'Southern Ways' stable northeast of Toronto.

Cone's equestrian knowledge and skills are based on the best of foundations. After one year of university, Cone, a former junior rider, decided he wanted to develop a career in the horse industry. First he travelled to New Jersey where he studied for three years under the internationally-known rider and horseman, George Morris. He then studied for another three years under the tutelage of the gifted United States team coach, Bertalan de Nemethy when he rode for the United States team for two years.

Eventually Cone started his own business – training horses and coaching riders. In 1978 he relocated in Canada.

Currently there are thirty horses from Southern Ways on the

show circuit. Cone's top hunter is Royal Hawk who is showing very successfully in the Working Hunter and Combined Conformation Divisions. His top jumpers are syndicate-owned Zantor, who is placing in the World Cup Qualifiers, and Pierre Levesque's Pessimist, who competes in modified Grand Prix and Speed Derby classes.

Eventually Cone would like Southern Ways to become a 'jumpers-only' stable.

ANSWER: Cone points out that it is very normal for a horse to change his behaviour once he leaves behind him the security of his home environment and enters the noise and commotion of the average show grounds.

Cone does not necessarily concentrate on a change of bit to control this different behaviour, but rather first looks at exercise and diet as two possible areas of influence that can have an altering effect. He makes the following suggestions:

Exercise:
• Increase your horse's exercise the day before the show.
• 'Wash him out'; that is, give him a good work out on the flat at the show before your classes begin. Cone prefers that the horse be ridden rather than longed, at a walk, trot and canter until, as he puts it, 'the horse gets everything out of his system.' At this point your horse will probably have worked up a good sweat all over his body. Give him a thorough wash, then tack him up again and start your day afresh.

Diet:
• Cut the grain back or take it away completely. Cone explains that because each horse is totally different he has no hard and fast rules about changes in feed, but bases *how* and *how much* he cuts back on the individual horse and his temperament. With certain horses Cone gives them no grain the night before a show, lets them go through the first day of a show and then gives them grain on the night of the first day after they have competed. They then stay on full rations all

the way through the show. Of others, Cone says, 'You never can just get to the bottom of them and keeping the grain away does help.' These (hunters only) he would keep off grain throughout the whole show. Cone stresses, 'We always have a big fat, full hay net hung up in their stalls where they can have all the hay they want.'

He adds with a chuckle, 'The way I see it, God didn't put sweet feed trees out there for them. We're the ones supplementing them with unnatural things. Horses are basically grazing animals, so if I cut the grain back on one that's a little bit wild, I don't feel I'm being inhumane.'

Cone refers to increased exercise and reduced diet as *preventative medicine;* that is, they prevent or lessen the chances of changes in the behaviour of horses at shows. He sums up, 'Get to *know* your horse and *exactly* where you're happy as an individual with his temperament and then just *set up a pattern* to get him to be exactly where you want him to be (behaviour-wise).'

Bits: Cone explains that at Southern Ways the hunters and the jumpers usually have what he calls 'a working bit' or 'a hacking bit' as well as 'a show bridle'. Most or eighty per cent of the time, the show bridle is a more severe bridle than the working bridle. Cone prefers to use different types of snaffles rather than a bridle which requires two reins because he feels two reins are just that much more complicated, particularly in competition when it helps to have things as straightforward as possible.

He does not feel that loose rings on a bit are appropriate on a hunter.

Your Full Cheek Snaffle and How It Works: You mention that you are using a full cheek snaffle. That name can apply to many different kinds of snaffles. Cone takes it that you are using a plain full cheek snaffle; that is, one with a fairly 'fat' mouthpiece which in the middle has a very loose joint that allows the bit not only to fold in half but also to go up and down. He refers to such a bit as 'a very, very mild, wonderful working bit.'

He likes the full cheek application because he feels it really helps in the turning of the horse. The presence of the bar at the top and the bar at the bottom of the bit put a lot of pressure on the opposite side of the horse's face to the rein that is being pulled. The horse responds to the pressure on his face by turning away from it. If the rider is pulling on the left rein, for example, the bar presses against the right side of the horse's face and he turns away from that pressure; that is, he turns left.

Suggested Series of Bits in Increasing Severity:

• The 'fat' or thick, jointed full cheek snaffle that you currently use.
• A thinner version of the full cheek snaffle or a 'D' ring. (The 'D' ring acts in the same way as the full cheek because of the tall bars top and bottom – there because of the straight back of the 'D.')
• Varying degrees of thickness of the mouthpiece of either a full cheek or a 'D' ring snaffle. (The thinner the bit, the more severe it is.)
• A 'twist' mouthpiece. The twist adds to the severity of the bit at the corners of the mouth.
• Varying degrees of thickness of the mouthpiece in the twist.
• A 'port' bit. Cone explains, 'It's a plain full cheek with a fat mouthpiece but instead of being jointed, there's actually a little port which would be like a curb bit but as it's only on a snaffle rein you don't have a long shank that you're pulling on. What this does, instead of only applying pressure to the corners of the mouth, is put a little pressure on the tongue and on the roof of the mouth because of the port mouthpiece.'
  Cone finds this type of bit very effective on a horse that has an extremely insensitive or 'numb' mouth.
• Varying degrees of thickness of the mouthpiece of the port bit.
• The edge bit. In the snaffle department, this is the most severe type of bit that Cone ever uses on a hunter. The bit has a plain full cheek sidepiece but the mouthpiece is built more like a triangle. The edges of the triangle work against the corner of the mouth when the horse is being turned. The more rounded the edges of the triangle, the less severe the bit within this group. The sharper the edges of the

triangle, the more severe the bit. Cone cautions, 'With the edge bit I can't stress enough that the rider *must* make sure that if it starts to cut the mouth a little, she must cut back to something less severe.'
• Varying degrees of sharpness as described above.

General Comments on Bits: Cone explains that only one hunter at Southern Ways requires an edge bit and that the rest go in much less severe bits. To quote Cone, 'The edge bit is very much the exception, not the rule.' He advises that unless you are with a very good trainer or you, yourself, are a very good trainer, you would not be wise to use a severe edge bit in your horse's mouth, especially if your only reason is just because he might be a little fresh. 'An edge bit,' says Cone, 'can be very much a razor in a monkey's paw.'

As Cone points out, his list of bridles includes a variety of thirty to forty different bits from which you can choose. He reiterates that from this selection he picks suitable snaffles for his jumpers as well. He adds that ninety-five per cent of the jumpers around the world go in a one-rein bridle because in the middle of challenging competitions, it's much easier not to have to worry about whether or not you are on the curb or the snaffle.

In Summary: Cone suggests that you might want to use a more severe bit on the first day of the show and then return to your plain full cheek snaffle for the remainder of the show. Sometimes a change such as that on the first day of competition is all that's necessary to have your horse behave well for the entire show.

Road Hacks and the Nervous Horse

QUESTION: I do a lot of cross country riding. Often this involves one or two miles of riding along country roads to get to other properties. Some of the roads are paved and some are gravel. My horse is very nervous of cars and to make matters worse, some cars don't even slow down. He often is so frightened that he shies into ditches or fences that are at the side of the road. If he sees a truck or a tractor his reaction is worse. I am worried about having a bad accident one day.

What I need to know is how can I get him more used to traffic without endangering myself at the same time?

EXPERT: Born in Germany, Captain Werner Wagner, grandson of cavalry officers, grew up in the world of horses and learned breaking, training, driving and riding at an early age.

Years later, after a four-year apprenticeship under Commander Lynch of the English Army Riding School in Hamburg, he was examined by the German Association for Riding Masters and put in charge of a riding school. For several years he trained students who competed successfully in all three riding disciplines.

In Canada, Wagner has been an active organizer of shows such as the former Sunnybrook Park Equestrian Event, a Director of the Canadian Combined Training Association and a member of the Governor General Horse Guards. As well, he is a Senior Judge.

It is his extensive background in riding quadrilles in which precision and accuracy coupled with his experience in riding escort in heavy noise situations that make him an ideal expert for this particular question.

(As a matter of interest, Wagner and I each played the parts of knights in a television commercial for a red and a white wine. We were on horses and saddles supplied by Werner. The horses were extremely well-mannered despite the flapping adornment they wore, the armour we had on and the lances we had to raise – all for the benefit of the cameras. What a day it was! Without the help of such thoroughly schooled horses, we would have had a much more difficult time during the day's shoot.)

ANSWER: Wagner feels that only good riders on fairly responsive horses should attempt to ride on the road. Failing such a combination, at least one of the pair should be experienced. He stresses the safety aspect and points out that an inexperienced rider on a green horse is really putting his own life and that of his horse in jeopardy when he attempts roadwork before he and his mount are ready. So, before you venture out to encounter traffic, make sure your horse is responding properly to your aids. Remember, when you have your horse 'well onto your aids' your requests will be occupying his mind and the more he is thinking about what you are asking of him, the less he will be thinking about approaching vehicles.

Many people tend to turn their horses towards the object. Wagner strongly advises against so doing; instead, he advocates *flexing your horse away* from an oncoming object. Such a flexion is accomplished by increasing the pressure of your outside leg (closest to the ditch) and bending your horse around this leg. The leg pressure must be supported by very firm contact with the outside rein and supportive contact with the inside (vehicle side). Thus the horse will still see the object but he will be prevented from swinging his hindquarters around too much and escaping from the rider's aids.

Naturally, if necessary, be prepared to bring in the inside leg in order to prevent the horse from drifting towards the path of the oncoming vehicle.

If the object is stationary, flex him away as you approach it. After passing, retrace your path two or three times to help teach the horse that the object won't hurt him and to aid the horse in gaining confidence about it.

To help in the actual introduction of your horse to traffic, Werner suggests some procedures you might follow:

• When your horse is going well, take him to a field adjacent to the road and ride him parallel to it with the fence or trees or whatever, between you and the vehicles on the road. (He calls this procedure, 'learning by degree'.) You and your horse are still exposed to the noise and the movement of a vehicle but you have some protection in the form of the barrier between you and the road. Using this as a 'first step', your horse will have a good chance to 'get a pleasant taste' from this experience.

• Before going out on the road make sure your horse has already done a substantial amount of work so that he does respond to aids and has expended some of his 'steam' and energy. Of course don't overdo your preparatory workout because you don't want to work your horse too hard.

• When you are ready to make your debut in traffic, if riding a particularly nervous green horse, always go out first with an older, quieter horse who hopefully will be a stabilizing influence.

When it comes to road safety, Wagner stresses one other important consideration: If you are riding at dusk or when it's dark, add some reflective device, as do the mounted police, so that traffic will be able to see you.

Cross Country Hacks and the Badly Behaved Horse

QUESTION: I own a five-year-old sorrel pony gelding. Lately, well now that I think of it, for the past while, I have been having problems with my pony.

He has absolutely flawless manners in the barn and for general handling (grooming, feeding, turning out, etc.), but when I ride him (I am his only rider by the way), he often acts up. When the wind blows strongly he tends to freak out, and starts to prance around, toss his head and bolt. Also he tries to bolt in certain areas. We go out on the trails and generally ride in the same places. I try to do different paces in different areas so he doesn't connect certain spots with galloping and the like. Also he shies or spooks a lot.

Several days ago he spooked and bolted down a hill. I stayed on down the hill but at the bottom he jumped sideways and literally out from underneath me and I fell off. Due to injuries from this spill, I missed a few days off work (I have a part-time job and am in Grade Ten). But we go on the same trails and he's seen everything plenty of times and yet he still spooks. I have tried to be patient with him but I'm slowly becoming black and blue!

Last year, in an accident on him, I had to be hospitalized for about a week and I just don't know what to do anymore. I don't want to sell him because I do like him a lot and have owned him several years. My family and I suspect that he may have a hard mouth ... is there any way to repair that? If it helps any, we use an English saddle, plain snaffle bit and snaffle bridle. He seems to spook at nothing.

EXPERT: Jane Holbrook has a wide background of equine experience. Beginning her riding career at the age of eleven, she showed extensively as a junior rider. Her best mount at that time was a fourteen hand, two inch Thoroughbred.

In the sixties, Holbrook was a member of the Canadian Equestrian Team. In the seventies she became an 'A' examiner for the Pony Club and for eight or nine years travelled across Canada to test Pony Club instructors. In the eighties she has been in demand both as a judge and as a steward on the 'A' Circuit. Holbrook breeds Canadian Sport Horses, Thoroughbreds and Trakehners at Rivergreen which she runs with her partner, Sheila Macleod.

ANSWER: A horse instinctively runs to save himself from real or imagined dangers. It is that very instinct that has helped the horse to survive as an animal species for thousands of years.

Unfortunately, because your pony has been successful in shying and bolting, his success will have reinforced these tendencies; in other words, because he has got away with such behaviour, he will be more likely to continue.

Holbrook, however, has made numerous suggestions which should prove helpful to you.

• First of all, she suggests that you cut down on the amount of grain that your pony is getting; in fact, give him no more than a cupful just to keep him happy while his stablemates are being fed. Do make sure though, that he is getting good quality hay.
• Turn your gelding out before you ride him so that he has a chance to get rid of his excess energy. The more paddock exercise he gets, the better. Actually, it would be perfectly acceptable to turn him out most, if not all, of the time.
• Ride him in a controlled area such as a riding ring or a paddock where he cannot run too far away with you.

At the same time Holbrook suggests that you should do the following:

• Get a professional rider or trainer to try out your pony and find out whether or not he has a hard mouth. Even if he does, you would probably still be wise to use your plain jointed snaffle. Switching to more severe bits can become a non-stop practice.

You write that you have had your five-year-old pony for several years. Does that mean that you trained him yourself? If so, it is quite possible that your horse needs some thorough basic training. Possibly the experienced rider or trainer who tries out your pony's mouth could give him schooling that will help to make him more obedient to the aids.

• Have your veterinarian check your pony's eyes and mouth to make sure he has no physical problems which might be causing him to behave badly.

• When you eventually do go out on trails, ride with someone who is on a really quiet, well-behaved horse. Better yet, suggests Holbrook, let a capable rider on a quiet horse 'pony' you. To 'pony' you and your mount, the other rider would have to hold one end of a lead in his or her hand with the other end attached to your pony's halter, which could be left on underneath his bridle. If you are being led, or 'ponied', your mount will not be able to bolt with you and you will therefore be much safer. As well, your pony has to learn that he cannot always spook and run when he feels like it, but must follow human commands. Hopefully, he will become accustomed to slower outings and thus become easier for you to control in the future.

• Last of all, it sounds as if you may be going out hacking under very challenging conditions. Many horses will act up on windy days because of the sheer exuberance they feel. As well, because the wind will sometimes lift and blow objects such as leaves and branches around, your horse is more likely to be spooked.

• It also sounds as if you are riding up and down hills and through valleys. Such terrain often makes it more difficult to control horses, because downhill they have a tendency to become heavier on the forehand and run to keep up with themselves, and uphill they find it easier if they have gained the momentum to carry them to the top. Too, a rider is more likely to be caught off balance when riding up and down hills because he or she is in the forward seat position; hence the rider, leaning forward, falls off more easily. When you do go out on trails, choose warm, calm days and travel over flatter land until you have more control.

9. SHOWING YOUR YOUNG HORSE 'ON THE LINE'

The late Dick Day was a master at standing up a horse 'on the line'. In this photograph, Day would have preferred that the hind leg closest to the camera would have been about two to three inches further forward.

How to Prepare your Young Horse
For a Conformation Line Class

QUESTION: I am the owner of a really good-looking young foal who is out of an approved Hunter Foundation Stock mare and by a registered Thoroughbred stallion. He has the potential, I think, to do well in hunter line classes; in fact, I would like to prepare him for eventual entrance in the Governor General's Cup. As I have never had any real experience with young stock prior to this foal, I need to learn as much as possible about such things as:

- Feed
- Veterinary attention
- Farrier attention
- Exercise and training
- General show information.

EXPERT: Born into a 'horsey family' in England, the late Dick Day spent well over sixty years in the business of horses – breeding, training, riding and showing. To Day, however, horses were more than a business. He had an expert eye for spotting a good horse and an expert knowledge of caring for horses. He loved a good horse; in fact, his eyes absolutely lit up when he saw one.

Winner of *seven* Governor General's Cup awards, Day was always one of the best at developing a horse to its true conformation potential.

Day was the father of Jim Day who is not only a former Olympic gold medalist on Canada's jumping team but one of the leading Thoroughbred trainers at racetracks in Canada if not North America.

ANSWER:
Eligibility: First and foremost Day pointed out that it is necessary to make sure that the foal is *eligible* to enter such shows as the Royal. Both the brood mare and the stallion must be approved by the

Canadian Sport Horse Association. In order to enter a Sport Horse (Hunter) line class, a foal must be registered with the Sport Horse Association. Application for inspection and registration may be obtained from either The Canadian Sport Horse Association, or The Canadian National Livestock Records.

Day suggested that if you are interested in showing in Sport Horse classes it is best to become a member of the Canadian Sport Horse Association. The Association issues newsletters that list shows which have Canadian Sport Horse classes (usually six or seven per year) and also has speakers who lecture on various topics of interest to horsemen.

If your foal is out of a mare who is a registered Thoroughbred as well as a Canadian Hunter Foundation Stock mare, your foal might also be eligible to show in Thoroughbred line classes at the Royal.

Suitability: Once you have made sure that your foal is eligible to show, your next consideration should be whether be appears to have enough *promise* to make showing worthwhile.

A tiny, 'weedy' offspring stands little or no chance of placing. Day cautioned however, that sometimes a foal which does not look that great in his first year can turn into a beauty by the time he is in his third year.

Generally speaking, these are the qualities which Day always looked for in a foal:

- A lot of bone – a lot of substance
- A nice head
- A lot of front
- A short back
- A lot of depth (through the chest)
- Short cannon bones
- Depth at the quarters
- Straight movement
- Absence of cow hocks or sickle hocks.

By the way, an *early* foal (February or March) stands a much better chance of doing well in line classes because of its extra growth and maturity.

The First Year: Day stressed the importance of the care and handling which the foal experiences in his first year. Correct feed, veterinary and farrier attention, paddock exercise and handling all contribute to the foal's progress.

• Feed: The foal should be encouraged to eat a little grain when he is only two to three weeks old. A 'foal creep' that the mare cannot reach is the best way to allow the foal access to grain. The other alternative is to tie the mare up for awhile while the foal eats.

Give the foal a chance to make friends with another animal, perhaps a pony. Then, when it is weaned at about five months of age, the foal has a friendly companion and tends to miss his mother less.

Day recommended 'Big Un' or 'Frisky Foal' and let the foal eat as much as he likes up until about nine months of age. As a supplement, Day fed a vitamin and mineral pelleted combination and, for the freshly weaned foal, added a tiny amount of cod liver oil. The aim, of course, is to encourage as much growth as possible and to help achieve this aim, good nutrition is essential.

Caution: If the foal is not getting outside much, he should not be given as much feed. As well, a very close eye must be kept on the foal's fetlocks and legs. If he starts to stock up even minutely he should be cut back on his feed so that he does not run into such growth problems as contracted digital flexor tendons or epiphysitis.

• Veterinarian Attention: A foal should be checked by a veterinarian as soon after birth as possible and given the required shot(s). Barring any accident requiring a tetanus needle, Day did not recommend that any other needles be given until the foal reaches eight months. What Day did emphasize however, is the importance of deworming. He first had a foal dewormed at six weeks of age and then dewormed every following six weeks until the cold weather set in. Remember: bad worm infestation cannot only stunt the foal's growth but also cause colic at some later time in the young horse's life.

• Farrier Attention: Day recommended that a farrier check a foal's feet when he is six weeks old. If the foal is not travelling straight a good blacksmith can do a lot to help improve way of going. The foal should receive farrier attention every six weeks.

241

• Exercise and Handling: Day believed in putting a halter on a foal the day it is born because it is easier to handle the foal then and, in turn, it makes the foal easier to manage from then on. He was a firm believer in handling the foal as much as possible, including picking up his feet when he is only two or three days old.

He was highly in favour of getting a foal outside as much as possible – from morning to night if the weather is good. Freedom to move around at a walk, trot or canter helps the foal to develop.

As far as grooming is concerned, 'A really good cleaning for a foal is just about as good as a good feed,' said Day. He stressed the fact that grooming stimulates good blood circulation and in so doing improves the coat. Remember, the recommended cod liver oil also helps the foal coat and a shiny coat will look more attractive then a dull one in a line class. Finally, the foal benefits from the handling aspect of grooming.

• Direct Preparation for Showing: As far as actual preparation for a show is concerned, Day suggested that you make a point of getting a foal used to loading on a van so that on the day of the show, shipping will be easy. Make sure that the foal and mare are used to being out of hearing range of each other because for the line class at the Royal the foal must enter and compete alone.

Since the foal will need to stand while being judged, teach the foal to *stand properly*. Day, a master at showing a horse in a line class, outlined the way he liked a horse to stand. Rather than all four feet square, Day liked the appearance given by one hind foot perhaps six inches behind the other. He also suggested such a spread with the front foot, pointing out that when the judge is on the near side of a horse, if the near front foot is six inches in front of the other, it gives the shoulder a better angle. If the same leg is back instead, the shoulder tends to look straighter.

Teach the foal to walk on the lead. Not all, but some judges do ask that you also trot the foal; so to be safe, make sure he is used to doing both.

• Showing: To quote Day, 'It makes quite a difference if an *experienced* person shows a horse on the line, rather than someone who has never done it.' As long as a foal has been taught the basics of standing properly and walking and trotting 'in hand', a professional handler can take over a horse 'cold' before a class.

If the handler you choose is already spoken for, show the foal yourself rather than settle for someone mediocre.

Finally, make sure that your youngster is beautifully turned out on the day of the show. Braids should be both neat and numerous. He should be wearing tack that suits his head and the tack should be clean and oiled.

A personal note: The exposure experience is good for a foal so if you think your foal has some potential, give showing him a try. As well, showing on the line gives the owner a chance to show his youngsters to potential buyers.

IO. VETERINARY

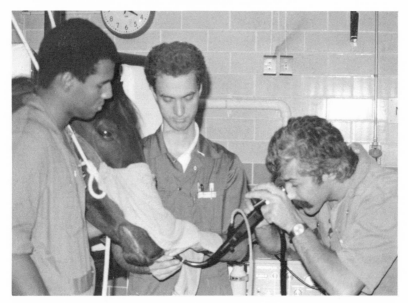

Veterinary research has led to improved techniques and has furthered understanding, but there is much yet to be learned.

Here, Dr. Laurent Viel, a respiratory specialist at the Ontario Veterinary College, uses a bronchoscope to examine a horse's respiratory tract.

A First Aid Kit for Your Stable and What to Do in Common Equine Emergencies

QUESTION: Help! Recently I moved my two horses to a stable close to home. The trouble is, the owner of the stable has a full-time job which takes her away from the property all day. I shall be seeing my horses just about every day so I can check on them to make sure they are okay. (They will be turned out in a large field with three other horses during the time the stable owner is away.) The owner of my previous stable always used to look after any emergencies and I'm not sure I would know the correct thing to do if something happens to them while no one but me is around. Can your experts give me any advice about first aid supplies I should keep in my tack box and give me some help about how to look after scrapes, cuts, bites and maybe kicks?

EXPERT: Dr. Mary Bell is that invaluable combination of equine veterinarian and rider. Because of her experience in owning and showing hunters and, more recently, dressage horses, she is very aware of all the worrying injuries that can befall horses.

An American, Bell graduated from the University of Pennsylvania, did an internship in large animal surgery at the Ontario Veterinary College, and became an assistant professor in large animal medicine. Returning to the United States for a three-month period, Bell worked under Dr. Fegin in large animal cardiology at the New Bolton Center.

In 1977 she established herself in private practice in the Guelph area in Canada. Her practice operates under the name Mannington Veterinary Services.

ANSWER: First and foremost Bell strongly suggests that you contact your own veterinarian, find out *what* he or she would suggest that you have on hand and also, even more important, *how* he or she would suggest using it.

She cautions that it can do more harm than good to use drugs and other supplies unless you really know what you are doing.

Bell advises *her clients* to have the following supplies on hand:

- Antiseptic Soap such as either Betadine or Hibitane
- Topical Spray such as Topazone or V-Sporin
- Clean Bandage Material such as sheet cottons or quilts
- Sterile Cotton such as Johnson & Johnson
- Flannel Bandage Material or Commercial Leg Bandages
- Gauze Pads (usually four by four inches) of the type found in drug stores
- Vetrap™ (a 'stretchy' material bandage that adheres to itself. It is put over cottons as a pressure bandage.)
- Antibiotic Ointment such as Furacin dressing
- Colic Drench (see cautionary notes)
- Tranquilizer such as Atravet granules
- Opthalmic Ointment (see cautionary notes)
- Tape or Pins Used to fasten bandages. If using tape, make sure that it is not put all around the leg and overlapped.)
- Kopertox for thrush
- Zincofax
- Poultice Dressing
  Animalintex for open wounds
  Phlo-Go for non-cut areas
- Rubbing Alcohol
- Absorbine or other leg brace
- Rectal Thermometer
- Oral Antihistamine
- Antibiotics (see cautionary notes)
- Water Hose
- Bran
- Scissors.

Cautionary Notes:
- Betadine should never be used over sensitive areas such as the vulva, the scrotum or the eyes.

248

• Many eye problems are underestimated by horse owners. Most eye difficulties should be examined by a veterinarian.

• Colic drench should only be used in consultation with a veterinarian as there are times when colic drench should not be administered.

• Antibiotics to be given by needle are best avoided unless given following consultation with your vet.

Bell encourages her clients to make up charts for the various emergencies which might occur and suggests that you 'try to garner some hints' from your own veterinarian as to his or her preference regarding method of treatment. Bell explains that there is frequently more than one correct way to treat a problem.

For *initial treatment only* Bell recommends the following:

A Deep Cut: Deep cuts frequently occur on the lower leg and the best way to handle such cuts in Bell's opinion (as long as the cut is not a body cut or near a joint where it is suspected that there has been a penetration of a joint capsule or penetration of a body cavity such as the chest or the abdomen) is to provide some irrigation with clean water, preferably hose water rather than that from a bucket. After irrigating the cut, if your veterinarian is *not* going to be arriving within the hour, spray with Topazone. Next, apply a pressure bandage; that is, one held directly to the wound or bandaged onto the wound. The best and cheapest material to use on a deep cut is a sanitary pad. Cover this smoothly with a sheet of cotton and finish with Vetrap™. To make sure that the bandage does not provide uneven tension or pressure on the leg, apply the pad, cotton and Vetrap™ *evenly.*

If the wound is bleeding profusely, do *not* use irrigation but do use a pressure bandage as outlined. If the bleeding persists, *resist* the temptation to keep removing the bandage and checking on the wound; instead, stress the urgency of veterinarian attention as soon as possible. Another cautionary point Bell makes is that you *avoid* moving a horse with a profusely bleeding wound any more than is absolutely necessary.

A Surface Wound: Assuming that you are referring to an abrasion, first remove the dirt with an antiseptic soap such as Hibitane if the wound is around the head or sheath or vulva, or Betadine if it is around the body. (Remember to rinse off Betadine very thoroughly.) Next, pat the area dry and then apply ointment such as Hibitane, Zincofax or Furacin. Bell, herself, uses a combination of one-half Furacin and one-half Zincofax on most occasions. You will find that Zincofax helps the Furacin to adhere to the abrasion.

Swelling from a Kick: Bell suggests cold therapy such as cold water or ice packs for thirty to forty-five minutes. Remember, this is an initial treatment only.

Swelling(s) from Insect Bites: Use rubbing alcohol or witch hazel over the swollen area(s). Your veterinarian will make a decision as to the administration of antihistamines.

A Wound from a Horse Bite: Either the treatment for a deep cut or a surface wound (see above) would apply to this problem, the only additional factor being that a wound from a bite frequently involves a lot of pressure, and therefore you should protect against the future sloughing of skin by using an ointment rather than a spray. If the wound is a penetrating one, then follow the recommendation for a deep cut; if not, follow that for a surface wound.

Penetration of a Hoof by a Sharp Object: Call your veterinarian! And know *precisely* where the object penetrated. Bell frequently recommends a poultice. The odd time a horse steps on wood and it can penetrate quite deeply. If you pull the wood out, there is a chance that splinters might be left in the hoof. Therefore, if the wood appears to be imbedded deeply, have someone hold up the foot while you contact your veterinarian for instructions.

A major concern in all of these recommendations involving penetration of the skin is tetanus. Shots should always be up-to-date and for any deep injury, a booster shot is advisable.

Finally, Bell sums up her advice with the following caution: 'You shouldn't give anything or use anything that you don't fully understand or use it in a circumstance that you don't fully understand!'

The Severe Vaccination Reaction

QUESTION: I have a three-year-old gelding and a near two-year-old filly (a recent addition) which I plan to show this year. The D.V.M. I was using at the time suggested both horses be given influenza and rhino shots prior to the show season. They should get a preliminary shot sixty to ninety days before the start of the show season, and a booster shot just before the first show. Since both horses were also due for their tetanus and rabies shots I decided to have these done at the same time, thereby saving money on additional veterinary calls.

The filly was being brought down from a stable sixty miles away, and the gelding transported twelve miles to a stable closer to us. The filly had just been purchased and as such a vet exam was needed for insurance purposes. Since the vet was coming for the insurance exam, I decided to have the necessary shots given at the same time. The D.V.M. injected the rhino and influenza vaccine on one side of the neck and the rabies and tetanus on the other. This was at nine-thirty in the morning. His examination of the filly showed her to be extremely sound.

At five-thirty the same day I received a call from the stable manager informing me that the filly wasn't doing too well. She had a large lump on her neck and was shivering badly. The gelding appeared to be fine. When I arrived at the stable some thirty minutes later I noticed the gelding also had a large lump on his neck and was shivering as well. By six-thirty both horses were stiffening up and shivering badly. The filly was having trouble bending her neck and couldn't reach her hay on the floor. She was trying desperately to keep herself up. She looked like she would buckle any second. She leaned against the wall to stay up. The gelding began doing the same.

When the vet finally arrived at ten o'clock, three hours after I called and requested he come over immediately, he shrugged his shoulders and told me some horses react to the influenza shot that way. Both horses had temperatures of 102°F. Nonetheless, he administered a muscle relaxant (to stop the severe stiffening of the neck and legs) and an antihistamine. He played the politician (running around what might be the true cause of the reactions) and made a hasty exit.

The horses both seemed to perk up after the two shots (both in the neck again), but by the next morning the symptoms had worsened. That afternoon another D.V.M. examined the horses. The gelding had a temperature of 104°F and the filly wasn't far behind. The swelling on the neck was rather large and both horses looked bad. Penicillin was given (in the rump this time) and bute for five days. A neck sweat was recommended for the gelding to help reduce the lump on the neck.

By the third day after the penicillin was administered both horses had broken the fevers and had temperatures within the normal range. At the time of this writing both seem fine but are to be given reduced rations and rest for the next two days.

What caused the violent reactions? Have any of your readers had similar problems with reactions of this nature? Keep in mind both horses came from two different stables (one a cooler barn and the other a warmer -- one had a winter coat, the other none) sixty miles away. They were not in the same stable long enough to 'pick up' anything, and none of the other horses in the barn were sick. Both horses had had shots earlier and had never reacted to any of them. The first D.V.M. used new syringes on both horses, so there was no chance of them being infected by a dirty needle, etc. The rhino and influenza is pre-measured in a single dose in an individual syringe (no vials to use) and the tetanus in individual vials. The rabies used was in a bulk vial, I am told.

Your feedback and ideas will be greatly appreciated, since we will have to give the flu and rhino boosters soon and want to know what to expect.

EXPERTS: George Shaw is the former Manager of Technical Services in the Veterinary Division of Ayerst, a supplier of these types of vaccines which, in the case of Ayerst, are manufactured by Fort Dodge Laboratories, Inc. of Iowa.

Veterinarian Dr. Gus Thorsen is a Professor of Virology at Guelph's Ontario Veterinary College.

ANSWER: Shaw, although expressing an interest in which side of the neck the swelling was on, cites rhinopneumonitis as being the probable cause of the problem(s).

He suggests that within the last two months the horses possibly had been exposed to rhinopneumonitis in the two stables from which they came and therefore had a high antibody count. Their reaction would be caused by an interaction of the antigen that is in the vaccine with the antibodies which the horses had previously developed.

Thorsen, who also expresses interest as to which side the swelling developed, refers to the problem(s) as a hypersensitivity reaction to the influenza and rhinopneumonitis combination, and goes on to say that such a reaction is not all that unusual.

He agrees with the initial diagnosis and approach to therapy which your horses were given, but does suggest that 'It may have needed to have been pursued more vigorously, particularly the antihistamine component.'

Thorsen adds that once the initial hypersensitivity reaction had been set up, there may have been an infection in the form of some sort of abscess to cause the continuing problem and the febrile response (temperature). If such was the case, then the second treatment which utilized antibiotics 'was on the right trail too.'

On the subject of revaccination, Thorsen anticipates that the same adverse reaction is likely to happen. In other words, once a horse had reacted badly to a vaccine, it is more than likely that he will do so again, possibly even severely. As well, as to why these horses

253

would react so drastically when they had had shots before, Thorsen says he would have been surprised by their reaction if they had *not* had shots on an earlier occasion.

Why? Apparently some horses become sensitized to the combination of the components of the virus and the adjuvant (a light oil substance in the case of rhinopneumonitis and influenza ... included to enhance the response of the vaccine) and once this happens, the chance for an adverse reaction increases every time.

Thorsen suggests two ways of handling this sensitivity in the future:

- *Do Not Vaccinate.* Take a chance on the horses contracting either rhinopneumonitis or influenza and treat accordingly if either occurs.
- Revaccinate, but start with antihistamines at the same time and follow up with a prolonged course of antihistamines to try to control the reaction. (Antihistamines, by the way, will not interfere with the vaccine response.)

In Summary: Thorsen, if he were the owner of the horses, would take his chances on the infection rather than risk an even more severe reaction to the vaccine.

Shipping, a new 'home' and all those shots at the same time create stress which could have worsened the reaction.

You might have been wise to space out the vaccinations, even though it would have increased your veterinary bills. As it turned out, your expenses were probably considerable.

Respiratory Work-Up and
The Bronchoalveolar Lavage

QUESTION: When a horse is taken into the O.V.C. for a respiratory check, what procedure is followed, and what can be determined?

EXPERT: Quebec-born Dr. Laurent Viel received his D.V.M. from the University of Montreal. He acquired a graduate diploma in large animal internal medicine from the University of Guelph in 1978 and later earned his M.SC. and PH.D. Viel is currently an Assistant Professor of Large Animal Internal Medicine at the Ontario Veterinary College.

His area of specialization is in the field of respiratory diseases of horses. Viel has pioneered the development of the bronchoalveolar lavage for horses. His is presently pursuing research on equine respiratory viral diseases, foal broncho-pneumonia and exercise-induced pulmonary haemorrhage (EIPH) in racing horses. Viel is frequently requested to speak on his area of specialization.

ANSWER:

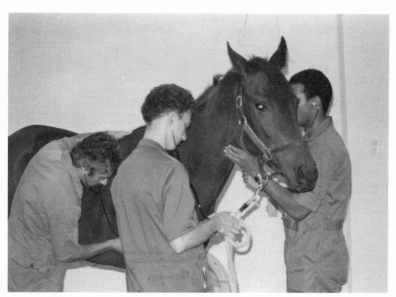

Step 1: The horse is taken to a soundproof room where the clinician listens to the animal's lungs.

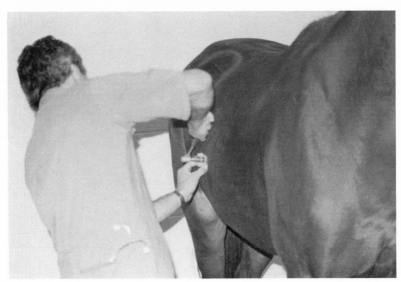

Step 2: A percussion hammer or plexor, and a flat plate or pleximeter are used to check the sounds bounced back to the listener. A dull sound means that fluid is present in the lungs.

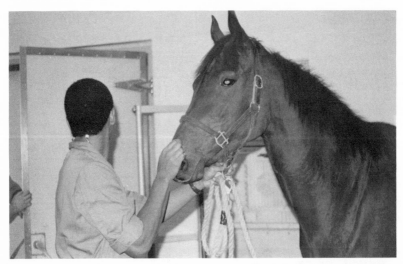

Step 3: Nostrils are pinched to prevent the inhalation of oxygen. When the nostrils are released, lung sounds are emphasized and thus easier to recognize.

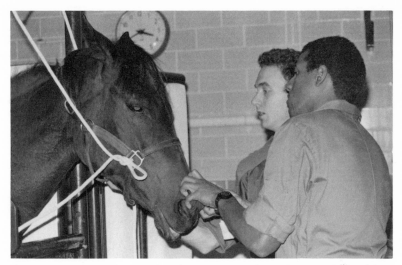

Step 4: Taken to the stocks, the horse is relatively immobilized by a padded frame. With only his head protruding out of the stocks, he is fairly controlled. A local anaesthetic is given to block the sensation of the bronchoscope passing up the nostrils.

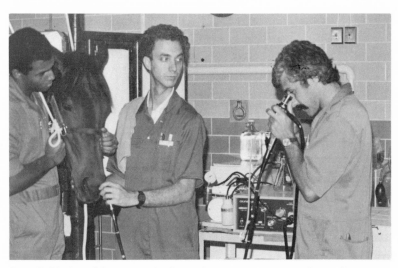

Step 5: Viel is able to see the horse's respiratory tract from the upper airways to the bronchi. Here he examines the larynx. Various signs tell the story of the condition of the respiratory system.

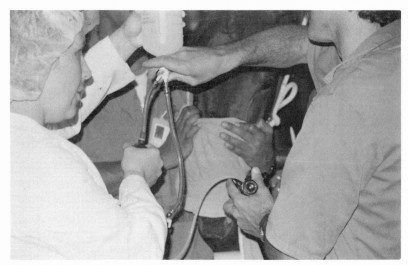

Step 6: Saline is passed down the tube of the scope into one small section of the lung.

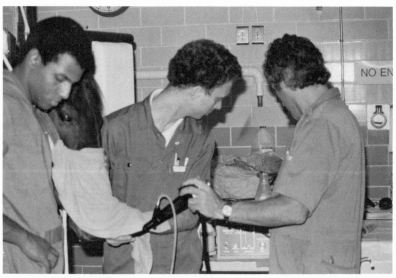

Step 7: The saline is then aspirated into the bottle without being contaminated by bacteria present in the upper respiratory tract. The fluid will be examined for the presence of various bacteria, etc.

Final Step: An appropriate antibiotic will be administered specific to any bacteria detected.

Respiratory Problems

QUESTION: I have a very sick horse and have had three different answers to her problem. She was a horse in excellent shape with fall hunting and daily exercise all winter outside and indoor training once a week. In February 1978, I noticed a cough at a hard workout and loss of ability during a workout. One morning she had a bad breathing problem and I called my vet. He said she had the 'heaves' and treated her for two weeks. Two times he let her off medicine and she had more heavy breathing and coughing.

So we then took her to the University of Guelph where they said she had advanced influenza and put her on medication for six weeks by which time she was to be completely recovered.

She didn't recover and I got another vet to look at her. He said she had an allergy to something in the barn.

This mare is breathing very heavily from forty to as high as seventy-five times per minute. She has lost a lot of weight and still does a lot of coughing especially on a wet day which seems like every day since she first got sick. She eats well but doesn't gain any weight. Can your experts give any answers to my problem?

EXPERT: Dr. Russ Willoughby is a very respected specialist in the field of respiratory problems. A 1957 graduate of the Ontario Veterinary College, Willoughby worked in a mixed practice for four years in Saskatchewan, after which time he returned to Guelph for one year and worked in the farm service clinic. His next stop was Cornell University where he studied for three years for his PH.D. In 1965 he became a faculty member of Guelph University. His main professional interest is the influence of the environment on the animal – a subject which he feels plays a large part in veterinary medicine. Willoughby, who was one of the driving forces behind its existence, is presently the Director of the Equine Research Centre at the University of Guelph.

ANSWER: According to Willoughby one must be initially aware that horses are susceptible to a lot of virus infections, the main one being influenza. Because the influenza virus does not penetrate the body very deeply, immunity is very short-lived, perhaps as short a time as two to seven months. As a result the horse conceivably could experience two or three infections a year.

The influenza virus invades two types of cells. It enters cells which produce mucus and also cells which have fine hair-like projections on them called cilia whose function is to clear the mucus. As a result of the invasion of the influenza virus, the former type of cell produces *excessive* amounts of mucus while the second type is *unable to get rid of the mucus* because the cilia have become damaged. Normally the fine hair-like projections or cilia that are on certain cells sweep the mucus that's produced, up from the lower airways, up the trachea and into the pharynx or throat and the animal swallows the mucus material. Unfortunately, the influenza virus disrupts the cilia and thus the horse's ability to clear the mucus is impaired. Therefore, when the horse inhales the normal amount of dust from hay or from sweeping the floor or from its own haircoat, it inhales this material and has difficulty clearing it because of the cilia's inability to function properly. As a result, the horse accumulates more debris which it can't clear; hence a vicious reaction is set up within the animal.

Horses' lungs are anatomically and physiologically very much like those of humans; in fact, they develop almost exactly the same diseases as humans. Just as we develop chronic bronchitis very easily, so do horses.

Willoughby prefers the term 'chronic bronchitis' to that of 'heaves' because the word 'heaves' has a hopeless connotation to it. 'Heaves' and 'emphysema' tend to be more synonymous as both are thought to be 'end of the line illnesses'. The sequence of events which leads to heaves or emphysema is as follows. Chronic bronchitis leads to a plugging of the airways by accumulated mucus. Hard breathing and coughing occur next and then coughs rupture the small and delicate alveoli or air sacs. This rupture forms a lesion called emphysema and the horse has much more difficulty in getting air. All you people with chronic smoker's cough beware! Once the small airways rupture they can never be replaced. The body does not repair them and although there are a great many, once about thirty per cent of them are damaged, problems begin to show themselves.

Another aspect of chronic bronchitis is the allergic one in which the horse is allergic to something in its environment. There is no question of the association between dusty hay and the onset of bronchial spasms. Certain feeds are more likely to induce bronchial spasms than are others. Willoughby cites it as a case of 'Which comes first, the cart or the horse?' He feels that the influenza virus comes first and damages the horse's ability to clear particulate material in the normal fashion. As most of that particulate material is capable of causing an allergic reaction, the problem worsens.

To zero in on the particular problem as outlined in the question, it could be said that there is truth in each of the three diagnoses. Willoughby is worried that possibly the seriousness of the case is not fully realized by the owner. A treatment scheduled to last six weeks indicates a very severe case. He points out that the fast respiratory rate and the weight loss show extensive involvement of the airways. He also is concerned over abnormalities on an electrocardiograph. As the influenza virus can affect the heart muscle, he suspects these abnormalities also indicate 'pretty severe influenza infection'.

Willoughby outlined the following procedure for this mare. First she should again be taken to the 'Large Animal Clinic' at Guelph to be reassessed to see if the lungfield has expanded. If the lungs start to occupy a greater than normal percentage of the chest, this expansion is a sign that the airways are obstructed by mucus and the lungs cannot deflate normally. If the horse has already received treatment and there has been a recent expansion of the lungfield then the indication is that the treatment is not keeping ahead of the illness.

Once there has been a reassessment of the lungfield, the following treatment is advocated:

• Minimize the work that a chronic bronchitic has to do – that is work in terms of clearing particulate material from its airways. In other words keep dust away from the horse as much as possible by keeping the horse outside. (In winter provide some shelter that the horse can wander into if necessary.) Moisten all bedding and all feed to aid in the reduction of floating particles. When grooming, use a 'wee bit of oil' on a cloth to keep the hair coat a 'trifle oily'. A grooming vacuum cleaner is another possible dust reducing aid.

• Rest a horse suffering from influenza and any ensuing complications.

• Under veterinary guidance, treat the horse with the following drug medication:

a. *Iodides* – Use iodides to decrease the stickiness or viscosity of the mucus. Large amounts of iodides must be given over a long period of time so that the horse can not only get rid of the mucus that is there now but also dispose of the mucus which develops until the cells stop producing an excessive amount.

b. *Levamisol* – This drug stimulates the production of antibodies and thus might give a slight boost to a horse not capable of coping with the influenza virus by itself.

c. *Long Acting Penicillin* – This drug will get rid of most common bacterial infections that might co-exist along with the virus infection.

According to Willoughby there is no practical treatment for controlling influenza infection because it is a viral infection. The only thing one can do is try to minimize the stress on the animal, give the horse as much of an advantage as possible and hope that the animal will be able to cope with the virus infection.

Willoughby can easily understand why horse owners become confused about respiratory problems. Some horses only have a mild infection or have a good defence mechanism and are thus able to recover. Others are fortunate enough to receive help before too much damage has occurred.

In Summary: Willoughby pointed out that the horse is naturally prone to chronic bronchitis and in our climate where horses have to be housed, are consequently exposed to one another and influenza infection and on top of these factors are surrounded by lots of dust, it is no wonder that respiratory problems develop. Even the changeable weather (hot to cold to wet to dry) we experience in Southern Ontario makes matters worse. It stops the cilia activity for ten to fifteen minutes – just long enough for the influenza virus to penetrate airways, enter cells and cause fullblown infection. Is it any wonder that respiratory ailments are so prevalent?

An Effective Treatment for Chronic Bronchitis or Heaves

QUESTION: I have a horse that progressed several years ago beyond chronic bronchitis to emphysema or heaves. The treatment prescribed three years ago involves:
- outside from 8 A.M. to 5 P.M.
- dampening of hay
- iodides.

My horse seems to be *much* worse in the spring. Could flowering plants be triggering an allergy?

I would appreciate any help you could give me on this subject.

EXPERT: Dr. Russ Willoughby (see Chapter 10, Question 4).

ANSWER: Willoughby suggests that *in addition* to what you are already doing, there are three areas of treatment worth considering for a horse who has had this type of problem for several years. The three possible treatments are:
- Bronchodilator drugs
- Allergy drugs
- Desensitizing drugs.

Bronchodilator Drugs: The smooth muscles in the airways of horses with a severe respiratory problem contract or go into a spasm making breathing more difficult. In addition, in the airways, there is more mucus present that the cilia (fine hair-like projections) are able to sweep up out of the airways.

Bronchodilator drugs do two major things to help. Not only do they *relax* the smooth muscle spasms in the airways, but they also *increase the movement* of the cilia that are so necessary to propel the mucus up from the lower airways, up the trachea, and into the pharynx or throat where the horse can swallow it. Obviously in so doing, these new bronchodilators do *exactly* what is necessary to help alleviate the problem without the adverse side effects (decrease in saliva production, pupil dilation, etc.) that some of the old drugs caused.

There are quite a few new bronchodilators that are effective but Willoughby considers Clenbuterol the best one. Studies carried out a few years ago at the O.V.C. showed that it has the following advantages:

- Its effectiveness is long lasting.
- It is very potent, so only a small amount is needed.
- It can be given by injection.
- If given by mouth, horses don't seem to mind it.

A second bronchodilator that can be used is Salbutamal or, to use its counter name, Ventolin. This drug has to be inhaled by the horse, but the procedure to administer it is not difficult.

Willoughby describes how: You cut the bottom out of an old gallon jug, and clip the gallon jug up over the horse's face. As the air blows out through the neck of the bottle on your finger, you know he's breathing out. What you need to do is compress the inhaling apparatus when the horse breathes in.

Quite a number of people use this drug on their horses and find it not only effective but also quite inexpensive.

Allergy Drugs: The second possible treatment is the use of an allergy drug known as Cromolyn. This drug *blocks* allergic reaction, but it has to be given *before* the allergic reaction occurs. It does not work if it is given after the horse has been exposed to the allergies. Cromolyn must be inhaled, and an apparatus to administer it can be purchased.

Willoughby does *not* think that allergy drugs are really effective because there is very little evidence to suggest that horses are truly allergic to things. He feels that although the horse's reaction might appear to be allergic, it is much more likely that his 'ticklish' or sensitive airways are simply *aggravated* by dust and pollen.

Desensitizing Drugs: These drugs are given as injections, and are similar to the ones a person with allergies takes when he has a series of injections to try to counteract his sensitivity to the various allergens. Once again Willoughby does not feel these are particularly effective, because he feels that allergies are not what cause the problem.

In Summary: Willoughby states that evidence points to *viral infections* as being at the root of chronic bronchitis rather than allergies. As a result, he feels that bronchodilator drugs are the best drugs to use to alleviate the respiratory distress your horse suffers. He recommends Clenbuterol. If your horse is severely affected, the drug should be administered two or three times a day. Its effective action lasts for three to four hours, so giving it morning, noon, and night would be most helpful. If you plan to ride your horse, give him Clenbuterol in the morning and more just before riding.

Laryngeal Hemiplegia

QUESTION: My horse seems to be getting very tired when I ride him even when I don't work him very hard. His breathing seems to be abnormally loud as well. One of the boarders where I keep my horse said that she thinks he sounds like a roarer. She also told me that roaring is an unsoundness.

Can you give me any information about roaring? What causes it? Is there anything that can be done to help him get better? I would appreciate any help you can give me.

BREATHING

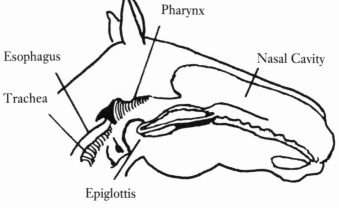

Pharynx

Esophagus

Nasal Cavity

Trachea

Epiglottis

SWALLOWING

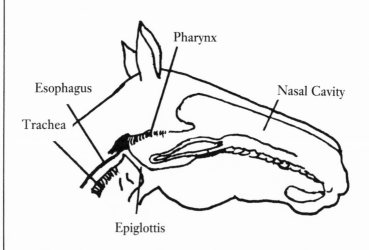

Pharynx

Esophagus

Nasal Cavity

Trachea

Epiglottis

In swallowing, the epiglottis closes off the air passage.

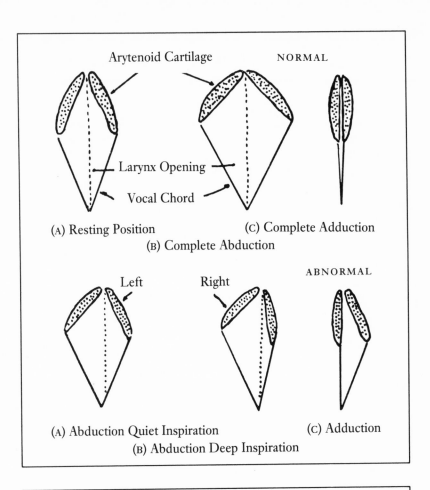

Arytenoid Cartilage   NORMAL

Larynx Opening

Vocal Chord

(A) Resting Position   (C) Complete Adduction

(B) Complete Abduction

Left   Right   ABNORMAL

(A) Abduction Quiet Inspiration   (C) Adduction

(B) Abduction Deep Inspiration

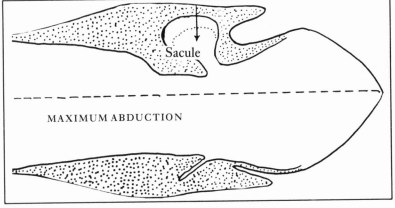

Sacule

MAXIMUM ABDUCTION

EXPERT: Dr. Michael Livesey is a surgeon in the Large Animal Surgery Department at the Ontario Veterinary College.

Trained in Scotland, he worked in a mixed practice in England for three years before immigrating to Canada. On arrival, he spent one year as an intern and two as a resident at the Ontario Veterinary College before becoming a surgeon on staff. Livesey is frequently called upon to speak at various veterinary and breed seminars.

ANSWER: Roaring is caused by a condition once known as laryngeal paralysis but now more commonly referred to as *laryngeal hemiplegia* (paralysis of one side of the larynx) which affects the amount of air that is able to pass to the lungs. It is definitely an unsoundness.

To fully understand the serious nature of laryngeal hemiplegia it is necessary to be familiar with the horse's respiratory tract which is comprised of nose, pharynx, larynx, trachea and bronchi. This tract permits air to pass quickly and freely both up and down the airway.

Larygeal hemiplegia occurs in the larynx – the narrowest part of the airway. The larynx, a valve-like structure of muscle and carti-lage, has three basic functions:

• It guards the entrance to the trachea by closing during swallowing to prevent food from passing into the trachea and down into the lungs. It is the epiglottis or thin plate of cartilage in front of the entrance to the larynx that actually closes over the larynx opening to prevent food from entering.
• It regulates the volume of air that passes to and from the lungs. To increase air flow, the larynx opening is dilated by two *abductor* (draw-ing away) muscles which lie on the *dorsal* (toward the back) surface of the larynx. These muscles act on the *arytenoid cartilages* (see dia-gram) expanding and opening from a diamond shape to that of a kite. The abductor and *adductor* (drawing toward) muscles of the larynx are supplied their motor power by the *recurrent laryngeal* nerve.
• It is the voice-box of the horse.

What Exactly is Laryngeal Hemiplegia? When laryngeal paralysis occurs it is the second function that is particularly impaired. The paralysis occurs when the recurrent laryngeal nerve ceases to work. This nerve supply, which controls the muscles which in turn control the arytenoid cartilage, is cut off resulting in the inability of the muscle to function. Because the muscles are inoperable, the arytenoid cartilage cannot be abducted. In the majority of cases, it is the left, and only the left, recurrent laryngeal nerve supply which degenerates; thus it is only the left arytenoid cartilage that is affected. This arytenoid cartilage hangs down and across the airway (to a greater or lesser degree depending on the severity of the paralysis) and thus obstructs the free flowing passage of air. Such an obstruction creates turbulence; hence cutting down that much more on the amount of air which is able to travel along the airways to the lungs. Obviously, the work required in order for the horse to breathe will be much greater.

Signs of Laryngeal Hemiplegia: Suspect laryngeal hemiplegia if you notice one or more of the following signs indicative of various degrees of respiratory distress:

• A high-pitched but quiet (slightly piercing) whistling noise on inspiration (breathing in).
• A harsher, more breathy, louder roaring noise on inspiration. (This noise is associated with serious laryngeal obstruction).
• A sudden attack of partial *asphyxia* (suffocation) often referred to as a gurgling, rattling or choking down when at fast exercise.
• Poor stamina. The horse tires more quickly when jumping a course, performing a dressage test or galloping across country, etc. Race horses may fade out in the last quarter.
• An unusual-sounding neigh.

It is interesting to note that a long-necked, big horse is much more likely to have laryngeal hemiplegia that is a smaller, shorter-necked horse. The reason for this is that the recurrent laryngeal nerve is longer and thus more susceptible to being damaged.

Examination of a Suspected Case of Laryngeal Hemiplegia: When a horse suspected of having this unsoundness is admitted to the Ontario Veterinary College, Livesey:

• Obtains a detailed case history pertinent to the respiratory problem.
• Palpates the larynx. Because the nerve supply is no longer causing the muscles to be used, these muscles atrophy or waste. A comparative palpation of each side of the larynx may reveal, to a skilled clinician, a difference in the muscle development.
• Examines the horse using a fibreoptic endoscope. A laryngoscopic examination provides an invaluable internal 'picture'. If laryngeal hemiplegia is present, there may be a sagging of the left arytenoid cartilage towards the mid-line and the absence of abductor or adductor movement on the affected side.
• Examines the horse at exercise. A horse with laryngeal hemiplegia will make a roaring or whistling sound on inspiration. (Conversely the most common but not the only cause of whistling and roaring is laryngeal hemiplegia.) Livesey, as well as listening for an abnormal respiratory noise, also assesses the difficulty the horse has in breathing and the degree to which it affects the horse's performance.
• Repeats the endoscopic examination after exercise. In cases of laryngeal hemiplegia, laryngeal asymmetry will be more noticeable because the full abducation or pulling back of the right arytenoid cartilage will emphasize any lack of abduction on the left.

What Can Be Done to Help a Horse Suffering from Laryngeal Hemiplegia? No cure exists! Nothing can be done to regenerate the laryngeal nerve although a new technique which involves transplanting nerve is being developed. According to Livesey the only treatment which exists at the present time is to 'improve the flow of air through the larynx by cutting down on the turbulence resulting from the dangling arytenoid cartilage.'

Such treatment involves surgery. There are two different types of operations which attempt to improve the air supply: a ventriculectomy, and an abductor muscle prosthesis.

• Ventriculectomy: When the larynx is opened up, a small sacule on each side of is pinched off, but neither is pinched off when the larynx is not fully opened.

If the left arytenoid cartilage is hanging down, the left sacule will not be closed off. The resulting area is one in which air can get sucked in and turbulence will occur. A ventriculectomy involves the removal of this little sacule (about the size of the end of a finger).

Livesey describes a ventriculectomy:

We make an incision at the ventral part of the throat. The muscles cleave at this point so we can part the cleavage and clamp the tissue apart. We incise through the membrane and locate the sacule. We dry the sacule with gauze. (The sacule, like the rest of the larynx, is coated with mucous membrane.) We insert a long burr (solid metal, pencil-like object with a rounded, rough 'burr' at one end) and pull the sacule up with gentle traction so that it doesn't slip off the end of the burr. We then grab the sacule with a clamp and snip it off using long scissors inserted into the wound. (The sacule, while still attached, cannot be exposed because we are working at depth.) The larynx contains a large number of bacteria so it is better if we leave the wound open to drain. The wound granulates quite quickly and before long you'll not even know it's been done. In the past it was believed that if the sacule on the problem side were removed there would be a resulting adherence or sticking together of the arytenoid cartilage to the thyroid; however, there is now some doubt that an adhesion does result. Actually it would be much better were there no adhesion because it would interfere with the normal function of the larynx which needs to be a mobile instrument in order to not only stop food moving down into the trachea but also alter the amount of air flow.

A ventriculectomy is a relatively common procedure taking only five minutes from the time of incision to the cutting off of the sacule.

271

Although there is some dispute among veterinarians as to the benefits of this operation, the general opinion of the clinicians at the O.V.C. is that it does definitely help to cut down on air turbulence and thus allows the horse more air with each inhalation.

Pleasure horses may be helped sufficiently to warrant only this operation.

• Laryngeal Abductor Muscle Prosthesis or Laryngoplasty: Sometimes referred to as 'a tie-back', this operation which takes about two hours, is far more complicated than the simple ventriculectomy. The surgeon is working at depth in a very small wound.

According to Livesey, the basic idea of an abductor muscle prosthesis is to mimic the muscle that is wasted as a result of the nerve supply having been cut off. A piece of nylon or elastic (a prosthesis) is inserted in the larynx. One end goes through the arytenoid cartilage and the other to the muscular process so that the arytenoid cartilage is 'tied-back'; that is, held partially open all the time.

The complications which may arise from an abductor muscle prosthesis are considerable:

a. The major complication is the danger of producing a horse with a chronic cough caused by food material entering the trachea.

'What you're doing,' Livesey explains, 'is tying back the cartilage into the position it should be in when the horse is exercising heavily and once it's tied back, it's fixed in that position and it can't close when the horse wants to swallow so it's possible for food material to go down the trachea.'

b. The suture material (nylon or elastic) of the prosthesis may cut through the cartilage allowing the arytenoid cartilage to fall back to its original position. Livesey explains, 'The cartilage is not big nor is it solid where the needle is put through so with two strands through it and with a lot of tension on it, the prosthesis can cut its way through the cartilage and then everything falls apart.'

c. A chronic infection and / or calcification may occur. According to Livesey, 'There's a very fine membrane adjacent to the cartilage which, if penetrated too far by the needle, results in bringing back infection with the needle. You can end up with masses of calcium forming in the larynx. The actual cartilage of the larynx can become calcified. Also you can end up with chronic infection around the suture material because the nylon or elastic is foreign to the body. The body tries to wall it off by laying down some fibrous tissue around the material. If an infection occurs in the suture material it just sits there as a chronic abcessation or it discharges to the outside. The cartilages themselves can get calcium laid down in them so they don't move naturally.'

Despite these potential problems, the success rate of the abductor muscle prosthesis or laryngoplasty when performed by a competent surgeon is as high as eighty per cent.

Current recommendations are that one and, preferably, two prostheses *plus* a ventriculectomy are necessary for optimal results. Race horses would definitely fit into the category of horses that would need this more involved surgical procedure.

New Technique: Doctors Ducharme, Horney, Hulland and Parlow of Canada's Ontario Veterinary College have been investigating the possibility of restoring function to the muscles which control the arytenoid cartilage by reinnervation; that is by implanting a new nerve supply.

The technique is more formally referred to as 'the technique of second cervical nerve end implantation into the denervated dorsal cricoarytenoid muscle.'

In fairly early stages of experimentation, this new technique for laryngeal hemiplegia has not, as yet, been very successful.

Choices: Livesey suggests that first of all you ask your veterinarian to examine your horse to determine whether or not he is a roarer or ask to have him referred to the nearest equine clinic or veterinary hospital for a more extensive examination.

At present, if your horse does suffer from laryngeal hemiplegia, you have two basic choices to make – reduced expectations as to your horse's future athletic career *or* surgery. If surgery is decided upon, then the existing choices are still only either a ventriculectomy

or an abductor muscle prosthesis with an accompanying ventriculectomy.

Teeth Flotation

QUESTION: I own a nine-year-old Anglo-Arab mare. She is in overall good health but, for some reason, she needs her teeth floated every three months. When her teeth are sharp, it is almost impossible to ride her. She tosses her head up and down repeatedly, comes above the bit and hollows her back. When her teeth become overly sharp, she packs up a cud of grass between her teeth and cheek. She is out at pasture during the day, and stabled only at night, so she has plenty of opportunity to chew and grind her teeth.

My question is how and why do her teeth need floating so often, and is there anything I can do to help alleviate this problem? I would be grateful for any information you could give me on this matter.

EXPERT: Dr. Howard Dobson was a clinician in the University of Guelph's Equine Field Service. He is now in the Radiology Department.

A graduate from Edinburgh in 1977, Dobson spent two years in a large animal practice in Britain, then did his intership in surgery at the Ontario Veterinary College. From there, he returned to England and spent five years in a horse practice near Newmarket. Dobson came back to Canada in 1985.

ANSWER: When we speak of 'floating' teeth, we are talking about getting rid of sharp points which develop on a horse's molars. These points develop for several reasons:
- Some horses' teeth are softer than others.
- Some upper and lower molars are more offset than others.
- Some horses chew differently than others; that is, some move their lower jaws in an up-and-down motion, rather than a round-and-round one. The latter, a circular motion,

is much better in that the teeth are going right over the edges of the opposing ones and wearing them down more evenly.

The points that develop cut the soft insides of a horse's cheeks as well as his tongue when he attempts to chew. As a result, he suffers considerable discomfort.

Generally, horses' teeth need to be floated only once a year, but there are some that need attention every six months. Obviously, in your horse's case, a more severe problem exists, as the need to float teeth every three months is most unusual.

Dobson suggests your horse might also have a slight parrot mouth ('slight' may be as little as one-eighth of an inch).

In a parrot mouth, the row of upper teeth extends marginally beyond the row of lower teeth at the front, whereas the lower row of teeth extends marginally beyond the upper row at the back of the mouth. As a result, a hook develops at the front of the top row and at the back of the lower row. These points can become very sharp and it can be quite difficult to get them floated off properly, particularly the ones at the back, because they are very hard to reach.

There is a chance that this might be the reason why you are having to float your horse's teeth so frequently. Dobson cited a case in which he found it necessary to give a horse a general anaesthetic in order to get far enough back in the mouth to properly float off the hook at the back. Once done, however, it solved the problem for that particular horse.

Dobson suggests that you have someone take a very thorough look inside your horse's mouth, and he advises that a general anaesthetic might be necessary in order to do so. If there is a hook at the back caused by a parrot mouth problem, then it can be floated off and your horse's problem will be resolved for several years. (It takes longer for hooks caused by parrot mouths to develop than it does for points caused by badly offset molars to form.) Naturally, once such a problem has been discovered, 'the person who floats the teeth must make one hundred and ten per cent sure that he reaches right to the very back of the horse's mouth!' advises Dobson.

In Summary: There is a very big difference between the sensitivity of individual horses to sharp teeth and Dobson explains that 'some horses can have absolute razors for teeth, and they are not the least bit concerned by them.' He puts such differences down to temperament when he summarizes 'some horses put up with an awful lot, and some are mostly "sucks".' Horses also have different pain thresholds, and some actually experience more pain than others.

As far as your horse is concerned, if his problem is not parrot mouth, there is a chance that one or more teeth are abnormally placed. This is something which you can do very little about. To quote Dobson: 'You may be just unfortunate, and have to grin and bare it!'

Poultices – Why? What Types Are There?

QUESTION: Very few people seem to know much about poultice bandaging. Can you do an article on poultices including such information as what you poultice for, how you poultice and what types of poultice there are?

EXPERT: Dr. Roger Footman, owner of Erin Veterinary Clinic, graduated from the Ontario Veterinary College fifteen years ago. His busy practice northwest of Toronto specializes almost completely in equine veterinary medicine.

ANSWER: Footman first of all emphasizes that it is essential that one understands the principal behind poultice and outlines two reasons for their use: to increase circulation and to draw. To use his words:

> You are attempting to draw out or remove fluid and its bacteria content found in the fluid build-up of an injury, so that the inflammatory reaction that is being produced behind it is coming in and continuing to irrigate it. That certainly does

happen because inflammatory cells come in to ward off
infection.

As far as choice of poultice is concerned, Footman has two basic
preferences: that they not be messy and that whenever feasible, they
be whatever poultice the horse owner has in his possession. Footman, in fact, carries the latter practical aspect one step farther and in
his actual poultice bandaging tries to utilize whatever is available in
the barn.

He cites the most common use of poultices in his practice as
being for the treatment of sub-solar abscesses in the foot and goes
on to say that such a problem is the type most frequently encountered by veterinarians.

To poultice a foot, Footman, adhering to his 'use whatever is
available' policy, suggests the following: Mix one cup of bran with
two tablespoons of epsom salts and add enough hot water to make a
paste consistency. Pack the foot with the bran poultice and cover
with a corner of a burlap bag (or strips of cloth plus a corner of burlap bag) to hold the dressing in place. Add a piece of plastic (either a
shopping bag or part of a nylon feed bag) to help contain the heat and
moisture. Finally, cover with a layer of burlap bag or perhaps a sock
to help protect the plastic from being worn through by the hoof.
Footman suggests changing the poultice twice daily – in the morning
and at night.

Another instance when Footman will suggest the use of a poultice
is during the 'hot cycle' of an alternating hot / cold series of treatments. Following two or three days of ice pack applications to
reduce swelling, a poultice might be used to increase circulation and
thus 'bring in the *phagocytes*' – cells which ingest micro-organisms or
other cells and foreign particles and in so doing reduce swelling.
After two or three days the cold cycle is begun again. Such a method
is used in the treatment of trauma-type wounds accompanied by
swelling and of strains and sprains, etc.

A poultice is also ideal in the treatment of an old wound that has
become infected. Not only does its drawing power help to cleanse

the wound but also it ability to increase circulation brings an influx of 'repair cells' to the area.

Footman does caution that many *antiphlogistic* (an agent that counteracts fever and inflammation) poultice products contain irritating ingredients which, if applied to open surfaces, will stimulate the growth of proud flesh and so must definitely *not* be used on open wounds.

Founder

QUESTION: My horses are on pasture all summer long. Although they have shade trees and there is often a breeze somewhere else in the pasture, they often stand during the heat of the day bunched together close to the south side of the stable in the bright sun. I don't know why they do this. Eventually I let them in the barn for a couple of hours and give them a little rolled oats. One day in June the fifteen-year-old Arabian mare was very slow in walking and seemed to be in great pain. I examined her hooves and feet for thrush or injury but found none. There were no changes in diet or feeding. The local veterinarian suspected sore muscles, gave her two injections and prescribed Butazone. I kept her in the stable more, but when she was out she did not walk with the other horses but stayed in a soft spot, usually the manure pile. After about one week I noticed that one hoof was always wet at the sole even though the ground in the barn and outside was very dry. I checked again and found a narrow crack in the sole of the left front foot. About one week later the same happened on the right front foot. When pressed with the fingers in the surrounding area, an almost clear, thick liquid came out. From then on I cleaned the sole daily, disinfected it with Creolon solution and painted the sole with Bluestone solution. About four weeks later I noticed that all four hooves started new growth at the coronet underneath the old hoof just like people grow a new fingernail when the original is damaged. It seems to me that all four hooves will gradually come off. (She was never worked hard or on hard ground.)

Although I feared at some time that I would have to put the mare down, she now walks and runs with the other horses and seems healthy. The soles are dry though at some points appear spongy. As bedding I use sawdust from fresh cut logs, that I pick up myself from a local sawmill. I do not think that PCP is involved here, but I sure wonder what caused this shocking ailment.

I would appreciate any help you can give me in clearing this 'mystery' and thank you.

EXPERT: Dr. Chris Little works in the Large Animal Surgery Department at the Ontario Veterinary College in Guelph, Ontario where he has lived since October 1988.

Born in Australia, Little graduated from veterinary school in Perth, spent six months in practice and then did an Internship in Equine Medicine and Surgery at Western Australia's Murdock University at which he stayed on in a faculty position for a brief period of time when his internship was over.

After moving to North America in the mid-eighties, Little spent four years at the University of Minnesota doing a Residency in Large Animal Surgery and then a Masters Degree.

Although not a horse owner himself, Little's academic and work interests lie mainly in the equine field.

ANSWER: According to the symptoms you describe, Little's diagnosis is that your mare had laminitis or founder.

Laminitis is inflammation in the foot. This inflammation severely restricts the blood supply to the laminar structures. Founder is the crippled condition caused by laminitis. The curved crack in the sole is typical of very severe laminitis which may result in permanent damage to the laminae. This permanent damage deprives the horse of his normal attachment of coffin bone to hoof wall. When the attachment is destroyed, the weight of the horse pushes down on the coffin bone which then rotates downward, puts pressure on the sole, and causes a crack. Sometimes, in the most severe cases, the coffin bone will actually protrude through the sole of the foot.

You mention that 'an almost clear, thick liquid' came out of the sole when it was pressed. This 'weeping', which is composed of a combination of serum and pus, is common in severe cases. The fact that all four feet are showing evidence of new hoof growth and almost trying to slough off the other part of the hoof is also a classic sign of laminitis.

The More Common Causes of Laminitis or Founder:

• Diarrhea: Although a direct cause, diarrhea itself is usually the result of a severe bacterial or viral infection, or of some form of stress such as being shipped, or a change in environment or work. When a horse is suffering from severe diarrhea, toxins from the bowel may be absorbed into the bloodstream.

Those toxins, by constricting the small blood vessels, will eventually affect the laminae which are fed by these vessels. Because the laminae form the attachment, it is then weakened or destroyed and laminitis results.

• Retained Placenta: A mare that retains placenta may get metritis (inflammation of the uterus) or infection of the uterus. Toxins from the uterus may then be absorbed into the bloodstream, once again leading to laminitis.

• Grain Overload: Horses that gorge large amounts of grain or grass change the normal bacteria in their bowels. Abnormal ones start growing. Toxins are absorbed from the bowel. Laminitis develops.

• Overweight in Ponies: There may be hormonal factors that pre-dispose little ponies to fat and at the same time predispose them to getting laminitis.

• Weight Overload: A horse that has a severe injury in one leg tends to avoid bearing weight on that leg. The foot of the leg that is sup-porting all of the weight, because it was not designed to do so, devel-ops laminitis.

What Could Have Caused Founder in Your Horse? You mention that there was no change in her diet nor in her feeding schedule. You also say that you get your sawdust directly from the mill. As you have already concluded, with none of your other horses ill, it is most inlikely that PCPs are involved.

Little wonders if you have had your mare for a long time. If not, he suggests that she may have had chronic laminitis before you acquired her and now something has occurred to trigger an acute phase.

It is most unfortunate but true, horses who have had laminitis are very prone to having it again. They are also prone to recurrent foot problems such as abscesses and infections because they have this weakened, abnormal attachment between the coffin bone and the hoof wall.

Why are Horses that Founder More Prone to Abscesses in the Foot? The abnormal connection, which exists in horses with chronic founder, between the hoof wall and the coffin bone means that they no longer have the normal defence mechanisms and the normal tissue up in that area. This weakened connection allows dirt and manure, and thus bacteria, to invade the area and abscesses form.

Did the Creonin and Bluestone Help? Little explains that they would not help founder itself but could help in dealing with secondary infection on the sole and in foot abscesses.

You might be interested to know that until recently the immediate treatment for a horse suspected of having foundered was to stand the animal in a bucket of ice. Cold (ice or cold compresses) is analgesic or pain-relieving.

Today, at the Ontario Veterinary College, alternating hot and cold treatment is used – five minutes of cold to constrict the peripheral vessels (those that carry blood to the outer parts of the body such as the legs) and five minutes of heat to enlarge the vessels. This constriction and enlargement creates a pumping action which helps to move blood through the vessels.

Little sums up his comments about your mare with the following suggestion:

If this horse truly does have laminitis or founder, it would be worthwhile getting x-rays of the feet to see if indeed there is rotation of the coffin bone and if there is, to realize that the horse is predisposed to recurrent episodes of laminitis and predisposed to abscesses. If there is coffin bone rotation, consult a veterinarian and a farrier as far as corrective trimming is concerned.

He suggests that you not try to treat the spongy areas of the sole until you have the feet x-rayed.

Splints – What Are They?
What Can You Do About Them?

QUESTION: I have a five-year-old Arab gelding which has two massive splints on either foreleg about one and a half inches below the knee on the inside. Besides surgery, how would you get rid of these? I have heard internal blistering is effective but is not recommended. Why not?

EXPERT: Dr. George Badame (see Chapter 1, Question 3).

ANSWER:
What Are Splint Bones? Originally the horse had five digits (fingers or toes). The two outer ones were lost through evolution, and the remaining two outer ones are in the process of disappearing. The centre bone is the cannon. The vestiges of the two, adjacent to the cannon bone, are the splint bones. They do not make contact with the ground, and are held to the cannon bone by an interosseous ligament (little ligament that binds it to the cannon bone).

How Do Splints Occur? Splints usually occur as the result of a rotary movement or twist that ruptures the interosseous ligaments and pulls the periosteum (a specialized connective tissue covering all bone of the body) away from the bone. As all bone repairs occur through the periosteum, the injury results in calcium and other minerals being laid down; hence, instead of the interosseous ligament bridging the gap between the cannon bone and the splint bone, you have mineral deposits.

Signs of a Splint: When a splint injury occurs, it is usually first noticed when the horse trots lame. Careful palpation by a knowledgeable person might reveal some heat and soft swelling at the site of the injury, but if a horse is not being worked or observed at a trot it is possible for the problem to go unnoticed until the splint 'bump' appears; that is until the mineral deposits show visibly.

Treatment: It is important that a horse with a new splint stop work and be treated because splints can become bigger, at which point it is possible that they could interfere with the suspensory ligament which 'sits back of the splint bone.' To reduce the acute inflammation, splints should be cooled out using antiphlogistic packs or cold bandages. Once the splint is cool, the treatment Badame prefers – being a veterinarian at the track where time is money – is firing, a process which speeds up healing and usually permits the horse to be back in training in about ten days. In the hunter and jumper world, where blemishes such as firing marks are considered unsightly, firing is not recommended. Blistering would be a preferred method of treatment, but Badame points out that the recovery time is longer. In essence, what one is doing in using either of these treatments is stimulating the area to speed up healing. Given time, nature will take care of it herself.

Badame enlarges on this by explaining:

> When nature heals bone, it mineralizes or lays down calcium quickly and haphazardly with what we call osteoblasts (new bone cells which lay the calcium down). But other cells called osteoclasts smooth the rough 'job' over and take away the excess calcium so that in time, even though a splint might be there for a horse's lifetime, it will get smaller as he gets older because of nature's gradual moulding job. What

283

you want is ankylosis or fusion in the splint area, and it is the minerals that accomplish that, not the blistering or firing. These two methods of treatment just increase the circulation to that area so you get a quicker repair process.

Not 'True' Splints: A six-year-old horse, for example, cannot get a 'true' splint because by the time the horse is six the repeated minor stresses his legs have endured will have caused the interosseous ligaments to have filled in with minerals resulting in a fusion of the three bones – the cannon and the two splints. What this horse, and any other horse of any age can get, is a 'bump' resembling a splint. Remember, a true splint comes between the splint bone and the cannon bone; however, damage to the periosteum from a blow of some kind will cause mineralization to occur.

Splint Removal: In terms of cosmetic effect, no product changes the appearance of a splint. It is possible for a surgeon to chip off the excess minerals, but if the periosteum is disturbed, there is a strong possibility of another splint being produced.

A personal note: I have had great success diminishing a large 'trauma bump' by applying the product 'Splintex' on a three-day-on, three-day-off basis.

What Are True Curbs?

QUESTION:What is a curb? How do curbs occur? What type of hock springs a curb?

EXPERT: Dr. Huw Llewellyn (see Chapter 3, Question 6).

ANSWER:
What is a Curb? A curb is a result of a *strain* on the rather short plantar tarsal ligament which runs down the back of the hock holding the point of the hock in line with the cannon bone. The strain results in a

swelling which creates a bulge in the back of the hock. Although this swelling will subside, a residual thickening known as a curb remains.

How Do Curbs Occur? Curbs occur mainly in young horses at the beginning of their working career when they are called on to do strenuous hindquarter-type work such as racing or jumping before their bodies are physically ready. Curbs may also occur in young horses at play.

What Type of Hock Springs a Curb? When looking at the profile of ideal hocks, one sees a straight line from the back of the hock down the cannon bone; however, if a horse's lower hind leg does not have this straight line, it does not necessarily mean that the horse has a curb. Some horses have a prominent head to the splint bone. Such a prominence looks like a curb but in reality is not. Careful palpation reveals to the observer that the 'bump' is actually the head of a bone. The hock which is likely to be prone to developing a curb is one that curves at approximately the location that a curb appears. (In an average-sized horse that location would be about five inches below the point of the hock.) This curve, bend or bulge exists because of an improper alignment of the tarsal bones with the cannon bone. Often, this curve is mistaken for a curb but the thickening which develops in a true curb, is not yet there. A curb may also occur in a hock which appears to be perfectly normal. Young foals sometimes have a bend in the area between the hock and the cannon bone. Such a condition occurs when little bones in the hock collapse – a situation thought to be caused by an iodine imbalance and which is irreparable. Such animals are not lame until they begin to work but when x-rays show *tarsal collapse*, euthanasia is recommended, although such animals could be used for breeding, as the damage was caused by diet rather than hereditary weakness.

Treatment: Several different methods are used in the treatment of curbs:
- Blistering is one option. If a mild blister is used, the horse should be rested for two to three weeks.

• Pin firing is often used at the track as it is a method which requires only a very brief rest period.

Some of the more recent methods of treatment are:
• Cyrosurgery which involves using liquid nitrogen to freeze the area and destroy the nerves in that region, thus making a curb less painful.
• Laser treatment which reduces inflammation. Time is still necessary for actual healing of the injury.
• Internal blistering.
• Injection of cortisone.

Prognosis: Curbs, once sprung, are much like splints that have popped; that is, if the horse has been allowed sufficient recovery time, although unsightly, they do not affect the horse's performance.

Breeding: Although there is an hereditary susceptibility, mares or stallions that have performed well in spite of their curbs, may be used for breeding as long as the mate has exceptionally good, strong hocks.

All About Bows

QUESTION: I would like as much information as possible about bowed tendons because I have been offered a chance to buy a horse with a 'cold' bow. I don't know how the injury occurred, but is it likely to happen again? Some people say that a leg that has bowed is stronger than a normal leg. Others say that a leg with a bowed tendon is more susceptible to injury. Which is true?

This horse was a successful hunter and if I buy him I plan to show him. Are there any precautions I should take to try to prevent further injury?

EXPERT: Dr. Darryl Bonder (see Chapter 5, Question 3).

ANSWER: You ask for as much information as possible about bowed tendons. To fully understand a bow, it is helpful to be aware of the anatomy of the tendon. Made up of a number of very strong fibres which are arranged in a linear pattern, the tendon has an outer covering, known as the peratenon, attached to it. It is a loose connective tissue that allows the tendon to move within its sheath. The outer covering or tendon sheath is made up of two synovial layers.

The tendon, being a flexor, controls the movement of the limb in a flexed position.

In appearance, the bowed tendon looks like a swelling (in the shape of an archer's bow) on the back of the cannon bone. It may bow out towards the back or thicken from side to side. An outpouching of the flexor tendon, it is painful and carries a lot of heat. Overextension (or other causes listed below) leads to actual tearing of the tendon fibrils, disorganizing their linear pattern. Blood and edema flowing into the tissue spaces between the fibres lead to swelling and heat, both of which are the outward signs of acute tendinitis. If the tendon sheath becomes involved, the condition is known as tenosynovitis. Because the sheath is synovial-secreting membrane, when damage to it occurs, a greater secretion of synovial fluid is produced, resulting in a thickening or outpouching of the peratendonous area.

You mention that you do not know what caused the bowed tendon in the horse that you are thinking of purchasing. There are a number of possible causes:

• Hyperextension of the Limb: If the limb is overly-extended and the tendons stretch beyond their normal range of 'stretchability', a bow may occur.
• Improper Bandaging: A large number of cases are the result of too tight a bandage or insufficient padding underneath a bandage.
• Direct Trauma to the Tendon: The horse over-reaches very badly or falls and traumatizes the tendon directly with the hind foot. Possibly he might catch his leg in a fence, etc. and directly injure the tendon causing it to bow.

- Faults in Conformation:
  a. A horse with a very long, weak pastern will be predisposed to stretching the tendon area.
  b. A horse that is badly back at the knee (calf-kneed) will have excessive curvature of the forelimb and be predisposed to tendon problems.
- Forced Training When the Horse is Fatigued: An animal that is fatigued can no longer properly control its muscle movement and, if the muscle and the tendon are not prepared to take on weight-bearing, something gives way.
- Long Races When a Horse is Not Conditioned: When muscular control is gone, injuries are likely to occur. (Most racing injuries occur towards the end of a race.)
- Improper Shoeing: If a horse is left with a tremendously long toe and a low heel, he is predisposed to over-extension which in turn injures the tendon.

Note: Of major concern to you would be any faults in conformation which could lead to further injury.

To quote Bonder on the subject of the strength of the tendon that has bowed:

> It is a fallacy that a bowed leg is stronger than a normal leg. That is ridiculous! Scar tissue is never, ever stronger than normal tissue. The risk of injury is higher in a leg that has previously had a bow.

The original severity of the bow will influence just how this bowed leg will stand up. Have your veterinarian thoroughly check out the leg to determine whether the suspensory ligament was affected.

Probably the most accurate method of evaluating a tendon or ligamentous injury is through the use of sector scanning ultrasonography. This sophisticated technology allows the veterinarian to painlessly observe the soft-tissue structure of the limb. The on-board computer will also give accurate measurements of not only the structures, but any defects found within the structures. Tendon fibrils can be observed for any disruption in linearity; defects such as tears within tendons can be observed and measured; hard copy print-touts can be readily obtained, and, therefore, accurate assessment can be made as to the healing process within the tendon. In other words, veterinarians can predict, with great accuracy, exactly how well the tendon is mending, how soon it will be before the horse is able to work again and exactly how much work he can take. This can be a real help to you in your decision to purchase the horse because you can determine just how well the leg has mended and how much work the horse will be able to withstand in his career. The sector scanning ultrasonography unit has been added to the armamentarium at Humber College and has proved to be invaluable in assessing soft tissue lesions.

As far as precautions are concerned, Bonder suggests that you avoid terrain that is very deep or sticky as this type of going will predispose the horse to over-extension. Some examples of such footing might be excessively deep footing in an arena or a slick, muddy outside course.

Bandaging may be beneficial if done properly, but a bad bandage job is extremely dangerous; therefore, unless you know that you bandage well, you would be well-advised not to bandage.

Jumping is obviously going to be more traumatic than flat work because the hyperextension of the fetlock joint on landing puts stress on the flexor tendon and on the suspensory ligament, so do avoid high or particularly stressful jumping.

Acupuncture

QUESTION: What is acupuncture?

EXPERT: Dr. Dubro Zerajic graduated in Veterinary Medicine from the University of Zagreb in 1963 and immigrated to Canada in 1967.

A rider from the age of eleven, Zerajic was an amateur jockey in

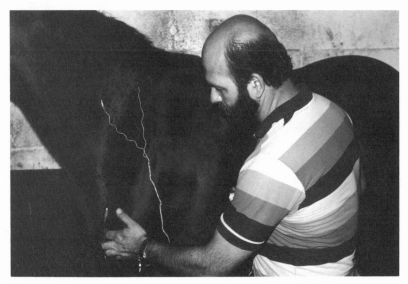

Dr. Dubro Zerajic

flat racing and steeplechasing in his native country and has continued his riding involvement in all forms of equestrian sport.

Zerajic first became interested in acupuncture almost by accident, but his fascination with this form of treatment has led him even to the Orient where he studied for a short time. According to Zerajic, 'If we put all our theories about acupuncture to one side, we realize we learned everything we need to know in our first year of physiology.'

He stresses that 'the success of acupuncture depends on the accuracy of the diagnosis of the problem.' Extremely compassionate in his handling of horses, Zerajic's special interests are acupuncture and sport injuries.

ANSWER:

What is Acupuncture? It is an ancient Chinese system of medicine involving, as its name reveals, a piercing (puncturing) of the skin to a depth of a few millimetres with a fine needle (acu).

On What Theory did the Ancient Chinese base Their Reasoning?
Put very simply:

Yin (negative and passive) and Yang (positive and active) constantly interact with, and react to, each other in order to attempt to achieve a *balance*. Yin and Yang flow in the form of ch'i along meridians which link all the body organs to each other and the surface of the body. Acupuncture tries to keep a body balance of Yin and Yang through the manipulation of ch'i by the needle.

What is a Typical Acupuncture Treatment Like? Naturally there is some variation depending on the particular problem being treated. The majority of Zerajic's acupuncture treatments involve the relieving of discomfort caused by aching muscles and by muscle spasms.

A Typical Case:
• Patient: A young horse who suffers from tired, sore muscles.
• Examination: Zerajic watches carefully to see how the horse moves as he is walked, first away and then towards the veterinarian.
• Equipment:
 a. A small electrical stimulator containing a nine volt battery.
 b. Sterilized acupuncture needles. (The number used varies, depending on the horse and his problem.) In this case four needles were used.
 c. Connecting cables.
• Method: Zerajic starts on the left side of the patient. He inserts the four needles into different points on the horse's neck and connects the needles to the stimulator with clamps. At this point, the muscles start quivering in a spasmodic fashion. This procedure is used, following different points all over the horse's body. Surprisingly, the patient takes very little notice of what is being done to him with the exception of one area which Zerajic says is a particularly sore one. The entire treatment takes about three-quarters of an hour.
• Result: The horse, who had been lying down, looks very relaxed and at ease when we leave.

• Explanation: Acupuncture, in this case, was used to stimulate the muscles and give an 'internal massage' similar to the external massage given by physical therapists.

• Evaluation: As Zerajic points out, if a horse is not lame, the problem is usually not considered serious, but when a horse who is suffering discomfort competes, the aches and pains make a big difference in his performance. When relieved of discomfort he becomes a 'different' horse with much freer movement.

How does Acupuncture Help a Horse Suffering from Sore Muscles? When a horse is suffering pain he starts to walk differently, thus making the muscles even more cramped. Acupuncture relieves pain not only by 'internally massaging' but also by causing the body to produce certain hormones called *endorphins* (similar to morphine) which kill pain and give a feeling of well-being.

What Problems does Zerajic Treat with Acupuncture?
• The relief of aches and pains as described above.

• Foal Pneumonia: When certain acupuncture points are stimulated, white blood cells are increased up to fifty per cent. One might say that acupuncture is stimulating the body's *natural defence mechanism*. (Zerajic always backs up acupuncture for foal pneumonia with Western medicine's antibiotic treatment.)

• Castration: Stimulating certain points causes the *blood vessels* to *contract*, thus helping to seal off bleeding.

• Founder: Zerajic has had great success when using acupuncture in the first twenty-four hours of a founder situation. By working on certain acupuncture points for ten to twenty minutes he has been able to cause the foot to become cold and circulation to return to normal.

In this instance acupuncture is *stimulating circulation* and, as long as no permanent damage has been done, within half an hour the horse moves normally.

(Although some veterinarians such as Dr. Klide, one of the authors of *Veterinary Acupuncture*, claim success with chronic founder, Zerajic has done little work in that direction.)

• Colic: Acupuncture points are stimulated to encourage the *stomach* to *work faster* or *slower* whichever is needed.

When Does Zerajic Not Use Acupuncture?
• When a horse is on heavy doses of steroids, acupuncture is not successful.
• If a leg has a bowed tendon or chips, etc., time is the most important factor in tissue healing and acupuncture cannot change this time factor.
• If the horse needs to have an analgesic before it is treated, Zerajic points out that acupuncture would be too time consuming when an area can be so quickly frozen, for example.

In Summary: Acupuncture, like anything else, *has to be done properly* in order to achieve successful results. It is essential that one knows at what point to puncture the skin in relation to what disease and to gain such knowledge takes time, effort and assistance. To quote Zerajic on the status of acupuncture: 'I think acupuncture is not superior to Western medicine, but in certain types of diseases, Western medicine does not have as much success as Eastern medicine or acupuncture does!'

11. BREEDING

A very special moment in the life of a brood mare owner.

'You'll *never* get her in foal!' – Never Say Never is the end result of careful brood mare management.

Basic Information for the Novice Breeder

QUESTION: Frequently novice breeders ask me such questions as 'What stallion do you like best?', 'Who are you going to breed your mare to this year?', 'What stallion is most popular?' or even 'Who do you think I should breed my mare to?'

So many people seem to want to hop on the popularity bandwagon of a stallion hopes that the foal they get will be perfection itself. What is so frequently forgotten is that the foal will not be a clone of the stallion; in fact, the mare contributes at least fifty per cent towards the foal and there is certainly evidence to support the supposition that she probably contributes ten or even fifteen per cent more.

For an in-depth look at suggested solutions to these breeding choice uncertainties, I approached a person who has both veterinary and practical experience in this field.

EXPERT: Dr. Peter Birdsall, author of three books on hunter and jumper bloodlines, writes articles, lectures and acts as a consultant – all on the subject of breeding as it relates to performance bloodlines.

Birdsall worked as a veterinarian in a general practice from 1965 to 1981 and from 1973 to 1980 ran his own breeding farm. In 1981 he accepted a position with Agriculture Canada, a position which has left him with more spare time to pursue his intense involvement with the breeding of sport horses. Outside of work hours, he travels extensively, mostly to the United States where he is involved in various research projects which are concerned with transported semen, frozen semen and embryo transfer. All such research is geared toward the breeding and development of top performance horses.

Birdsall decries the deplorable lack of records on the bloodlines of performance horses in Canada and in his capacity as President of the Horses in Sport Federation he is working diligently to change this situation.

ANSWER: Birdsall stresses the importance of knowing what you want to breed for *before* you select the mare. Once you know what *type of foal* you want to produce, you are ready to look for a mare that is suitable.

General factors to take into account when choosing a mare to breed are: type, quality, size, production record and bloodlines, but many of these qualities must be specifically suited to what you hope to get. In other words, a suitable hunter brood mare should possess different qualities than a suitable dressage or jumper mare.

Thus, what Birdsall is suggesting is that you decide whether you want a hunter, a dressage or a jumper-oriented foal. Then look for the mare most likely to produce that type.

For Hunters: You are looking at a Thoroughbred or Thoroughbred-type mare – one who is very attractive, a good mover and a good size. She can be more flat moving, even a little more on the forehand.

It helps if there are successful hunter performers in her bloodlines. A horse like Sir Thomson that Rodney Jenkins showed in the United States twelve or fourteen years ago, not only was a successful hunter himself, but also has had successful hunter and hunter futurity offspring.

According to Birdsall, Warmbloods, who have not in the past been suitable as hunters, are getting more Thoroughbred and are now 'knocking on the door'.

For Dressage: Movement is very, very important whereas prettyness is not. Parentage is extremely important; therefore, Birdsall feels that European horses are probably the most desirable. A good temperament is helpful as it makes a horse easier to get along with and thus more manageable. Although it is easier to sell larger offspring, Birdsall feels that a lot of dressage riders are overmounted as far as size is concerned. He suggests that a rider should consider his or her own physique and aim for a totally harmonious picture of horse and rider.

For Jumping: Birdsall stresses either the mare's performance record or, if she did not show, that she must possess talent or athletic ability. She does not have to be an exceptionally good mover and she does not have to be a great-looking mare, but she should have a combination of things that point her towards jumping ability.

A different kind of conformation is suitable for a jumper as opposed to a hunter. The point of balance is somewhat different as the jumper often has an erect neck set and jumps off of his hocks.

Birdsall points out that at the higher jumper levels there are very few Thoroughbreds these days. At big shows in the United States there might be three Thoroughbreds out of forty or fifty horses. The Warmbloods have really taken over mostly because they have been selectively bred.

Desire plays an important role in the success of an athlete, perhaps most importantly in the success of a jumper. Birdsall considers desire to be hereditary rather than learned behaviour. Jumpers, he feels, have to have a strange combination of attitudes. First, they must be bold – bold enough to jump anything they are aimed at. Secondly, they must be sensitive enough not to want to hit anything. Boldness by itself is not enough and being sensitive can be a problem. What is needed is a balance between the two. The horse must jump yes, but he must also want to jump clean. The old Bonne Nuit line was classic in that regard and the trait was passed down to later generations.

Are there Any Characteristics which Birdsall Avoids in a Brood Mare?
One characteristic in particular that he makes a point of avoiding is 'back at the knees'. He does not care too much for a short neck nor for long thin cannon bones, but he won't turn a really good mare down for one of them necessarily. Reproductive tract conformation faults such as a tipped vulva or a weak musculature in the vulva area – two problems found sometimes in older Thoroughbred mares also concern him. He does not mind a horse a shade long in the back and likes a neck to be well-attached and fairly long.

All in all to quote Birdsall, 'There are a lot of things you look at and don't like but then you see some pretty good horses that have them. A basic rule of thumb when out looking for a mare is "Stay away from an exaggeration of the normal." '

Improving on What One Has in a Mare: Birdsall points out that it depends on existing genes. If you breed to a stallion that does not have a conformation fault that your mare *does* have, it is possible to get a correction of it. That is certainly the rationale for breeding to a stallion that is good where your mare is weak. It does not guarantee that you are going to correct it, but it does improve your chances.

Again and again Birdsall comes back to the subject of performance and stresses that good performance bloodlines are the key to breeding good stock. As he puts it, 'Basically your horse is what his bloodlines say he is and more and more, the sport horse is becoming like the race horse – he comes from a very small genetic pool.'
Birdsall has good advice for the novice breeder.

Right now you have to be very selective. The days of indiscriminate breeding are gone. You have to know the market and what type of horses are winning. You have to know what type of horses people want and the lines which these horses come from. Just like any other business, you really have to research sport horse breeding, map out a strategy and then go with it.'
The better mare you can get, the better chance you have in the market. With stallion selection you have a lot of choice but with a mare you're putting all your eggs in one basket. The weakness of a lot of people's breeding programme is in the mares.

For the novice breeder who has a pet riding mare and wants to breed a foal as a future pleasure horse for sentimental reasons, this information if not designed to discourage that intention. For the person interested in breeding to later sell at a profit, this information hopefully will give that person motivation to do a great deal of research before taking 'the big step'. And that is exactly what it is. Make no mistake. Breeding a mare and raising a youngster is a costly undertaking. If that young horse is not really marketable, there will be a significant financial loss as well as a certain amount of mental anguish. What do you do with a young horse that no one wants to buy as you watch the bills mounting up? Try to avoid that situation by making *informed* decisions. There is still no guarantee that you will get just what you want, but you certainly can improve the odds.

Preparing Your Brood Mare for the Stud Farm

QUESTION: What can be done to best prepare the brood mare for a successful visit to the stud farm?

EXPERT: Dr. Neale Savage, although not my own veterinarian, was the person who successfully took over the treatment process for a 'problem' brood mare I owned.

A 1979 graduate with a Bachelor of Veterinary Science from Australia's University of Queensland, Savage came to an Internship in Large Animal Medicine and Surgery at the Western College of Veterinary Medicine at the University of Saskatchewan here in Canada. He was granted a Diploma of Internship before starting a residency masters programme in the reproduction section. In 1984 he was granted a Master of Veterinary Science Diploma. Meanwhile he had moved to Ontario as a faculty member at the Ontario Veterinary College. In 1987 he did a Specialty Board Certification and became a Diplomate of the American College of Theriogenology.

At present Savage is an Assistant Professor in the Theriogenology Section in the Department of Population Medicine. That he is a highly qualified expert in the field of veterinary reproduction is obvious and he is frequently called on to lecture on the subject at various seminars.

ANSWER: A brood mare should be in what Savage refers to as *good breeding condition*; that is, not to fat, nor too thin but with at least 'good fleshing' and, as well, fit or well-exercised.

She should have her four basic vaccinations – rabies, tetanus, flu and rhino. Savage stresses Pneumobort K for the rhino as it is a killed vaccine and thus the only recommended one for pregnant brood mares. Mares who have never had a rhino shot should be vaccinated before going to the stud farm preferably with Pneumobort K. In some areas of Canada, a Western and Eastern encephalitis vaccination is also recommended. As well, she should be on a regular worming programme.

Next, most stud farms request that a current negative Coggins certificate accompany the mare and finally, that a uterine swab be done either at home or when the mare arrives at the stud farm. At the same time that a swab is carried out, the conformation of the vulva should be evaluated. At such time it can be determined whether or not a Caslick's operation will be necessary after breeding.

Brood mares, although the same in many ways, have different potential for problems, all depending on their breeding history. Savage, to clarify these different types of problems, divides mares into three categories:
- The Pregnant Mare, or mare with foal at foot – (also called 'The Wet' Mare)
- The Barren Mare – (a term Savage dislikes as it is an arbitrary term which might preferably be categorized)
- The Maiden Mare – (one never bred).

The Wet Mare: This category of mare is probably the easiest one to deal with because her reproductive status was obviously good enough to get her in foal the preceding year and to deliver a live, healthy foal in the current year.

The most critical aspect of breeding this type of mare is good quality handling at the stud farm. Proper teasing is very important because often these mares do not show well. Particularly at the foal heat stage, they are more interested in protecting the foal at foot than in showing to the stallion. A good cover at breeding time is also essential for the same reason.

People wonder about the advisability of breeding on the foal heat. Savage has no reservations about breeding at that time as long as the uterus, cervix and vulva are in good condition; however, he actually favours letting the mare go through the foal heat and then short-cycling her at seven days to bring her into heat before her next regular heat cycle. This way, the foal heat cleans up the uterus, tones it and makes it easy for the veterinarian to evaluate the uterus while only seven days are 'lost'.

Savage cautions that there is one type of wet mare which fails to show heat signs and to get in foal. The management procedure for such a mare who has a history of getting into foal every *second* year is to take the foal and foster it onto another mare. Without the foal, the mare will usually start showing heat signs and become pregnant.

The Barren Mare: A detailed history on this type of mare is important. Whether she has not foaled for several years or for only one, is significant for example. A uterine biopsy should definitely be done on this mare. Such a biopsy will show whether any infection she might have had has damaged the uterus. It will give a clear indication of the condition of an aged mare's uterus. In short, it will enable the veterinarian to give a fairly accurate prognosis of just how likely it is that the mare will be able to get in foal. From a monetary point of view, such information is important as it gives the owner some guidance re whether or not to try to breed.

Brood mare management is extremely important with the barren mare. She must be teased well and bred as few times as possible. Frequently the minimal contamination technique is used. This technique involves infusing the mare prior to breeding with an antibiotic semen extender which hopefully will kill any bacteria in the semen and keep the uterus in good condition until the ovum travels down to it.

The Maiden Mare: The maiden mare's problem may be a psychological one. She simply is not tuned in to the stud farm nor to being bred. She has difficulty adjusting to such breeding activities as teasing, palpation and breeding. Usually she does not show well nor does she stand well for breeding. These problems are particularly true of the maiden mare fresh off the track. Often such mares not only are highly excitable but also have problem heat cycles due to the use of steroids or hormones.

Savage makes the following suggestions for maiden mares:
• Get them accustomed to being with other groups of horses.
• Allow them to psychologically settle down.
• If possible, accustom them to being teased before they go to the stud farm.
• If necessary, that is, if they do not seem to come into heat, set them up with some sort of hormonal therapy before they go to the breeding farm so that they are in a stable state when they arrive.
• Once they go to the stud farm, tease them but do not breed them until later in the season so that they are psychologically comfortable.

Early Breeding: For those mare owners who wish an early breeding for their mares, Savage recommends either the use of lights or some form of progesterone therapy.

If lights are used, they must be started in December to give the best results. Sixteen hours under a two hundred watt incandescent bulb has been the common practice but just recently it has been discovered that one hour of light about eight or nine hours after dusk is every bit as effective as a straight sixteen hours. Mares under lights shed their winter coats, thus it is necessary to rug them if turning them out for long periods of time.

If some form of progesterone therapy such as 'Regumate' is used, it establishes what might be considered an artificial corpus luteum. The body believes it is in diestrus so when the progesterone is taken away, the mare starts to cycle and cycles regularly afterwards.

Your Brood Mare May Have a Problem

QUESTION: I'm having a lot of trouble getting my mare in foal. I hear there are several different problems a mare's reproductive system can have. Will you please explain what these different problems are?

EXPERT: Dr. Neale Savage (see Chapter 11, Question 2).

ANSWER: In order to help you understand more about the reproductive aspects of your mare, Savage outlines each part of a mare's reproductive tract, describes problems that may be encountered in each part and makes suggestions as to how these problems might be avoided or at least dealt with as effectively as possible.

A mare's reproductive tract is made up of the following separate parts:
- Ovaries
- Uterus
- Cervix
- Vagina
- Vulva.

Ovaries: It is in the maiden mare category that a problem in the ovaries is most likely to exist. Obviously, wet and barren mares are less likely to have a severe ovarian problem as they have already proven themselves capable of becoming pregnant.

Occasionally, chromosomal abnormalities exist where the horse is female in external appearance but not in the ovaries; that is, the ovaries do not have XX chromosomes so they can not produce normal follicles. Usually, such mares exhibit antagonistic behaviour which is almost stud-like in certain instances. Hormones and drugs given when females are racing can also cause similar problems.

One ovarian problem which can exist in all mare categories is the presence of tumours. They are usually easy to detect on palpation. Normally, a mare's ovaries should be freely mobile and, in breeding season, about the size of a small kidney-shaped apple. A mare with very large ovaries and irregular heat cycles could very well have an ovarian tumour – the most common of which is the granulosa cell tumour. Other possibilities are haematomas (large blood clots) or abscesses.

Uterus: The uterus is the site of the majority of reproductive problems. Of the three categories of mares, it is the wet mare and the barren mare who most commonly have problems in this area.

a. *In the case of the wet mare:* On examination during the foal heat it can be determined whether the uterus of the wet mare has sufficiently recovered from her last pregnancy to carry a fetus. If a stud farm veterinarian recommends waiting until the next heat cycle or short cycling her with prostaglandin then Savage suggests that the mare owner follow that advice.

b. *In the case of the wet mare and the barren mare:* If a uterine swab shows that infection is present in the uterus, a culture is needed to determine the type of bacteria present and its sensitivity so that the correct antibiotic can be used for treatment.

It should be pointed out that although a sterile uterus is preferred for breeding, there are some mares who have present a very, very low number of bacteria which are probably only normal flora. It is when a significant growth of bacteria is seen that an infection is likely to be present, but as well, it should be stressed that if there is any doubt that vaginal or any other contamination occurred during the swabbing process, then swabbing should be redone.

If a uterine infection is present, then it should be treated immediately as it is a fact that the longer infection is present, the more damage is done to the uterus, and, as a result, pregnancy capabilities are reduced. On the other hand, Savage cautions against overtreating these mares. Some mares are treated with antibiotics and an environment is established that is very susceptible to the development of a different type of bacteria which in turn is treated leaving an opportunity for a third type to develop. Going from bad to worse, eventually a fungus infection, which in mares is extremely difficult to eradicate, might develop.

Remember, each infection damages the uterus further. Fibrous tissue develops and cuts down on the amount of healthy lining in the uterus – healthy lining which is necessary for fetal survival. It is a merry-go-round from which it is very difficult to get off. (Believe me, I know! One of my mares has gone through countless infusions, biopsies, etc. over the last few years.)

Fortunately, however, the majority of mares respond well to antibiotics. As well, today, recent developments involve the use of colostrum, plasma or whole blood in place of antibiotics. It is felt that these three types of infusions encourage development in the mare of her own antibodies to fight the infection, thus eradicating the risk of the totally open and susceptible environment which antibiotics produce. Savage has an open mind concerning which of these three types of new treatments might be preferable as little controlled research information has been published on them yet.

He concludes on the subject of infection that any mares who have been infected should be treated as 'potentially easily-infected mares' and bred using the minimal contamination method or artificial insemination (A.I.). Good breeding management with all such mares is essential.

Cervix: The use of a vaginal speculum to examine the cervix will enable a veterinarian to determine its condition. Evidence of bruising and damage discovered on a foal heat evaluation are often used to determine suitability for breeding. If the cervix has been damaged and some fibrosis is present, it may be impossible for the cervix to close properly. This inability of the cervix to act as an effective seal, renders the mare completely infertile, although recent work from Pennsylvania holds promise for surgical repair of some of these cervical problems.

Vagina: Prior to breeding, a maiden mare should be checked to see if she has any vaginal strictures such as a persistent hymen which is a reasonably common problem in horses. If the tissue is quite firm and fibrous, Savage suggests snipping it so that the stallion can penetrate more easily.

Leaving it intact could cause a mare and / or stallion to associate breeding with pain and therefore create future breeding problems.

All categories of mares should be checked for any growths, trauma or tearing – any of which may have to be treated prior to breeding.

Vulva: The most common aspect to consider here is whether or not the mare needs a Caslick's operation: that is, a suturing from the top of the vulva to just below the floor of the pelvis. (Suturing should not be continued past this point or urine may pool because lack of space may make passage difficult.)

Mares with tipped vulvas either because of poor conformation in that area or of age which slackens the muscles around the anus allowing them to sink in and change the normal angle, are ideal candidates for a Caslick's operation. Such an operation reduces the chances of the mares becoming infected due to fecal material collecting around the vulva and being windsucked in.

A sutured vulva must be opened prior to breeding, or the stallion can really damage himself trying to breed and prior to foaling or the sutured section will form more of an obstruction than the shelf of tissue between the rectum and the vagina and the foal passes out that way causing third degree perineal tears – to quote Savage, '... probably one of the biggest disasters you can get.'

As well, management during breeding is very important. A vulva that has been opened for breeding must be either clamped or stitched between the time of breeding and the time of the pregnancy diagnosis. Savage recommends that any mare who needs a Caslick's operation should be managed well enough so that only one or two coverings are necessary.

Apart from possible problems in the reproductive tract, Savage outlines other factors to be considered.

Artificial Insemination: Savage is greatly in favour of artificial insemination used under the right circumstances. For those breed associations which allow it, he considers it ideal in the breeding of problem mares. He explains, 'We can monitor them regularly so we know when they're going to ovulate and we can breed them at the most opportune time with semen that has been extended in an antibiotic extender so that we get absolute minimal risk of introducing infection into the uterus.'

As well, Savage feels that using A.I., a society can quickly develop the desired type of horse. He cites the Canadian Sport Horse as an example explaining that it would only take about five years to standardize the breed!. He draws this from the recent evidence of the American Sport Horse situation where a standard type is being developed quickly using A.I. and embryo transfer.

Pregnancy Losses and Early Pregnancy Diagnosis:
• Of all mares bred, loss due to *chromosomal* abnormalities is postulated at around five to ten per cent. According to Savage there is nothing that can be done about such loss. Losses are also considered higher in mares bred at foal heat.
• Some mares go thirty to thirty-five days and lose their pregnancy. One question that has always existed is whether or not such a loss is due to progesterone deficiency; however, it has never been conclusively proven that a progesterone deficit leads to fetal loss. A healthy fetal-uterine-ovarian inter-relationship is necessary for pregnancy in all species. If it can be shown by serial blood samples that in one cycle a mare's progesterone level actually declines around twenty days, then that mare may be an ideal candidate to be put on progesterone.
• Savage stresses the importance of an early pregnancy diagnosis. With the advent of ultrasound, a diagnosis can be made as early as ten days. (If the mare *is* pregnant, she should be checked several days later to determine whether or not she is carrying twins. Ten days is too early to indicate the presence of twins.) Even using the palpation method, an experienced practitioner can detect a conception as early as twenty-one days.

Early pregnancy diagnosis can, for example, save a season or even the life of a mare who is carrying twins. Although if a mare conceives twins, there is a natural embryo reduction mechanism which can get rid of one of them, sometimes the system fails. If twins are still there at forty days, the mare may carry them through until the uterus can no longer deal with them and the mare aborts. The problem, of course, is that there is a risk of losing the mare as well. It is therefore up to the owner of a mare who has had twins diagnosed in the early stages of pregnancy to decide whether or not to have them aborted or whether or not one of the twins should be 'pinched off'. Early pregnancy diagnosis can also aid in detection of early fetal death.

• A very important aspect of breeding to remember is that pregnancy losses before forty days leave the mare's reproductive cycle capable of coming back into heat, whereas after forty days, endometrial cups which produce P.M.S.G. and which prevent the mare from returning to heat have formed and a whole breeding season is lost for that mare. This is termed a pseudopregnant state.

Actually we can divide pseudo pregnancies into two categories: Pseudo Pregnancy Type I, and Pseudo Pregnancy Type II.

In Type I, the mare loses the embryo between fourteen and twenty days (approximately) but does not come back into heat at the twenty-one day cycle. It is assumed she is pregnant and even determined with ultrasound: however, it is the mechanism of getting rid of the fetus that has caused the delay in returning to estrus. This mare will usually come back into heat after the fetus is reabsorbed.

In Type II, diagnosed as pregnant as late as forty-two days, the mare leaves the stud farm, shows no sign of heat for the rest of the season but produces no foal. It is the formation of the endometrial cups which prevents a return to heat. Nothing can be done to remove these structures and so the season is usually lost.

These are only an overview of the major problems. Others certainly exist and consultation with your veterinarian will usually yield useful answers.

The Uterine Biopsy

QUESTION: What is a uterine biopsy?

EXPERT: Dr. W.T.K. Basu is Professor of Theriogenology at the school of Veterinary Medicine in Madison, Wisconsin. Prior to this position he spent several years at the Ontario Veterinary College.

Considered an authority on the subject of equine breeding and reproductive problems, Basu is the author of several papers as well as a lecturer at various equine seminars.

ANSWER: To anyone involved in breeding horses, barren mares represent disappointment, frustration and lost dollars. Fortunately for mare owners, the field of veterinary medicine is becoming more and more knowledgeable in the ways to assess mare fertility and, in many cases, improve it. How? A histological test known as 'the uterine biopsy' gives a remarkably accurate 'picture' or indication of the condition of the endometrium or membrane that comprises the lining of the uterine wall.

What Kind of a Situation Warrants a Uterine Biopsy? Basu recommends uterine biopsies for the following:

• Infected mares who are showing signs such as pus at the vulva.
• Barren mares who have been bred over the past two or three seasons and have not caught.
• Mares who, when examined rectally, seem to have abnormal reproduction tracts such as enlarged or too flaccid uteri, etc.
• Mares that have a history of early embryonic death or fetal absorption.
• Anestrus mares – ones showing an absence of heat but who are not pregnant.
• Mares who are known to be barren but for unknown reasons. (These mares are different from the first group in that everything

seems to be satisfactory as far as such things as freedom from infection, choice of stallion, management at the time of breeding, are concerned.)

• Mares who show obvious vaginal and cervical abnormalities such as a torn vagina which may predispose secondary infections.

• Mares who are being purchased for breeding and who do not have a live foal at foot.

Basu stresses that it is the mares who belong in the first and second group that are the primary candidates for a uterine biopsy.

When is a Uterine Biopsy Done? A mare may be biopsied at any time but for simplicity, sample-taking during estrus (the period of time when a mare is receptive to a stallion) is facilitated by easier access to the uterus.

Whether or not a mare is in estrus at the time of the biopsy must be kept in mind during interpretation of the results.

What is the Procedure?

• A reproductive history of the mare must be obtained.

• The tail of the mare should be wrapped in a clean bandage and either tied or held out of the way.

• The mare's reproductive parts are physically examined by way of a rectal palpation. Questions to be kept in mind by the examiner are:

    a. How do the ovaries feel?

    b. How do the uterine horns feel?

    c. What is the size and tone of each horn? etc.

• The perineal region must be thoroughly cleansed with a mild disinfectant such as Betadine.

• Vaginascopy: A vaginascope is used to look into the vagina and to see the cervix. General characteristics and any abnormalities prove very helpful in diagnosis. Such things as the state of the walls, the appearance of the cervix (up and closed or down and relaxed and open) and the state of the mucus, are noted.

• A swab is taken from the endometrium in order to find out if there is infection in the uterus. A correct swab may be obtained *only* if the tip is guarded until it is in the uterus and before it is removed from the uterus.

• The device used in a uterine biopsy is the uterine biopsy forcep or punch. Because it is a rigid instrument it is very important that the mare be relaxed and still. The uterine biopsy forceps are directed into the body of the uterus by palpation through the rectal wall. Once at the site of implantation the inside hand pushes the uterus against the instrument while the outside hand controls the device. It is important that 'a little jerk' be given so that the forceps pinch or cut sharply rather than tear. According to Basu the mare feels no pain from this procedure.

• The forceps are withdrawn from the reproductive tract and the piece of tissue is dropped into a fixative solution. The tissue is sent to the laboratory where it is sectioned and returned to be examined for changes in the endometrium.

• Penicillin or a Furacin solution is infused into the uterus, not as part of any necessary treatment but as a precautionary step as any invasion of the uterus must be handled carefully because of the possibility of having introduced infection.

Results of the Procedures: The culture results name the type of organisms (if any) and suggest effective antibiotics to kill them.

For an evaluation of the biopsy, several things are done:
• An indication of the stage of the cycle is looked for and an attempt to match this stage up with the ovarian and cervical findings on examination.

• There is a search for evidence of infection and for indication as to whether the infection is acute or chronic.

• There is a search for evidence of fibrosis because extensive fibrosis (the formation of scar tissue from around the glands, thus reducing the ability of the mare to feed the fetus) will affect the mare's ability to carry a foal to full term.

Categorization: Basu stresses two important considerations which must be remembered when prognostications are made:

313

- The decision is never made in isolation but only after a combination of biopsy results, rectal examinations and history, etc. are studied.
- It is assumed that the stallion is normal, that breeding management is good and that there is no infection at the time of breeding. It is also assumed that the mare is bred at the right time.

So far in North America there are three categories which have been established for the sake of conformity:
- Category 1: The normal mare belongs in this category. The foaling probability is very high – eighty to ninety per cent. (Nature's own rule is that out of one hundred mares handbred, only sixty have live foals.)
- Category 2: The mare shows some evidence of abnormality (fibrosis or scar tissue) in the endometrium. These changes might affect foaling probability. With good management or with treatment the mare should be able to conceive and carry a fetus to full term. The foaling probability however is slightly reduced.
- Category 3: Changes in the endometrium appear to be very chronic. The mare's foaling probability is down to about ten per cent. Some of these mares will be able to become pregnant and carry to full term but they are the exception rather than the rule.

Based on these categories, a prognosis is made as to the fertility of the mare.

Fighting Uterine Infection

QUESTION: Once again I am bringing to you a problem which I personally have encountered, the solution to which I hope will prove as helpful to you as it did to me.

One of my mares, Dan's Harem, had developed an infection in her uterus. This infection kept recurring each time she was bred. Because Harem had been Grand Champion Hunter and Grand Champion Thoroughbred at the Royal in line classes and because she had already presented me with two excellent foals, I decided it was very worthwhile continuing to try to get her in foal.

Four years 'down the road', and countless antibiotic infusions and colostrum treatments later, the problem still existed. We just could not seem to get her in foal and each time we tried she became reinfected.

Three uterine biopsies had shown that her uterus was at a 'Grade 2A' and thus should be able to allow a foal to develop and be carried to full term. Nonetheless, we had no success.

Extreme disappointment, constant veterinary bills and the advice of friends who said that I would *never* get Harem in foal were wearing me down. Then the second foal that I had had out of Harem, Dune, won the Governor General's Cup at the Royal Winter Fair. I decided not to give up on Harem for at least one more breeding season.

By chance, I happened to be talking about my mare's breeding problems to a veterinarian who had a practice in Maryland. He told me of a veterinarian at the University of Florida, a Dr. Asbury, who was doing extensive research on mares with recurring infections. Apparently he was using plasma infusions as part of his therapy.

I asked my veterinarian to contact Asbury and find out all he could about these plasma infusions. He did. We tried Asbury's plasma research methods on Harem. The result was a foal that I named Never Say Never.

EXPERT: Dr. Neale Savage (see Chapter 11, Question 3).

ANSWER:
Normal and Abnormal Uterine Defence Mechanism: First of all, it is important to understand what normally occurs in a mare at breeding. One and all experience contamination. The healthy or resistant mare has a very rapid response to the bacteria that are put inside the uterus when she is bred. She responds to these foreign substances by flooding her uterus with neutrophils or white blood cells which, when the local antibodies from the uterine lining have bound them, engulf the bound bacteria that are then flushed out of the relaxed estrous cervix.

315

In the case of a mare that is susceptible to infection, there is something wrong with that uterine defence system. Numerous aspects of this decreased uterine resistance have been researched. It now appears that the problem is caused by a lack of complement, an opsonin, which when insufficient, affects the ability of the antibodies to bind up the bacteria; that is, to opsonize. If the bacteria do not become a bound complex, then the neutrophils can not engulf them all successfully and thus flush them from the uterus. In short, it appears that the mare is susceptible to infection because the opsonization process is out of order.

Problems Associated with Antibiotic Treatment: In the past, infected mares have been treated with antibiotics which have killed the bacteria and cured the infection. Unfortunately, as soon as the mare is once again exposed to contamination when she is bred, she becomes reinfected. Again, reinfection occurs because her uterine defense resistance is impaired.

Former methods of antibiotic treatment involved their overzealous use which in turn often led either to fungal infections which are very difficult to eradicate or, even worse, to strains of bacteria which are very resistant.

Colostrum Treatment – Theory and Problems: Colostrum is the first milk of the mare; it provides the newborn with protective antibodies and also acts as a laxative.

The theory behind colostrum treatment was the belief that an antibody deficit existed. Thus colostrum, which certainly is full of antibodies, is infused into the uterus to assist in the white blood cell attack, the binding and the elimination of the infection. The therapy works, but it does not work for the proposed reason.

In actual fact, what is probably happening, according to Savage, is that colostrum is so foreign to the uterus that its presence stimulates the uterus to respond by overreacting and pumping in lots of white blood cells or neutrophils. Thus everything is cleaned up and the desired response is achieved but indirectly, rather than for the supposed theory.

The problem with the use of colostrum is that it is very difficult to obtain. Breeding farms prefer to bank colostrum for foal use rather than for uterine therapy.

Plasma Therapy as Developed by Asbury of the University of Florida:
Plasma, which supports the cellular components of blood, is the liquid part. Plasma has in it antibodies, opsonins, clotting factors – all the things that are not actually identified as cellular components.

According to Savage, Asbury's work was initiated because, when searching for the reason why mares fail to be able to deal with uterine infection, his question was, 'Is there an inability of the mare to effectively opsonize bacteria, that is bind them and clump them up and then allow the neutrophils to get in and engulf them?' His research theory involved using plasma to help the mare effectively opsonize bacteria.

He believes that blood should be taken from the mare when she is two or three days into estrus (animals in estrus have increased ability to get rid of infections that are in the uterus), plasma spun from it and that the plasma be frozen in separate quantities of sixty to one hundred millilitres until it is required for use. (Some veterinarians feel that plasma obtained from the blood of any horse is acceptable to use but Asbury's research shows that the mare's own blood is preferable.)

Asbury's Method of Treatment:

• About one week after the mare has gone out of heat, short-cycle her with prostaglandin and begin treatment either after the prostaglandin has been given or when the mare begins to show signs of heat.
• Clean the uterus with a saline (or purified water) flush, and infuse the sixty to one hundred millilitres of plasma along with antibiotics afterwards.

Continue this treatment for three or four days of estrus, that is, until the follicle in the ovary is palpably close to ovulation.

- Breed the mare, using minimal contamination techniques in order to introduce as few bacteria as possible to the uterus.
- Use ovulating drugs so that the mare actually ovulates quickly after the invasion of semen to ensure that the mare does not have to be bred again.
- Continue for three or four days with saline flushes, plasma and antibiotic therapy so that the normal contamination that occurs with insemination is cleaned out.

(Because the reception of an embryo occurs around the fourth day after ovulation, Savage prefers continuing for only two or three days in order not to run the risk of actually intervening in a uterus that is just about to receive an embryo.)

Asbury's studies show that the addition of plasma results in improved opsonization with complement playing a central role. Improved opsonization appears to result in a 'clean' uterus.

Savage Adds Other Important Considerations:

- Identify whether there is something you can physically correct such as the need for a Caslick's operation. Examine her when she is in estrus as well as out.
- Consider having a uterine biopsy done because mares whose uteri fit into a 'Grade 2B' or 'Grade 3' category might not be worth continuing to try to get in foal.
- Try not to get hung up on time. It is more important that the mare be free of infection and ready to breed even in April or May than that she be bred when she is still in transition and not ready.
- When mares are in estrus their ability to fight contaminants is improved. Short-cycling her several times can be beneficial, with or without antibiotic therapy each time.
- Do an early pregnancy test with ultrasound. If the uterus is filled with fluid ten or twelve days after breeding, the mare is probably infected. She should be short-cycled and treated once again.